ASP.NET
Weekend Crash Course™

ASP.NET
Weekend Crash Course™

Rob Standefer III, et al.

Hungry Minds™

Best-Selling Books • Digital Downloads • e-Books • Answer Networks • e-Newsletters • Branded Web Sites • e-Learning

New York, NY • Cleveland, OH • Indianapolis, IN

ASP.NET Weekend Crash Course™
Published by
Hungry Minds, Inc.
909 Third Avenue
New York, NY 10022
www.hungryminds.com

Library of Congress Control Number: 2001089319
ISBN: 0-7645-4836-0
Printed in the United States of America
10 9 8 7 6 5 4 3 2 1
1B/RS/RQ/QR/IN
Distributed in the United States by Hungry Minds,
Inc.
Distributed by CDG Books Canada Inc. for Canada;
by Transworld Publishers Limited in the United
Kingdom; by IDG Norge Books for Norway; by IDG
Sweden Books for Sweden; by IDG Books Australia
Publishing Corporation Pty. Ltd. for Australia and
New Zealand; by TransQuest Publishers Pte Ltd. for
Singapore, Malaysia, Thailand, Indonesia, and Hong
Kong; by Gotop Information Inc. for Taiwan; by ICG
Muse, Inc. for Japan; by Intersoft for South Africa;
by Eyrolles for France; by International Thomson
Publishing for Germany, Austria, and Switzerland;
by Distribuidora Cuspide for Argentina; by LR
International for Brazil; by Galileo Libros for Chile;
by Ediciones ZETA S.C.R. Ltda. for Peru; by WS
Computer Publishing Corporation, Inc., for the
Philippines; by Contemporanea de Ediciones for
Venezuela; by Express Computer Distributors for
the Caribbean and West Indies; by Micronesia Media
Distributor, Inc. for Micronesia; by Chips
Computadoras S.A. de C.V. for Mexico; by Editorial
Norma de Panama S.A. for Panama; by American
Bookshops for Finland.
For general information on Hungry Minds' products
and services please contact our Customer Care
department within the U.S. at 800-762-2974, out-
side the U.S. at 317-572-3993 or fax 317-572-4002.
For sales inquiries and reseller information, including discounts, premium and bulk quantity sales,
and foreign-language translations, please contact
our Customer Care department at 800-434-3422, fax
317-572-4002 or write to Hungry Minds, Inc., Attn:
Customer Care Department, 10475 Crosspoint
Boulevard, Indianapolis, IN 46256.
For information on licensing foreign or domestic
rights, please contact our Sub-Rights Customer Care
department at 212-884-5000.
For information on using Hungry Minds' products
and services in the classroom or for ordering exam-
ination copies, please contact our Educational Sales
department at 800-434-2086 or fax 317-572-4005.
For press review copies, author interviews, or other
publicity information, please contact our Public
Relations department at 317-572-3168 or fax
317-572-4168.
For authorization to photocopy items for corporate,
personal, or educational use, please contact
Copyright Clearance Center, 222 Rosewood Drive,
Danvers, MA 01923, or fax 978-750-4470.

About the Author

Robert Standefer is a professional developer specializing in Web development using Microsoft products. He lives in Dallas, Texas, with his wife and cats.

About the Contributors

Mridula Parihar is a Microsoft Certified Solution Developer (MCSD). She has worked with NIIT Ltd. for two years. In her first year, she worked as a technical instructor in the Career Education Group (CEG) division of NIIT Ltd. She has been working with the Knowledge Solutions Business (KSB) group for the last 12 months. Here, Mridula has had the opportunity to work on many technical projects. Her work involves design, development, testing, and implementation of instructor-led training courses. In addition to the instructor-led courses, she is involved in textbook writing. Also, she handles the additional responsibility of ensuring ISO compliance.

Ashok Appu is a technical writer in NIIT. He has had formal training on various programming languages and operating systems. He has been working for NIIT for the past 15 months. Throughout his tenure at NIIT, Knowledge Solutions Business (KSB division), he has been writing books on technical subjects. His work involves design and development, testing, and implementation of instructor-led training courses. Apart from his growth as an ILT writer, he has also had experience as a textbook writer. In addition to all this, he has given support to the factory primarily on installing and using operating systems, such as Linux and Windows, effectively.

About the Series Editor

Michael Lane Thomas is an active development community and computer industry analyst who presently spends a great deal of time spreading the gospel of Microsoft .NET in his current role as a .NET technology evangelist for Microsoft. In working with over a half-dozen publishing companies, Michael has written numerous technical articles and written or contributed to almost 20 books on numerous technical topics, including Visual Basic, Visual C++, and .NET technologies. He is a prolific supporter of the Microsoft certification programs, having earned his MCSD, MCSE+I, MCT, MCP+SB, and MCDBA.

In addition to technical writing, Michael can also be heard over the airwaves from time to time, including two weekly radio programs on Entercom (www.entercom.com/) stations, including most often in Kansas City on News Radio 980KMBZ (www.kmbz.com/). He can also occasionally be caught on the Internet doing an MSDN Webcast (www.microsoft.com/usa/webcasts/) discussing .NET, the next generation of Web application technologies.

Michael started his journey through the technical ranks back in college at the University of Kansas, where he earned his stripes and a couple of degrees. After a brief stint as a technical and business consultant to Tokyo-based Global Online Japan, he returned to the States to climb the corporate ladder. He has held assorted roles, including those of IT manager, field engineer, trainer, independent consultant, and even a brief stint as Interim CTO of a successful dot-com, although he believes his current role as .NET evangelist for Microsoft is the best of the lot. He can be reached via e-mail at mlthomas@microsoft.com.

Credits

Acquisitions Editor
Sharon Cox

Project Editor
Andrea C. Boucher

Copy Editor
Elizabeth Kuball

Technical Editor
Todd Meister

Editorial Manager
Colleen Totz

Senior Vice President, Technical Publishing
Richard Swadley

Vice President and Publisher
Joseph B. Wikert

Project Coordinator
Nancee Reeves

Graphics and Production Specialists
Jill Piscitelli
Heather Pope
Jacque Schneider
Kendra Span
Jeremey Unger
Erin Zeltner

Quality Control Technician
Laura Albert

Senior Permissions Editor
Carmen Krikorian

Media Development Specialist
Angela Denny

Media Development Coordinator
Marisa Pearman

Illustrators
Joyce Haughey
Barry Offringa
Betty Schulte

Proofreading and Indexing
TECHBOOKS Production Services

Cover Design
Clark Creative Group

To my mentors: Jon Brown, Tim Green,
and Richard Wehman.

Preface

ASP.NET Weekend Crash Course™ helps you learn the basics of ASP.NET in one weekend. There are 30 sessions, with each session taking one half-hour to complete, between Friday evening and Sunday afternoon. Each session covers a different topic, and you have the opportunity to pause and rest between sessions.

A New Way to Create Applications

The world changed when Netscape released the first commercial Web browser back in 1994. While in 1994 it was an achievement just to have a Web page, and HTML "programmers" were writing very buggy code, today's world is different. We have Web applications, complete software systems that depend on different server-side environments but that are accessible via a Web browser on (for the most part) any platform.

Programming for the Web in 1994 and programming for the Web now are like night and day. Companies such as Microsoft have simplified and compartmentalized the development process and made it available to all kinds of programmers. With the introduction of .NET, Microsoft has cemented the partnership between Windows developers and Web developers, applying its tried-and-true tools and methodologies for development on the Windows platform to creating applications for the Web.

One part of Microsoft's .NET initiative is ASP.NET, which is an environment for building and deploying Web applications. ASP.NET is free and easy to learn, and it doesn't require any special tools. It just requires a program running on a server and a text editor, such as Notepad, for creating the script pages and editing configuration files. You can even deploy an entire ASP.NET application with the xcopy command.

What's in This Book

This book is intended for the beginner or intermediate reader. It does not assume any prior experience with ASP or programming. Programming experience always helps, however, and I've included a chapter dedicated to helping you learn how programming works.

The book starts out with a discussion of .NET and what it's designed to do, and then moves on to building a foundation for coding ASP.NET pages. Once you're through that, you'll learn about VB.NET and XML. The ASP.NET-specific material is presented in a large chunk, leading into Web forms and working with databases. As you go through each section starting with Saturday afternoon, you build a chunk of code that will be added to a total application at the end of the book.

If you already know ASP, much of the material may seem like old hat, and you can skip to the VB.NET chapters. ASP developers should take particular note of the discussions throughout the entire book of how ASP.NET differs from ASP.

How to Use This Book

ASP.NET Weekend Crash Course follows a one-weekend format. The idea is to start Friday evening and finish on Sunday afternoon. This format is best for:

- The student needing to gain as much information as possible in a short amount of time
- The developer interested in learning the basics of .NET in general and ASP.NET in particular
- Anyone interested in learning a new technology

If you don't want to do all of the sessions in one weekend, you can read as much as you want and save the rest for later — just because the book is in a weekend format doesn't mean you have to cram it all in if you're not comfortable!

The book is separated into six parts, with each part containing four to six 30-minute sessions. Time markers in the margins help you keep track of your progress. Each lesson is followed by a review and a set of review questions to help you determine your comprehension of the material.

Overview

ASP.NET Weekend Crash course is composed of six parts split up into four to six chapters each.

Part I: Friday Evening

Part I helps you get the basics you'll need to understand and work with .NET. It covers the evolution of server-side scripting and programming and then shows you how to set up your ASP.NET environment.

Part II: Saturday Morning

Part II prepares you for programming with the .NET Framework. XML, the Common Language Runtime, and VB.NET are all covered in Part II.

Part III: Saturday Afternoon

Part III gets you into the nitty-gritty of ASP.NET, including managing session state and creating ASP.NET pages.

Part IV: Saturday Evening

Part IV shows you one of the most exciting parts of ASP.NET — creating Web forms.

Part V: Sunday Morning

Part V covers working with databases in ASP.NET with ADO.NET.

Part VI: Sunday Afternoon

Part VI shows you how to configure and deploy your application and covers some advanced topics. The code you wrote in the previous parts will be combined in Part VI for the skeleton of a complete application.

Accompanying CD-ROM

This book includes a CD-ROM in the back. The CD-ROM contains self-assessment software and all the code and examples from the book. For more information about the CD-ROM, see Appendix B.

Layout and Features

It's important to pace yourself while you are working through this book. If you think you need more than 15 hours, go ahead and take as long as you need. At the same time, don't rush yourself through the book or you'll find that you have missed key concepts.

To help you keep track of the time spent in each chapter, these icons appear in the margins:

30 Min.   **20 Min.**   **10 Min.**   **Done!**
To Go   **To Go**   **To Go**

These handy icons let you know how far along you are in a chapter and help you pace yourself. In addition to the time icons, a few other icons alert you to important pieces of information:

This is an important piece of information that you should make note of for later reference.

This alerts you to something you shouldn't do under any circumstances.

This is helpful advice on how to do something or a bit of information to help you in your programming travails.

This refers you to information on the CD-ROM included with the book.

When covering a key concept of ASP.NET or VB.NET, I'll highlight it as such:

Web.config contains one open tag and one close tag:

```
<configuration>
. . . Configuration info here . . .
</configuration>
```

Conventions Used in This Book

Other than the icons and syntax formatting, the following typographical conventions are used in the book:

- All code is presented in a monospaced font. Code within a sentence is presented like this:

To execute code when an ASP.NET page first loads, use the Page_Load function.

- Code within its own code block is presented like this:

```
Function ExecuteTask(strTask As String)

. . .

End Function
```

Occasionally, I'll refer to code that isn't presented in the book but exists on the CD-ROM. When I need to do this, I'll use the CD-ROM icon mentioned previously.

What's Next

Find a quiet place to read and turn to the first lesson!

Acknowledgments

Thanks to:

- Sharon Cox and the folks at Hungry Minds for their patience and diligence
- Andrea Boucher for her immeasurable help in bringing this book to fruition
- Todd Meister for his excellent suggestions, attention to detail, and lightning-fast turnaround
- My wife, Amanda, for taking care of me
- The ACES project team for listening to me talk about .NET in endless meetings

Contents at a Glance

Preface ix
Acknowledgments xiii

FRIDAY **2**
Part I—Friday Evening **4**
Session 1–Introducing .NET 5
Session 2–The Evolution of Server-Side Scripting 11
Session 3–Programming Basics 19
Session 4–Setting Up ASP.NET 29

SATURDAY **36**
Part II—Saturday Morning **38**
Session 5–Working with the .NET Framework 39
Session 6–Choosing a .NET Language 49
Session 7–Understanding XML 57
Session 8–Programming with Visual Basic .NET 67
Session 9–Building the Guts of a Program 75
Session 10–Working with Objects 85

Part III—Saturday Afternoon **96**
Session 11–ASP.NET versus ASP 97
Session 12–Introducing ASP.NET 107
Session 13–Using Namespaces and Classes 117
Session 14–Building ASP.NET Applications 125
Session 15–Managing Session State 135
Session 16–Building Your First ASP.NET Page 145
Part IV—Saturday Evening **158**
Session 17–Introducing Web Forms 159
Session 18–Working with Controls 167
Session 19–Validating User Input 177
Session 20–Building a Web Form 187

SUNDAY **198**
Part V—Sunday Morning **200**
Session 21–Understanding Databases 201
Session 22–Setting Up Your Database 211
Session 23–Using the Data Controls 225
Session 24–Understanding ADO.NET 235
Session 25–Working with Data 243
Session 26–Building a Data Aware ASP.NET Page 249
Part VI—Sunday Afternoon **262**
Session 27–Configuring ASP.NET Applications 263
Session 28–Finding and Fixing Errors 271
Session 29–Some Advanced Topics 281
Session 30–Putting It All Together 289

Appendix A–Answers to the Part Reviews 301
Appendix B–What's on the CD-ROM 307
Index 309
End-User License Agreement 329
CD-ROM Installation Instructions 332

Contents

Preface ix

Acknowledgments xiii

FRIDAY..2

Part I—Friday Evening 4

Session 1–Introducing .NET 5

  What Is .NET? 5

     .NET approaches a broad set of problems 6

     Developers have special needs 6

  Software as a Service 7

  How ASP.NET Fits in All of This 8

Session 2–The Evolution of Server-Side Scripting 11

  Common Gateway Interface 11

  From CGI to ASP 12

     Perl 12

     NSAPI/ISAPI 13

     Internet Database Connector 14

  Active Server Pages 15

     The ASP objects 16

     VBScript 17

     ADO 17

Session 3–Programming Basics 19

  What Is a Program? 19

     Programming languages 20

     Compilers 20

     Interpreter 21

  The Programming Process 21

     Software development lifecycle 21

       Requirements analysis 22

       Design 22

       Specification 22

       Development 22

       Testing 22

       Production 22

       Maintenance 23

       Enhancement and evolution 23

     Software engineering 23

  How Programs Work 24

     Variables 24

       Types 24

     Loops 25

       For...Next 25

       Do...Loop 26

     Conditionals 27

       If...Then 27

       Select...Case 27

Session 4–Setting Up ASP.NET **29**
   System Requirements **29**
   Installing ASP.NET Premium Edition **30**
   Configuring Your Web Server for ASP.NET **34**

SATURDAY **36**
Part II—Saturday Morning **38**
Session 5–Working with the .NET Framework **39**
   The .NET Framework **39**
      Simplified application development 40
      A rich set of programming libraries 40
      Side-by-side execution with existing applications 41
      Increased scalability for distributed applications 41
   What Is the Common Language Runtime? **41**
      Common language specification 41
      Language interoperability 41
   How the CLR Works **42**
      Managed code 42
         No dependence on individual runtimes *43*
         Garbage collection *44*
      Unmanaged and unsafe code 44
      Intermediate Language 44
         .NET compilation process *45*
         Platform independence *45*
      Just-In-Time compilers 45
         Standard JIT *46*
         EconoJIT *46*
Session 6–Choosing a .NET Language **49**
   Why Choose? **49**
   Some .NET Languages **50**
      Python 50
      Eiffel 51
      COBOL 51
   The Built-In .NET Languages **52**
      C++ 52
      JScript.NET 53
      C# 54
      Visual Basic.NET 54
Session 7–Understanding XML **57**
   What Is XML? **57**
      XML document features 58
      Well-formed XML 59
      Valid XML 59
         Structural validations *59*
         Functional validation *61*
         Namespaces *62*
   Using XML in Web Applications **63**
      Document Object Model 63
      Simple API for XML 63
      Extensible Stylesheet Language 64
         XPath *65*
         XSLT *65*
      .NET technologies 66

Session 8–Programming with Visual Basic .NET 67
  The Genesis of Visual Basic .NET 67
  Visual Basic .NET Core Concepts 68
    Comments 68
    Variables 69
      Object variables *69*
      Multiple variables *70*
    Constants 70
    Defining procedures 70
      Sub *70*
      Function *71*
    Error handling 71
  Unsupported Visual Basic Syntax 72
    Gone forever 72
      DefType *72*
      Gosub *73*
    Visual Basic .NET compatibility 73
Session 9–Building the Guts of a Program 75
  How It's Possible 75
  Sending E-Mail 76
    The code 76
    How it works 77
  Uploading a File 78
    The code 79
    How it works 80
  File System Access 81
    The code 81
    How it works 82
Session 10–Working with Objects 85
  Foundations for High-Level Programming 85
    The evolution of structures 85
      Assembly addresses *85*
      Structures *86*
      Limitations *86*
    Third-generation languages and beyond 87
      What abstraction means *87*
      Adding classes to software *87*
  And Then There Was the Object 88
    General OOP concepts 88
      Abstraction *88*
      Encapsulation *88*
      Inheritance *89*
      Polymorphism *89*
    Anatomy of an Object 89
      Properties *89*
      Methods *90*
      Events *90*
      Collections *91*
    ASP.NET: The best of Object-Oriented Programming 91

Part III—Saturday Afternoon **96**
Session 11–ASP.NET versus ASP **97**
  Environment **97**
    Execution 97
      ASP *97*
      ASP.NET *98*
    Languages 98
      ASP *98*
      ASP.NET *98*
    Database support 98
      ASP *99*
      ASP.NET *99*
    Objects 99
      ASP *99*
      ASP.NET *100*
    Browser support 100
      ASP *100*
      ASP.NET *100*
  Deployment and Versioning **100**
    Configuration 101
      ASP *101*
      ASP.NET *101*
    Deployment 101
      ASP *101*
      ASP.NET *101*
    Versioning 102
      ASP *102*
      ASP.NET *102*
  Scalability and Stability **102**
    Scalability 102
      ASP *102*
      ASP.NET *103*
    Stability 103
      ASP *103*
      ASP.NET *103*
  Debugging and Error Handling **103**
    Debugging 104
      ASP *104*
      ASP.NET *104*
    Error handling 104
      ASP *104*
      ASP.NET *104*
Session 12–Introducing ASP.NET **107**
  What Is ASP.NET? **107**
    Full .NET support 107
    Simplicity 108
    Manageability 108
    Tool support 108
    Performance 108
    Customizability 108
    Security 108
    Scalability 108

How ASP.NET Works **109**
   Client perspective 109
   Server perspective 109
Page Structure **110**
   Code declaration blocks 110
   Code render blocks 111
   Directives 112
      @Page *112*
      @Control *113*
      @Import *113*
      @Register *113*
      @Assembly *113*
      @OutputCache *114*
   HTML control syntax 114
   Custom server control syntax 114
   Data binding expressions 114
   Server-side object tags 114
   Server-side include directives 115
   Server-side comments 115
Session 13–Using Namespaces and Classes **117**
How to Use Namespaces **117**
The Namespaces **118**
   System 119
      Exceptions *119*
      Classes *119*
      Structures *120*
   System.Collections 120
   System.IO 120
      Exceptions *120*
      Classes *121*
   System.Web 121
   System.Web.UI 122
   System.Web.UI.HtmlControls 122
   System.Web.UI.WebControls 122
Session 14–Building ASP.NET Applications **125**
What Is an ASP.NET Application? **125**
   Creating an ASP.NET application 125
   Deployment 126
Creating Application Level Logic **127**
   Application events 128
   Session events 128
Securing Your Application **129**
   Authentication 130
      Windows authentication *130*
      Passport authentication *130*
      Cookie authentication *130*
   Authorization 131
      File authorization *131*
      URL authorization *131*
   Impersonation 132

Session 15—Managing Session State **135**

  How Session State Works **135**

  Problems with ASP Session State **136**

    Process dependence 136

    Cookie dependence 136

    Server farm limitations 136

  ASP.NET to the Rescue **137**

    Process independence 137

    Cookie independence 137

    Server farm support 137

  Using ASP.NET Session State **137**

    What is Web.config? 137

    Configuring the session 138

  ASP.NET Session State Modes **138**

    In-process mode 139

    Out-of-process mode 139

    SQL Server mode 139

  Cookieless Session State **140**

  Are There Any Other Options? **141**

  What About Performance and Reliability? **141**

    In-process 141

    Out-of-process 141

    SQL server 141

  How Is Session Used in Code? **141**

Session 16—Building Your First ASP.NET Page **145**

  What Do We Want to Do? **145**

  Build the Page Skeleton **146**

  Write Your Functions **147**

  Integrating the Code **149**

  Calling the Functions **150**

  Exception Handling **152**

Part IV—Saturday Evening **158**

Session 17—Introducing Web Forms **159**

  What Is a Web Form? **159**

    A rich set of controls 159

    Browser independent 160

    Separation of interface and logic 160

  Web Forms and Visual Studio.NET **160**

  Web Forms Page Processing **160**

    The three stages of processing 161

      Page_Load *161*

      Event handling *161*

      Page_Unload *161*

    View state and state management 161

  The HTML Controls **161**

  Building a Web Form **162**

    An ASP form 162

    An ASP.NET form 163

  Code Behind Development **164**

    Using code behind 165

    Deploying code behind 166

Session 18—Working with Controls 167
  What Is a Web Control? 167
    Rich, consistent object model 168
    Automatic browser detection 168
    Event passing 168
    Data binding 168
  The Web Controls 168
    Common properties 168
      AccessKey 168
      Attributes 169
      BackColor 169
      BorderWidth 169
      BorderStyle 169
      CssClass 169
      Enabled 169
      Font 169
      ForeColor 169
      Height 169
      TabIndex 169
      ToolTip 170
      Width 170
    Displaying text 170
    Inputting information 170
      <asp:TextBox> 170
      <asp:CheckBox> 170
      <asp:RadioButton> 171
      <asp:ListBox> 171
      <asp:DropDownList> 171
      <asp:CheckBoxList> 171
      <asp:RadioButtonList> 172
    Performing actions 172
      <asp:Button> 172
      <asp:LinkButton> 172
      <asp:ImageButton> 172
      <asp:HyperLink> 172
    Displaying images 173
    Layout and interface 173
      <asp:Panel> 173
      <asp:Table> 173
      <asp:Calendar> 173
      <asp:AdRotator> 174
  Using the Web Controls 174
Session 19—Validating User Input 177
  Input Validation 177
  ASP.NET Validation Controls 178
    Multiple validation criteria 178
    Automatic implementation 178
    Separation of reporting 179
  The Six Validation Controls 179
    CompareValidator 179
    CustomValidator 179
    RangeValidator 179
    RegularExpressionValidator 179

RequiredFieldValidator 180
ValidationSummary 180
Using the Validation Controls **180**
CompareValidator 180
CustomValidator 181
RangeValidator 182
RegularExpressionValidator 183
RequiredFieldValidator 183
ValidationSummary 184
Session 20—Building a Web Form **187**
A Quick Recap **187**
Redefining the Requirements **189**
Designing the Form **190**
Text boxes 190
Dropdown list 190
Submit button 191
Writing the Code **192**
Form Validation **193**
The first value 193
The second value 194
The operator 194
The ValidationSummary 195

SUNDAY **198**

Part V—Sunday Morning **200**
Session 21—Understanding Databases **201**
Relational Databases **201**
Tables 202
Fields 202
Keys 203
Relationships 203
Queries 203
Create Your Database **204**
Inserting and Updating Data **206**
INSERT 206
UPDATE 207
Retrieving Data **208**
Deleting Data **209**
Session 22—Setting Up Your Database **211**
Preparing for SQL Server 2000 ....**211**
Acquiring SQL Server 2000 211
System requirements 212
Installing SQL Server 2000 ....**212**
Creating Your Database **219**
Session 23—Using the Data Controls **225**
Data Binding **225**
Binding to data from a database 226
The data binding code 227
Data Controls and Classes **228**
BoundColumn 228
ButtonColumn 229
DataGridColumn 229
DataGridColumnCollection 229
DataGrid 229

DataGridItem 229
DataGridItemCollection 229
DataGridPagerStyle 229
DataKeyCollection 229
DataList 229
DataListItem 229
DataListItemCollection 229
EditCommandColumn 230
HyperLinkColumn 230
TemplateColumn 230
Using the Controls **230**
DataGrid 230
   Data binding with DataGrid *230*
   Manipulating Columns *231*
   Editing, deleting, and sorting data *232*
DataList 233
Session 24—Understanding ADO.NET **235**
What Happens When I Modify Data? **235**
Four transactional properties 235
   Atomicity *236*
   Consistency *236*
   Isolation *236*
   Durability *236*
Updating a Recordset using ADO 236
Using ADO.NET to Access Data **238**
ADO.NET namespaces 238
Using the ADO.NET classes 239
   DataSet *240*
   DataTable *240*
   OleDbConnection *240*
   OleDbDataAdapter *240*
Creating and Filling DataSets **240**
Session 25—Working with Data **243**
ADO Revisited **243**
ADO Code Rewritten **244**
Session 26—Building a Data Aware ASP.NET Page **249**
A Quick Recap **249**
Redefining the Requirements, Again **252**
Building the Connection Code **253**
Using the ADO.NET managed provider 253
Defining the connection 253
Building the Update Code **254**
Tying It All Together **256**

Part VI—Sunday Afternoon **262**
Session 27—Configuring ASP.NET Applications **263**
What Is Web.config? **263**
The Web.config Structure **264**
Session 28—Finding and Fixing Errors **271**
Where Do Errors Come From? **271**
ASP.NET Error Handling **273**
Tracing **275**
Application-level tracing 276
Page-level tracing 278

Session 29—Some Advanced Topics **281**
  Web Services **281**
    How do Web services work? 281
    Supported protocols 282
      HTTP-POST *282*
      HTTP-GET *282*
      SOAP *282*
    What's next? 282
  SOAP **283**
    SOAP operations 283
      Document-oriented operations *284*
      RPC-Oriented Operations *284*
    Web Services Description Language (WSDL) and Web Services Meta Language (WSML) 285
  ASP.NET Caching **285**
    Why cache? 285
    Page output caching 286
    Page data caching 286
Session 30—Putting It All Together **289**
  The Application **289**
  The Changes **292**
    Too much code 292
    Performance enhancement 295
  The End Result **296**
Appendix A—Answers to the Part Reviews **301**
Appendix B—What's on the CD **307**
Index **309**
End-User License Agreement **329**
CD-ROM Installation Instructions **332**

ASP.NET
Weekend Crash Course™

☑ **Friday**

☐ Saturday

☐ Sunday

Part I — Friday Evening

Session 1
Introducing .NET

Session 2
The Evolution of Server-Side Scripting

Session 3
Programming Basics

Session 4
Setting Up ASP.NET

PART

I

Friday Evening

Session 1
Introducing .NET

Session 2
The Evolution of Server-Side Scripting

Session 3
Programming Basics

Session 4
Setting Up ASP.NET

SESSION

1

Introducing .NET

Session Checklist

✔ Understanding .NET concepts

✔ Approaching software as a service

**30 Min.
To Go**

A very wise software engineer once said, "The software development business is fraught with innovation." His double-meaning witticism has rung true; as each new programming marvel comes and goes, the software development industry gets freaked out because something new and innovative emerges.

The engineer's cynicism wasn't prepared for the arrival of Microsoft's .NET Framework. The .NET Framework is not a flash in the pan of excitement for fanboy software engineers; rather, it's essentially an old way of doing new things. It's a return to the tried-and-true concepts of sound software engineering that enables new platforms and new programming ideas. It supports both the old (COBOL) and the new (C#). In a metaphysical sense, the .NET Framework is a melding of two minds: One mind thinks in the old mainframe way, and the other mind thinks in the post-client/server Web programming way. When Microsoft brought the two worlds together, there was a virtual Big Bang and the .NET Framework was born.

What Is .NET?

So far, I've discussed how great the .NET Framework is and how it brings two worlds together. I also briefly mentioned ASP.NET. Before we get into a deeper discussion of the .NET Framework and, specifically, ASP.NET, let's take a look at Microsoft's .NET strategy as a whole. And if you're still wondering, .NET is pronounced "dot net."

In a nutshell, .NET is Microsoft's initiative, or strategy, for delivering software as a service. It's the backbone of Microsoft's idea of the new Application Service Provider business model. The key points of .NET are the Microsoft .NET platform, which includes .NET infrastructure (like the .NET Framework) and tools to build and operate the services, clients, and other software to run on a new generation of "smart" Internet devices; the .NET products and services, including MSN.NET, Office.NET (also known as NetDocs), and Visual Studio.NET; and third-party .NET services that are provided by a huge range of partners, developers, and associate organizations that will build vertical market applications on the .NET platform.

For all practical purposes, the .NET Framework is an environment for building, deploying, and running applications, and specifically, Web Services. The .NET Framework is made up of three main parts: the Common Language Runtime, the Framework Classes, and ASP.NET. Let's not get ahead of ourselves, though. The .NET Framework is just one piece of the whole .NET pie.

What all this means is that the .NET platform is so much more than just the .NET Framework, and the .NET Framework is just one small part of a complete corporate strategy. Thankfully, this book only covers the .NET Framework and ASP.NET specifically; a single book that covers all of .NET would have to exist in volumes. To help you better understand what problems are solved by the .NET Framework, let's examine what the .NET initiative is designed to do.

.NET approaches a broad set of problems

I find it easiest to sum up how .NET is poised to change things by mentioning a simple problem that has complex solutions: information exchange. Basically, .NET plans to join together communications with computing and enable developers to create distributed software that will make information available any time, anywhere, and on any device.

I mentioned previously that the .NET Framework combines the old with the new. If you look hard, you'll see that today's Web applications closely follow the paradigm of mainframe green-screens from years past. A single computer, the Web server (the equivalent of the mainframe), processes all the information and delivers it to the client via the Web browser (the equivalent of, say, a TN3270 terminal). The Web server controls access, and the Web browser is just a dumb terminal with some extra capabilities to render certain things client side, like Java applets.

This model is isolationist and a little xenophobic. Web sites can't communicate with each other in any meaningful way, too much is required of the user (for example, having to enter the same information, such as the customer shipping address, into the same sites over and over again), and the model is very much a server-centric one. When you get the data via HTML, you can't analyze, edit, or manipulate it in any way. This may be fine for sites like The Onion (www.theonion.com), but it's not great for e-business or the user experience in any Web application. The user has to know the technology, rather than the technology having to know the user.

Things get even worse when you use more than one kind of accessing device, like a PC and a wireless PDA. My PC and Macintosh are forever out of sync; my PocketPC PDA will never know the touch of my Macintosh. That's sad, because all of my e-mail is handled by Microsoft's wonderful Entourage product, and there is no version of Entourage for the PC (or PDA). Add to that the pain and suffering involved in surfing the Web with a PocketPC or Handspring Visor, and it's almost enough to convince me to trash it all and buy an oak desk and a bunch of pens.

Developers have special needs

It gets worse, of course. Everything I've mentioned so far adversely affects the user experience. Now, if you're reading this book, you're most likely a developer, and a whole list of limitations affects you.

Current generation Web development tools out there pale in comparison to their Windows development brothers like Visual Basic and Delphi. The simple event-driven development model in Visual Basic does not lend itself well to Web application development with tools like Active Server Pages (ASP) because HTML by design is static and loosely structured. It's difficult to generate server-side application code that adheres to an event-driven model.

Most Web tools focus on the graphic design aspect of Web applications. Within the realm of ASP, the pickings are very slim. None of the tools designed for ASP development focus on the software lifecycle; it's almost as if the tool vendors don't consider ASP-based applications as software. When I set out to build an ASP application, I design it, develop it, deploy it, and maintain it. That's pretty much the basic software lifecycle, but there is no single good tool that will handle all of this well, and I am aware of no tool that will allow me to write code for the PC and deploy it to a variety of devices.

Software as a Service

Now that you have a better understanding of what the .NET initiative is designed to do, you can begin to explore how it will help you solve your problems. The first part of understanding the .NET Framework solution is the concept of software as a service.

Software as a service can mean several things, depending upon whom you ask. The simplest idea is software as a service equivalent to telephone service or cable TV. You subscribe to these services, and you are able to pick and choose what features of the service best suit your needs. For example, you may choose call waiting and call block on your telephone, or a movie package and extra news channels in your cable TV service. As long as your payments are current and the devices are functioning, you are able to experience your service.

The correlation for software is that users can subscribe to the software they use, and select how much or how little of the software they want access to. Some users may only want to be able to create simple documents in Word, so they subscribe to a service that provides printing and saving capability. A computer book author, however, needs more, so the author picks template, add-in, and macro capability. It's all user-defined, and the users only pay for what they need. That's the idea behind software as a service.

Technologically speaking, the software could be downloaded off the Web and you would only pay for what you installed. Or, the software could exist entirely on the Web and you use your Web browser to access it, similar to a service such as Hotmail. You connect to the site, edit and manipulate your documents, and save them to your local hard drive or an online storage site, like X:drive.

Any time an upgrade is necessary, it would be handled on the server side and the patch would automatically be downloaded to your machine, or simply installed on the server, depending on which service model is in place. The cool part of this for the developers is that they are able to track which pieces are downloaded and used most often, and they can concentrate on those pieces of the application for upgrading and performance enhancements. If this sounds familiar, remember what I said about melding the old with the new: VAX and mainframe developers have been doing this stuff for years, but with the limitation of a single type of client.

You can also take the consumer out of the picture and imagine software as a service between businesses. I could provide a set of services that provide a certain type of programming logic, and you could subscribe to these services and use them in your own applications. It's akin to putting COM objects on a server and letting subscribers instance it for a fee, but they don't have to be on my server. A good example of this is the online payment systems for auctions. I often bid at sites like eBay, and I prefer to pay for the auction via PayPal. PayPal could expose its payment services to another application service provider and eliminate the need for custom modules to handle credit card payment. It does that to an extent now, but it's all handled through clunky URLs and patchy HTML code. It would be wonderful if I could send an XML document to PayPal via SOAP and have PayPal automatically handle billing. (SOAP is covered in Session 29.)

10 Min.
To Go

How ASP.NET Fits in All of This

ASP.NET is the next version of ASP. It's not really an evolution of ASP; rather, it's a whole new way of creating server-side Web applications. In late 1997, ASP was just a year old and Microsoft was releasing Internet Information Server 4.0 and the NT Option Pack. It was then that Mark Anders and Scott Guthrie started talking about what they liked and didn't like about ASP. They agreed that ASP was too complicated and that it forced the developer to write too much code. Further, ASP had no component model so it was impossible to just drop an encapsulated ASP component into another ASP page; the developer always had to write code.

In January 1998, Scott Guthrie created a prototype of a new version of ASP that eventually became ASP+, which was renamed to ASP.NET. Three years later, what began as holiday conversation between two Microsoft employees has become one of the hottest technologies ever to emerge.

ASP.NET isn't designed to be a cure-all by any means, but it is definitely a very powerful technology with a heritage steeped in sound object-oriented design and real-world practicality. Although ASP.NET is completely new, you don't have to throw out your previous knowledge of and experience in ASP. ASP.NET hopes to accomplish several things, including the following:

- **Language independence.** I mentioned the Common Language Runtime earlier; ASP.NET takes full advantage of this. (You can find more on this in the next session.)
- **Improved tool support.** ASP.NET is much more like Visual Basic. It's component based and event driven, which should allow tools vendors to produce some awesome tools. There's also the very exciting Visual Studio.NET.
- **Separation of code and content.** ASP.NET allows a developer to keep the code of the page separate from the formatting of the page. This feature should greatly simplify team development.
- **Simplified deployment.** An ASP.NET application can be deployed through a simple xcopy command.
- **Improved scalability.** Forget the problems you've had with session state in the past. ASP.NET changes everything.

ASP.NET has taken the simple page-based model of ASP and combined it with some of the best features of modern compiled languages, like Visual Basic and C++. In fact, Microsoft even created a new language to help C++ developers take advantage of ASP.NET. It's called C#, and I cover it a little later.

Keep in mind that although ASP.NET doesn't have to replace ASP; they can complement each other. You can run your ASP.NET alongside your existing ASP applications on the same machine. ASP.NET is backward-compatible. That means that most of your ASP pages will operate within the ASP.NET environment as they are, and you can add ASP.NET features to them as you see fit. You have several choices, and I cover them over the next several sessions.

Done!

REVIEW

In this chapter, you were introduced to Microsoft's .NET strategy and its parts, including the .NET Framework. You heard about how the .NET Framework offers developers new ways of developing Web applications. You learned about software as a service and the problems it hopes to solve, and this clarified how .NET fits into the grand scheme of things. Next you learned how ASP.NET is poised to help developers embrace the .NET Framework. Then you learned about what ASP.NET hopes to accomplish. Finally, you were reassured that ASP.NET won't force you to relearn anything, which is a welcome breath of fresh air.

QUIZ YOURSELF

1. What is the mainframe model of application deployment? (See "What Is .NET?")
2. What are the main goals of .NET? (See "What Is .NET?")
3. What makes up the .NET Framework? (See "What Is .NET?")
4. What is the idea behind software as a service? (See "Software as a Service.")
5. Name one thing ASP.NET does that ASP can't. (See "How ASP.NET Fits in All of This.")

SESSION

The Evolution of Server-Side Scripting

Session Checklist

✔ Understanding the genesis of server-side scripting

✔ Exploring earlier methods of developing server-side applications

✔ Getting a handle on ASP and its core features

**30 Min.
To Go**

Before jumping into the ins and outs of ASP.NET and all of the relative technologies, let's take a step back and examine the evolution of server-side scripting languages that eventually led to the development of ASP.NET.

In the early 1990s, the World Wide Web emerged as the new place to do business. Companies scrambled to build Web sites as quickly as possible to capitalize on the growth of the Web. Webmasters created Web sites using only HTML — no JavaScript, no ASP, no FrontPage.

It didn't take long for people to realize that they needed more interactivity in order to create more than Web sites. A thirst developed in the programmer community for something new called a "Web application." In order for something to qualify as an application, it had to perform some kind of processing, solve some kind of business rule. The days of the static Web had already ended; a new, dynamic Web was upon us.

Common Gateway Interface

Common Gateway Interface, or CGI for short, is the foundation upon which all current server-side scripting is based. CGI is a standard for running external programs from an http-compliant Web server. An application runs on the server separate from the Web server process, and CGI specifies how arguments are passed as part of an http request to the running application. The only requirement for the program is that it must be able to accept command-line arguments.

CGI can generate HTML that will be passed down to the browser, and it can request URL redirection. CGI allows the returned HTML to be dependent on the request. In other words, a CGI program can access information in a database and return the results to the client as HTML. This kind of functionality has proven enormously useful. Using CGI, Web pages can request information from a database and return the data formatted as HTML.

CGI programs typically take one of two forms: a compiled application (typically written in C) or a script (typically written in Perl or Python). It's all a matter of semantics, so think of the terms *CGI program* and *CGI script* as meaning the same thing.

From CGI to ASP

**20 Min.
To Go**

When CGI became ubiquitous and the de facto standard for Web applications, the only real choice to be made was what language to use to write the CGI scripts. Because UNIX was the predominant operating system for servers (more so then than now), it made sense to use a tool already offered by UNIX. As you'll see in this section, UNIX tools only briefly remained the sole choice for creating Web applications.

Perl

Perl is an open source, high-level programming language originally developed by Larry Wall in the late 1980s. It is based on several different languages, especially C. Perl offers incredible support for regular expressions matching and string manipulation, whether text or binary.

Regular expressions matching allows you to search for a string with a string that matches a specified pattern.

Perl has a highly flexible syntax that can be simultaneously powerful and very perplexing, especially to the less experienced. It also has been heavily modified over the years to allow for the advances in Web technology. Still, very many Perl developers are satisfied with their language of choice — but many others consider Perl a "tacked on" language that has gone the way of the dinosaur.

Perl code is generally stored in text files that are compiled into virtual machine code at run-time. This means it is "interpreted." Perl scripts are typically very fast in execution but difficult to create in a short amount of time. Perl is also not very well-suited for joint application development environments, which proliferated in the client/server boom of the early 1990s.

This is a sample Perl program that handles form-to-e-mail, a popular feature on many Web sites. This code is here to show you how Perl programs look and to familiarize you with the humble beginnings of Web application development:

```
#!/user/bin/perl
my $config = {
templates => '/usr/local/apache/cgi-bin/mailform/templates',
from => 'user@domain.com'
};
use CGI_Lite;
use Mail::Sendmail;
use Text::Template;
use strict;

my ($cgi, $form, $fi, $message, $template, %mail);
```

```
$cgi = new CGI_Lite;
$form = $cgi->parse_form_data;
exit(0) if $form->{template}=~/\.\./;
foreach (keys %$form) {
    $form->{$_} = join ',',@{$form->{$_}} if ref $form->{$_};
}

$fi = new Text::Template ( TYPE => 'FILE',
SOURCE => $config->{templates}."/".$form->{template}.".email");

$message = $fi->fi( HASH=> [ $form ],
     DELIMITERS => ['<%','%>']
     );

$form->{email}||=$config->{from};

%mail = ( To      => $form->{to},
          From    => $form->{email},
          Subject => $form->{subject},
          Message => $message,
        );
sendmail(%mail);

print "Location: $form->{redirect}\n\n";
```

This program utilizes a template file to format an e-mail message and then send the message to a specified address. Study the code carefully and try to figure out what each line
does.

Although Perl was once the king of CGI when UNIX was more prevalent, its use has
declined over the years as developers have moved to Microsoft platforms.

NSAPI/ISAPI

Regardless of the language used, whenever the server receives a CGI execution request, it
creates a new process to run the external program. If the process fails to terminate, or if
requests are received faster than the server can handle them, the server may be overloaded
with processes and CGI requests.

To combat this major performance problem, Netscape created NSAPI and Microsoft created
ISAPI. These standards allow CGI-like tasks to run as part of the server process. This helps
avoid the overhead involved in creating a new process to handle each CGI request.

NSAPI stands for Netscape Server Application Programming Interface. ISAPI stands for
Internet Server Application Programming Interface. The technologies are very similar; however, I'll focus on ISAPI for simplicity's sake.

ISAPI scripts, or *filters* as they are commonly known, are typically written in the C language. They are compiled DLLs that are loaded in an Internet Information Server application.
Like CGI, ISAPI code can access all the information in the client request, and generate HTML
output.

Most of Microsoft's Web developments have existed in the ISAPI universe. Even ASP runs
as an ISAPI DLL (asp.dll). More on that later.

Internet Database Connector

Microsoft's first foray into simplifying Web application development, specifically database applications, was called dbWeb. Although it offered a good set of filtering, searching, and formatting capabilities for working with data on the server, it was horribly slow and inefficient. It came and went almost as fast as Microsoft Bob.

After dbWeb, Microsoft created the Internet Database Connector, or IDC. IDC was a boon to developers who wanted speed and control, as well as simplification of development. IDC offered a more generic approach using templates. The templates allowed developers to adapt existing HTML pages and build new applications.

Similar to Perl, IDC requires two files. The first file is a script that defines the data access, and the second is the template to populate with data. Unlike Perl, there is no actual programming to output specific information.

The configuration file has an .idc extension and basically contains connection information and a SQL script:

```
Datasource: YourSampleData
Username: sa
Password: sa
Template: showstates.htx
SQLStatement:
+ SELECT State_Name
+ FROM State
+ ORDER BY State_Name
```

The second file has an .htx extension and contains the HTML code for the formatting. It's an ordinary text file, and because it's HTML, it could contain JavaScript, ActiveX controls, and whatever else a developer would want to put in.

The .htx file is generated after the server executes the .idc file. The .htx code corresponding to the .idc example is:

```
<!—HTML code here -->
<TABLE>
<TR>
<TD>The Fifty States</TD>
<TD>
<SELECT NAME="States">
<%BeginDetail%>
<OPTION VALUE="<%State_Name%>"><%State_Name%>
<%End Detail%>
</SELECT>
</TD>
</TR>
</TABLE>
<!—rest of HTML here -->
```

If you are an ASP developer, you will probably notice some similarities. Microsoft took the concept of IDC and combined it with the concept of a scripting language, and ASP evolved from that.

Active Server Pages

**10 Min.
To Go**

In 1996, Microsoft released Active Server Pages 1.0. Going by the moniker ASP, it introduced thousands of Visual Basic developers to Web application development.

ASP is equivalent to CGI, ISAPI, and IDC all rolled into one, with some extras thrown in. Instead of existing as a single language, it was offered as a container with a set of exposed objects that could be used by VBScript or JScript. This helped introduce Visual Basic developers to ASP while preventing alienation of JavaScript programmers.

 ASP also supported PerlScript and CScript through third-party plug-ins.

With the ability to execute code inline and its support of COM objects, ASP was both simple and powerful. Add to that its support of ActiveX Data Objects (ADO), and it was almost too easy to create full-featured, powerful Web-based database applications.

ASP 1.0 was an add-on for IIS 3.0. With the ability to open recordsets and output the data however you wanted, ASP gained fast acceptance. ASP allowed the developer to display data in any order, at any time, in a Web page.

Microsoft released ASP 2.0 in 1998 as part of the Windows NT Option Pack. This new release changed the way external components could be instantiated. ASP 2.0 offered support for MTS and out-of-process components. ASP 2.0 applications could be run in their own separate memory space.

By 2000, ASP had grown to ASP 3.0 and IIS had become IIS 5.0. MTS gave way to COM+, which is MTS merged with the core COM runtime. ASP 3.0 and IIS 5.0 offered a robust environment for powerful Web applications.

An ASP page is a text file that contains script code, HTML, or both. Before we get too deep into the ins and outs of ASP, let's take a look at a sample ASP page. This page returns a recordset from a database and outputs HTML code:

```
<%@ LANGUAGE="VBScript" %>
<%
Dim oConn
Dim oRS
Dim sSQL

Set oConn = Server.CreateObject("ADODB.Connection")
Set oRS = Server.CreateObject("ADODB.Recordset")

sSQL = "SELECT ID, FirstName, LastName FROM Users WHERE " & _
       "ID = 1;"

oConn.Open "DSN=UserDB;USER=sa;PWD="

Set oRS = oConn.Execute(sSQL)
%>
<HTML>
<HEAD>
<TITLE>Sample Page</TITLE>
```

```
</HEAD>
<BODY>
  <TABLE>
   <TR>
    <TD>First Name</TD>
    <TD><%=oRS("FirstName")%></TD>
   </TR>
   <TR>
    <TD>Last Name</TD>
    <TD><%=oRS("LastName")%></TD>
   </TR>
  </TABLE>
</BODY>
</HTML>
<%
oRS.Close
Set oRS = Nothing
Set oConn = Nothing
%>
```

This code is a simple example of connecting to a database and retrieving a record using SQL. First, some variables are defined. Then two objects are instantiated — one for connecting to a database and the other for storing the results of a query. After the objects are instantiated, the script makes a connection and populates the recordset.

From that point, it's straight HTML until you get to the <% %> code block. The <% %> means I'm using inline ASP code. This inline ASP code allows the direct reference to existing code within an HTML page. That way, I don't need to write custom script to output HTML.

Finally, the recordset object is closed and the objects are destroyed. It's important to destroy object references to save memory (although that is a point argued to death all over the Internet).

The ASP objects

If you look at the sample code, you'll see the Server.CreateObject statement. This statement is what lets the developer instantiate external objects. The first part of the statement, Server, is called an intrinsic ASP object (the other part is called a method, and we'll take about methods later on). There are five commonly used intrinsic ASP objects: Server, Application, Session, Response, and Request. Each of these objects has a very specific function.

- **Server:** The Server object exposes access to the server running ASP. The most commonly used method of Server is CreateObject.

- **Application:** The Application object allows the developer to work with the application as a whole. For example, the developer can create an application variable that exists throughout the existence of an application. The existence of an application begins the first time a user visits an ASP page. There is only one instance of a given application variable. For example, if you create an application variable called "servername", referenced as Application("servername"), that variable exists throughout the application.

- **Session:** The Session object is very commonly used to maintain state from one page to the next. Using Session variables, a developer can persist data through a set of ASP pages. Unlike application variables, session variables exist on a per-user basis. For example, each user can have a session variable called "username", referenced as Session("username"). Session state is a very important part of ASP and one of the greatest enhancements in ASP.NET. (I cover session state a little later.)

- **Response:** The Response object allows an ASP page to write out data. Response is most often used with the Redirect method to send a user on to another page and the Write method to display data on a page. Response is also used with the Cookies object to send cookie data down to the client.

- **Request:** The Request object allows ASP to get data posted from the client. Request exposes the Form object, which allows an ASP page to get to form data. Request also exposes the Cookies object, which allows an ASP page to read information from a cookie. The third most common use of Request is the Querystring object, which allows an ASP page to read data from a URL.

These objects, combined with VBScript and external COM objects (such as ADO), provide a powerful programming environment.

There is a lot more to the intrinsic objects than what has been discussed here, but it's not necessary to cover all of that. You just need to know how ASP is different from VBScript, especially because the two are erroneously considered the same.

VBScript

VBScript, also called Visual Basic Script, is a lightweight scripting language based on Visual Basic. VBScript offers a lot of the same functions, statements, and other syntactical elements of its older brother, but it does not offer variable typing (more on that in a bit).

Although ASP is a container for script, and it exposes an object model to work with and a way to move from page to page, VBScript is the actual code you write to glue it all together. That's the difference between ASP and VBScript: ASP is a bucket into which you pour VBScript.

VBScript is not supported in ASP.NET. It has been replaced by Visual Basic.NET, which eliminates all the problems faced in VBScript. I discuss these limitations and problems later.

ADO

The last major piece of the ASP pie is ActiveX Data Objects, or ADO for short. ADO comprises the objects used to access and work with databases in ASP. These objects facilitate connecting to databases, retrieving data, updating data, deleting data, inserting data, executing stored procedures, and more.

ADO eliminates the hassle of low-level database work through ODBC. It provides an object model for safely and easily working with databases. ADO is a replacement for Data Access Objects (DAO), an ancient technology that was difficult to work with.

The ADO objects an ASP developer principally works with are Connection, Recordset, Command, Parameter, and Errors. Each of these objects has a very specific set of tasks it can perform, just like the intrinsic ASP objects:

- **Connection:** The Connection object is the first ADO object a developer uses, as it allows for the connection to a database. Without a connection to a database, nothing can happen (obviously!). The Connection object offers an Open method for opening a database, and an Execute method for tasks such as retrieving a recordset. Open and Execute are the most commonly used methods of the Connection object.

- **Recordset:** The Recordset object, along with the Connection object, is very heavily used in ADO programming. The Recordset object stores the results of any queries executed against the database. It exposes a plethora of properties and methods that allow a developer to do just about anything needed to deal with data. Recordset objects come in different flavors, including dynamic and forward-only.

- **Command:** A Command object is used to retrieve Recordset objects and, more commonly, to execute stored procedures. A Command object has a text property that lets the developer define the command text (the stored procedure name or SQL script).

- **Parameter:** The Parameter object is used along with the Command object in dealing with stored procedures. The Parameter object is used to store the input and output parameters of a stored procedure.

- **Errors:** The Errors object is a collection of errors reported by any of the ADO objects. This object is obviously helpful in debugging.

ADO is a very powerful tool and very important to ASP developers. Being familiar with what ADO is and how it fits in the ASP world is important, because ASP.NET works with a new version of ADO called ADO.NET.

Although knowledge of SQL is not absolutely necessary in order to use ADO, it is very highly recommended. ADO exposes a set of methods that will allow you to bypass SQL altogether

Done!

REVIEW

This chapter set out to describe the evolution of scripting languages culminating in ASP. CGI, Perl, and the Internet Data Connector were discussed as precursors to ASP. We moved on to a discussion of ASP and its history. We discussed how ASP works, then moved on to what makes up an ASP page. The intrinsic objects were discussed, then VBScript and its relation to ASP.NET. Finally, we covered ADO and its core objects. The discussion of ASP was designed to prepare you for discussion of ASP.NET, which we're steadily moving toward.

QUIZ YOURSELF

1. What is CGI? (See "Common Gateway Interface.")
2. What is the most popular CGI language? (See "From CGI to ASP.")
3. What does ISAPI stand for? (See "NSAPI/ISAPI.")
4. What is needed to use IDC? (See "Internet Database Connector.")
5. What are the major intrinsic objects in ASP? (See "The ASP objects.")

Programming Basics

Session Checklist

✔ Defining programming

✔ Exploring the differences between languages, compilers, and interpreters

✔ Understanding the software development lifecycle

✔ Learning how programs work

**30 Min.
To Go**

Now that you have learned *about* ASP.NET, it's time to start learning how to *do* ASP.NET. The first step is building a foundation, if you don't already have one. This session covers some programming concepts to prepare you for the sessions on VB.NET, which is used in all of the ASP.NET samples in this book. VB.NET is very easy to learn and use as long as you have the basics down. If you already know a programming language, you can safely skip this session and move on.

What Is a Program?

Although the term *program* is slightly outdated, it still represents any piece of software, whether a simple script or a complex application.

A computer program is a set of instructions for a computer to carry out. The instructions can be just about anything, whether it's keeping track of mileage on an automobile or monitoring the heart rate of a patient in a hospital. A computer follows this set of instructions precisely; it never makes a decision on its own to do something else.

Computer programs consist of two major parts: the source code and the executable (or interpretable, depending on the language used). Source code is written in a programming language, and then compiled into an executable program. The programming language can be part of an integrated development environment (IDE) such as Microsoft Visual C++, or just a command line compiler. Programming is a very flexible task; a programmer has many choices of operating systems, programming language, IDEs, editors, compilers, and libraries.

Programming languages

A programming language is the means by which a programmer issues a set of instructions to a computer. Programming languages take on many forms. They can use English words like *print* and *open,* and they can use human-unreadable text (Perl is famous for this).

There are thousands of programming languages to choose from. Some are popular, like Visual Basic, C++, Java, and C. Some are more academic, like Smalltalk and Modula. Others are designed for more specific tasks, like Ada (defense computing, avionics), Eiffel (software engineering), and FORTRAN (scientific computing). Alternative programming languages (such as Dylan, Mumps, and Modula) are considered alternative because they achieve the same results as a language such as C++ or Visual Basic but aren't in widespread use.

A subclass of programming languages is the scripting language. Scripting languages are useful for creating small programs that are controlled by another program. For example, Active Server Pages is a program running on a server (an ISAPI filter called asp.dll); the ASP ISAPI filter serves ASP pages that contain scripts. The ASP ISAPI filter processes these scripts, written in scripting languages. Scripting languages are often used to quickly create small programs that don't need to be compiled. They're text files processed by a scripting engine. Popular scripting languages include Python, Perl, and Tcl.

Compilers

A compiler translates source code into an executable program. The compiler is what provides the programmer with an easier way to create programs for a computer. If there were no compiler, the programmer would have to write programs in a language the machine can understand, aptly called *machine language.* Machine language is a series of numbers that are meaningless to most humans. Machine language looks like this:

```
368A
BADE
24A3
```

From looking at that, most people wouldn't be able to figure out that that code does something meaningful, like calculating 2 + 2. People are more comfortable with writing code in a programming language and letting the compiler do the hard part. Consider this code:

```
Print 2 + 2
```

Figuring out what this code does should be easy. The compiler will take this human-readable code and translate it into machine-readable code. The way it performs this task is not magic; it's actually a very simple design.

Let's say you're using Visual Basic. You have a source program written in the Visual Basic language and you are ready to turn it into a program. When you tell Visual Basic to make an executable, the Visual Basic program is taking your code and compiling it into an object. It then links the object with a runtime library and whatever else it needs and makes an executable.

In the true sense of the word, a compiler only performs one task in the process of making an executable from source. However, using the word *compiler* to represent the tool performing all the work has become acceptable.

After Visual Basic has compiled and linked your code, an executable is created. This executable is entirely different from the original source code in format, but it achieves the desired results, assuming no bugs have been introduced.

Interpreter

An interpreter is different from a compiler in that the interpreter program processes the source code line by line, and does not generate a machine-language executable. Interpreted languages, such as LISP and most scripting languages, are popular for their portability and ease of use.

An interpreter translates a high-level language (meaning, a human-readable language) into an intermediate form. The interpreter then executes this intermediate form. This is how the .NET Common Language Runtime works.

Compiled programs typically run faster than interpreted programs; however, an interpreted language does not need to go through compilation to be executable. This is an advantage for the interpreter because the compilation process can be time-consuming if the program is long. The interpreter can immediately execute any program, regardless of its length.

Interpreters are popular for prototyping applications, and they're often used in education, because they allow students to get up and running very quickly. The best part of an interpreter is that it can allow for language independence.

> To remember the difference between compilers and interpreters, think of those people you see on TV translating foreign languages in interviews. They are translating each sentence as it is said. That's an interpreter. When a translator translates an entire book for a foreign market, that's a compiler.

The Programming Process

The process of programming naturally follows a cycle. This cycle can be implied, or it can be specified. An *implied programming cycle* is one that follows common sense; you must write code before you can test, you must test before you deploy. The other type of programming cycle is called a methodology. A *methodology* is a more formal approach to software development. When you are creating ASP.NET pages, you must decide for yourself which approach you want to take. When creating ASP.NET applications, such as a billing application or content management system, adopting a formal methodology is highly advisable.

Software development lifecycle

The software development lifecycle (SDLC) is the concept behind creating sound software applications. It defines a set of steps to take to develop software. The SDLC extends from the most basic of scripts all the way to the most complex software applications.

The software development lifecycle consists of eight steps. Each of these steps maintains its own importance within the cycle. If a step is skipped, its absence affects the other parts of the project. For instance, if testing is skipped, then buggy software will be deployed to production.

Requirements analysis

The Requirements Analysis phase of the SDLC emphasizes the requirements of a particular piece of software. The Requirements Analysis asks the questions for the software; it presents the problem the software will be designed to fix. Requirements Analysis exposes all the details of the business problem and is used as the blueprint upon which the design is based. User input is imperative in this phase.

Design

After the requirements have been gathered, the developer forms the basis of the software in the form of a design. A design can be a model, a prototype, or a bunch of screenshots. User input is highly recommended in this phase.

Specification

The specification, or *spec* as it's commonly known, is the true blueprint of the software system. It represents everything that has been accomplished in the previous two phases of the SDLC. A solid specification has many advantages, including:

- It allows the client and the developer to agree on exactly what will be delivered in the application.
- It provides accurate cost budgeting and delivery schedules.
- It demonstrates the developer's understanding of the project's requirements and design.
- It addresses technical issues at the beginning of the development process.

The specification will require the most amount of work prior to the coding process.

Development

After the requirements have been gathered, the application has been designed, and a spec is in place, coding can commence. The development phase of the SDLC is typically the longest. It encompasses all aspects of actual coding, including code documentation and immediate debugging.

Testing

When development is complete, testing can begin. The testing phase in the SDLC represents the alpha...beta approach. Testing done in-house is called alpha testing. After a somewhat stable release is ready, it enters beta testing, which is performed by the client or some other outside party. Alpha testing is done primarily to discover bugs; beta testing is to work out the kinks.

Production

After everything has been coded and tested, and after it meets the requirements, the software project is rolled out.

Maintenance

The maintenance phase begins as soon as the deployment to production occurs. Maintenance encompasses post-production bug fixes, routine upgrades, and refurbishment. Performance upgrades are often part of maintenance.

Enhancement and evolution

After the system has been installed, users will invariably find new ways to enhance it. Interface changes and new functionality are typically the most requested enhancements. Software needs to evolve as users' needs evolve.

The SDLC is a sound approach to developing software. While you are creating ASP.NET pages and applications, keep this iterative process in mind. If you are more of a by-the-book type, then software engineering may be right for you.

**20 Min.
To Go**

Software engineering

Software engineering is a more involved type of software development, but some of its concepts can prove very useful to even the newest of programmers. Software engineering is the application of engineering concepts to the development of software. Software engineering goes beyond programming; it encompasses all aspects of creating a software project, including resource management, versioning, and modeling.

Software engineering takes the software development lifecycle and extends it through the use of methodologies. Methodologies are defined approaches to software engineering. Rational Software, a vendor of tools to aid in software engineering, defines a methodology called the Rational Unified Process. The parts of the Rational Unified Process are:

- Requirements
- Analysis and Design
- Business Modeling
- Implementation
- Test
- Deployment
- Configuration and Change Management

If you compare this to the standard SDLC, you'll see some major similarities. Rational has taken the SDLC and extended to a process that takes advantage of their software. The Rational Unified Process includes a part called Business Modeling. This is not defined explicitly in the SDLC; Rational added this step because they are firm believers in the idea that software modeling adds value to software development.

Software engineering is definitely an advanced topic. Don't worry if you don't understand the methodologies and processes. The discussion is presented here to let you know it exists; it's not a requirement for creating ASP.NET pages.

How Programs Work

For as long as programs have been created, they have worked a certain way. Programs have almost always been made up of three things:

- Variables and constants
- Loops
- Conditionals

These are considered to be part of a programming language's syntax. Programs can have much more than these three building blocks, including objects, methods, properties, events, user-defined types, collections, and so on.

Variables

Any information your program must store is put into a *variable*. A variable is a section of memory designated by the compiler (at compile time) to store whatever data you want to store in it. A variable can store whatever you want. Input from a user, a calculation, or a list of IQ scores — these are all candidates for storage in a variable.

Every variable has a name and a type. The name is the designation for the variable, and the type is the kind of data the variable will store. Types let the compiler know how much memory to allocate for your variable. Each compiler offers its own types and type syntax.

A constant is a variable whose value doesn't change.

Types

A language that supports types is called *strongly-typed*. Strongly-typed languages, such as VB.NET, have advantages over non-typed languages, like VBScript. Declaring a variable type is the first way to harness performance gains in an application; with no variable type declared, all variables default to a variant type. When a variable is declared as a specific type, the compiler determines memory allocation for the variable based on that type. For example, the Boolean type is two bytes; when you declare a variable of type Boolean, the compiler knows to set aside two bytes of memory for that variable.

Because VB.NET is a strongly-typed language, the Visual Studio.NET environment keeps track of your variable usage when you are creating VB.NET programs (or writing VB.NET code in an ASP.NET page). The Visual Studio.NET environment will catch incorrect type usage (for example, putting text in a numeric data type).

VB.NET supports 13 different variable types:

- **Boolean:** Boolean stores a 2-byte value representing True or False.
- **Byte:** Byte stores a 1-byte value ranging from 0 to 255.
- **Char:** Char stores a 2-byte value ranging from 0 to 65535.

- **Date:** Date can hold an 8-byte date ranging from January 1, 1 Common Era to December 31, 9999.

- **Decimal:** Decimal can hold a 16-byte value ranging from +/- 79,228,162,514,264,337,593,543,950,335 with no decimal point.

- **Double:** Double (double precision floating point) is an 8-byte value capable of storing values from −1.79769313486231E308 to −4.94065645841247E-324 for negative values, and 4.94065645841247E-324 to 1.79769313486231E308 for positive values. (Those are some big numbers.)

- **Integer:** An integer is a 4-byte value capable of storing −2,147,483,648 to 2,147,483,647.

- **Long:** A long (long integer) is an 8-byte value that can store a value ranging from −9,223,372,036,854,775,808 to 9,223,372,036,854,775,807.

- **Object:** An object is a 4-byte value that stores any type that can be stored in a variable of the object type.

- **Short:** Short is a 2-byte value storing values from −32,768 to 32,767.

- **Single:** Single is a 4 byte value storing 03.402823E38 to −1.401298E-45 for negative values, and 1.401298E-45 to 3.402823E38 for positive values.

- **String:** A string can contain 0 to approximately 2 billion Unicode characters. A string variable is used to contain text. A string variable is 10 bytes + 2*string length.

- **User-Defined Type:** A user-defined type size is the sum of the sizes of its members. It can contain any of the other variable types.

Variables of these types can usually be converted from one type to another using one of VB.NET's built-in functions. Changing a variable's type after it has been populated is called *casting* the variable.

These variable types will be explained in further detail as you use them in later sessions. Don't worry about trying to memorize all the maximum values. Deciding which variable type to use comes from experience.

10 Min.
To Go

Loops

As you write programs, you will discover that you need some kind of repetition. You may wish to loop through a list of names, for example.

For...Next

For...Next lets you loop through a specified number of items. The For...Next loop is the most commonly used loop. Between the For and Next are the instructions that are repeated.

```
For n = 1 to 8
i = i + 1
Next n
```

In this example, n is the counter variable. The loop will run 8 times, starting at one and ending at 8. Through each iteration of the loop, i will increment by 1.

Do...Loop

Do...Loop is more flexible than For...Next. Do...Loop repeats a block of statements while a condition is True, or until a condition becomes True.

There are four ways to use Do...Loop: Do While...Loop, Do Until...Loop, Do...Loop While, and Do...Loop Until.

Do While...Loop

Do While...Loop evaluates the condition before it enters the loop. If the condition evaluates as False, the loop isn't executed.

```
Do While x < 4
...
Loop
```

Do Until...Loop

Do Until...Loop does the exact same thing as Do While...Loop, but expresses it differently. Consider this code:

```
Do Until x = 4
...
Loop
```

You can consider it one of those "glass is half empty, glass is half full" kind of things.

Do...Loop While

Do...Loop While puts the comparison at the end of the loop. That means that the loop will always execute at least once.

```
Do
    i = i + 1
Loop While i < 4
```

The loop will execute at least once.

Do...Loop Until

Do...Loop Until is the same as Do...Loop While, just expressed differently. Refer to Do Until...Loop for an example.

Don't let yourself create endless loops. Always make sure your loop will have some kind of out; check to make sure that its condition will evaluate. Endless loops use up a lot of resources and are very frustrating.

Conditionals

There is often a need to compare values when programming. To do this, you use a conditional. The two most popular conditionals are If...Then and Select...Case.

If...Then

If...Then takes a condition and evaluates it. It's best explained by example:

```
If y < 4 Then
    MsgBox "Success!"
End If
```

This code says, "If y is less than 4, then execute a message box statement." You can add to it by adding an else:

```
If y < 4 Then
    MsgBox "Success!"
Else
    MsgBox "Failure!"
End If
```

This code says, "If y is less than 4, then execute a message box statement that indicates success. Otherwise, message box a failure statement."

An If...Then...Else statement can be very useful when evaluating user input. The only disadvantage to using If...Then is the proliferation of spaghetti code, which is code that is very hard to read and debug. Nested If...Then statements, which are If...Then statements that contain If...Then statements, can be very difficult to traverse. Try a good indentation scheme to offset your If...Then statements.

Select...Case

Select...Case functions much the same way as If...Then, but they can take several conditions in one statement:

```
Select Case IQ
Case 100
    MsgBox "You have an average IQ."

Case 140
    MsgBox "You're a genius!"

Case Else
    MsgBox "I don't know how to tell you this..."
End Select
```

As you can see, the Select statement takes a conditional (IQ) and evaluates it. It checks it against each Case; when a match occurs, it carries out the statement for that case. If no match is found, it defaults to Case Else.

Select...Case can be a very useful tool when evaluating several potential values of a variable. I use it most often in error handling, where I have an error number in a variable and I want to display custom messages for each error.

Done!

REVIEW

In this chapter, you learned about programming. You learned what a program is and how programs are created. You learned about programming languages, compilers, and interpreters. We then moved on to the programming process, covering the software development lifecycle and software engineering practices. We jumped into how programs work, covering variables and constants, loops, and conditionals. In the next few sessions, you will learn more about VB.NET and how to write code using it.

QUIZ YOURSELF

1. What is a programming language? (See "Programming languages.")
2. What does a compiler do? (See "Compilers.")
3. What is the point of the software development life cycle? (See "Software development lifecycle.")
4. What's the difference between a variable and a constant? (See "Variables.")
5. What is an endless loop and why is it bad? (See "Loops.")

Setting Up ASP.NET

Session Checklist

✔ Installing ASP.NET Premium

✔ Configuring your Web server for ASP.NET

**30 Min.
To Go**

S o far, you've learned about what .NET is and how ASP.NET works into it. At this point, you're probably anxious to start coding. Before you can do that, you have to set up your ASP.NET development environment.

Remember that ASP.NET pages don't run in your browser like an HTML page. Instead, they're executed on the server and the results are sent to the client. So that means you have to install ASP.NET on a machine capable of serving pages to client browsers.

System Requirements

ASP.NET Premium Edition contains everything you need to build, deploy, and run ASP.NET applications. It includes the .NET Framework, containing the Common Language Runtime, .NET Framework class libraries, ADO.NET, a command-line VB.NET compiler, a command-line C# compiler, a command-line JScript.NET compiler, and core ASP.NET support.

ASP.NET Premium Edition runs on Windows 98, Windows NT 4.0, Windows Millennium Edition, Windows 2000, and Windows XP. A Microsoft Web server is required. Suitable Microsoft Web servers are Personal Web Server and Internet Information Services (IIS), version 4.0 or above. To install IIS on Windows NT, you'll need the Windows NT Option Pack from Microsoft. IIS 5.0 is typically installed by default on Windows 2000, but you will need to confirm its presence (and install it if necessary). In the Add/Remove Programs control panel, click Add/Remove Windows Components. You should see a window that looks like Figure 4-1.

Make sure the checkbox next to Internet Information Services (IIS) is checked. If it isn't, click the box to make it checked and then click Next to continue the installation of IIS. If it is checked, click Cancel; you already have IIS installed. After IIS is installed, or confirmed to be installed, you can move forward with the installation of ASP.NET Premium Edition.

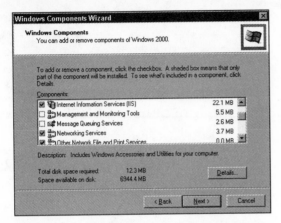

Figure 4-1 *Add/Remove Windows Components*

Personal Web Server is available on the Windows 98 and Windows Me CD-ROMs.

You'll also need Microsoft Internet Explorer 5.0 or better, and Microsoft Data Access Components (MDAC) 2.6 or better.

*20 Min.
To Go*

Installing ASP.NET Premium Edition

Now that you have your Web server up and running, you're ready to install ASP.NET and the rest of the .NET Framework.

ASP.NET Premium Edition is available for download from `http://msdn.microsoft.com` as a 17.8 megabyte file. ASP.NET is also available with the Visual Studio.NET distribution, but this chapter assumes you are installing ASP.NET Premium Edition. If you have the Visual Studio.NET distribution, run its setup program, and ASP.NET will be installed.

After you download the ASP.NET Premium Edition distribution from Microsoft, browse to the folder you chose during the download process. Double-click the setup.exe file, and you will see the first ASP.NET Premium Edition setup screen (see Figure 4-2).

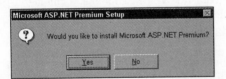

Figure 4-2 *ASP.NET Premium Edition Setup*

Click Yes, and ASP.NET Premium Edition will commence by copying the setup files to your hard drive (see Figure 4-3).

Figure 4-3   *Setup files are copied.*

When the initial copying of setup files is complete, one of two things will happen. Depending on your operating system's configuration, you may be prompted to install the updated Windows Installer components (see Figure 4-4). If you already have the updated Windows Installer components, you'll see the second ASP.NET Premium Edition Setup screen (see Figure 4-5). If you see what's shown in Figure 4-4, click Yes to install the updated Windows Installer components.

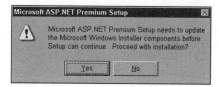

Figure 4-4   *Update Windows Installer Components*

After this is complete, the second ASP.NET Premium Edition screen (see Figure 4-5) appears.

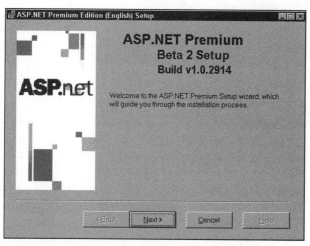

Figure 4-5   *ASP.NET Premium Edition Setup*

The second ASP.NET Premium Edition Setup screen shows what version of ASP.NET you are installing. In my case (refer to Figure 4-5), I'm installing beta 2, build v1.0.2914. When you install ASP.NET, you may see something completely different as the product goes through different versions.

10 Min.
To Go

Click Next to proceed. You'll be prompted with the License Agreement screen (see Figure 4-6).

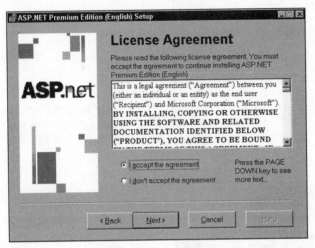

Figure 4-6   *ASP.NET Premium Edition license agreement*

Click the radio button next to "I accept the agreement" to make it active, and then click Next. You are then prompted to choose a destination folder for the ASP.NET Premium Edition distribution (see Figure 4-7).

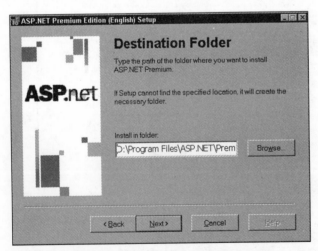

Figure 4-7   *Choose a destination folder.*

You can accept the default or specify a folder for the ASP.NET Premium Edition installation. When you have chosen your destination folder, click Next. The setup program will then install the ASP.NET Premium Edition components (see Figure 4-8 and Figure 4-9).

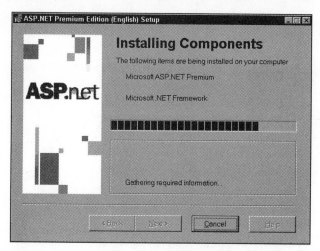

Figure 4-8   *Preparing to install components*

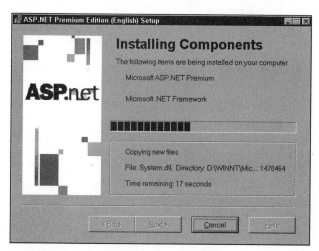

Figure 4-9   *Setup installs the components.*

When setup has finished copying files, it indicates completion with a notice, as shown in Figure 4-10.

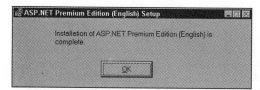

Figure 4-10   *Setup is complete.*

Click OK. Now all you have to do is restart your computer (see Figure 4-11) by clicking Yes, and ASP.NET Premium Edition is installed.

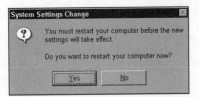

Figure 4-11 *Restart Windows after installation.*

Configuring Your Web Server for ASP.NET

You don't have to do anything! ASP.NET is all set up and ready to go.

Done!

REVIEW

In this chapter, you installed software you need to run ASP.NET. Specifically, you:

- Installed ASP.NET Premium Edition
- Configured ASP.NET by doing nothing

Your environment is ready to go. Onward to the next chapter!

QUIZ YOURSELF

1. Where do ASP.NET pages execute? (See the chapter opening.)
2. What versions of Windows support ASP.NET Premium Edition? (See "System Requirements.")
3. What are suitable Web servers for ASP.NET? (See "System Requirements.")
4. Do you need to install the Visual Studio.NET beta to use ASP.NET? (See "Installing ASP.NET Premium Edition.")
5. What do you need to do to configure your Web server for ASP.NET after ASP.NET Premium Edition is installed? (See "Configuring Your Web Server for ASP.NET.")

PART

I

Friday Evening
Part Review

1. In one sentence, what is the .NET Framework?
2. What "two worlds" does the .NET Framework bring together?
3. What is the distinction of the .NET Framework from .NET as a whole?
4. Name a simple example of software as a service.
5. Does ASP.NET replace ASP?
6. What qualification must something meet to be termed a Web application?
7. What are Perl's main strengths?
8. What is the difference between NSAPI and ISAPI?
9. What does an ASP text file contain?
10. What do the ASP Request and Response objects do?
11. What is a computer program?
12. Name some popular programming languages.
13. Describe the difference between compilers and interpreters.
14. How many steps are in the Software Development Lifecycle?
15. What can Select...Case do that If...Then can't?
16. Do ASP.NET pages run in a browser like an HTML page?
17. What platforms support the .NET Framework?
18. What do you have to do to configure your Web server for ASP.NET?

☑ Friday

☑ **Saturday**

☐ Sunday

Part II — Saturday Morning

Session 5
Working with the .NET Framework

Session 6
Choosing a .NET Language

Session 7
Understanding XML

Session 8
Programming with Visual Basic .NET

Session 9
Building the Guts of a Program

Session 10
Working with Objects

Part III — Saturday Afternoon

Session 11
ASP.NET versus ASP

Session 12
Introducing ASP.NET

Session 13
Using Namespaces and Classes

Session 14
Building ASP.NET Applications

Session 15
Managing Session State

Session 16
Building Your First ASP.NET Page

Part IV — Saturday Evening

Session 17
Introducing Web Forms

Session 18
Working with Controls

Session 19
Validating User Input

Session 20
Building a Web Form

PART

II

Saturday
Morning

Session 5
Working with the .NET Framework

Session 6
Choosing a .NET Language

Session 7
Understanding XML

Session 8
Programming with Visual Basic .NET

Session 9
Building the Guts of a Program

Session 10
Working with Objects

Working with the .NET Framework

✔ Learning about features of the .NET Framework

✔ Understanding the Common Language Runtime

**30 Min.
To Go**

S o far, you've learned that Microsoft has created something called .NET, and it's supposed to help solve all kinds of different problems. You've also learned about the genesis of scripting languages and how ASP.NET fits in. Now you're ready to get into the
meat and potatoes of the .NET Framework, which is the technology that makes all the .NET
greatness possible, including ASP.NET.

The .NET Framework

The .NET Framework is a set of tools, programming libraries, and applications to facilitate
application development under the banner of Windows DNA. It simplifies development of
distributed applications.

The .NET Framework is component-based; it's made up of a bunch of different parts, each
reusable and interoperable. The Framework can provide a set of services that are built-in and
accessible by your applications. These include

- Simplified application development
- A rich set of programming libraries
- Side-by-side execution with existing applications
- Increased scalability for distributed applications
- A multi-language runtime engine

When you install the .NET Framework, you're getting several different things, including
ASP.NET and all the files it needs to work. Although ASP.NET is a big part of the .NET
Framework, the .NET Framework doesn't exist solely for ASP.NET. The .NET Framework acts as
a base for all kinds of applications built on the Windows platform. Figure 5-1 illustrates how
the .NET Framework provides for ASP.NET applications.

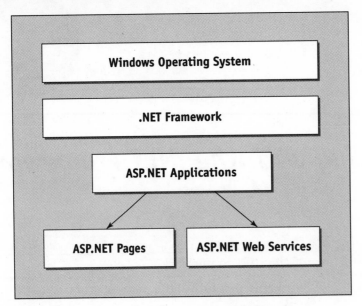

Figure 5-1 *.NET Framework provides ASP.NET services.*

The Windows operating system is the base for all application services. The .NET Framework runs under the Windows operating system; it provides a host for ASP.NET applications.

Simplified application development

The .NET Framework acts as an interface between applications and the Windows operating system. This ensures a consistent approach to software development by ensuring that applications use the operating system in a standard way.

The .NET Framework facilitates ease of development by encapsulating key features that the programmer or the programming environment had to provide. Things like reusable objects, garbage collection, and application security are all provided by the .NET Framework so the programmer doesn't have to implement it in a specific way.

A rich set of programming libraries

The .NET Framework offers a set of programming libraries, or classes, that can be used to build applications that work within the Framework. These classes facilitate code reuse and provide a standardized environment for developing applications across different languages. The classes provide the key functionality of the .NET Framework from a programming standpoint; they are covered in more detail in Chapter 12.

Side-by-side execution with existing applications

Applications coded against the .NET Framework can run side-by-side with existing Windows and Web applications. If your Web server is configured to serve ASP pages, and you install the .NET Framework, your server will be able to serve ASP and ASP.NET at the same time.

ASP pages have a the filename extensions .asp and .asa, and ASP.NET pages have the filename extensions .aspx and .asax. As long as you keep these file-names intact, your server will not have a problem knowing the difference between the two.

Increased scalability for distributed applications

As your Web site grows in usage, it must be able to scale to allow the larger number of users and concurrent requests to be handled without returning a bunch of "Server Too Busy" messages. The .NET Framework runtime detects errors and overloads and responds by restarting and managing the applications that are in use at the time. This prevents memory leaks from bringing the server to a screeching halt.

**20 Min.
To Go**

What Is the Common Language Runtime?

One of the most exciting parts of .NET is the Common Language Runtime (CLR). The CLR facilitates ease of programming within the .NET Framework. Whereas ASP was severely limited in language choices for development, ASP.NET supports three different languages, with the possibility for many more. This is possible through the CLR.

The Common Language Runtime is a .NET component that provides language interoperability and simplified development within the .NET environment. The CLR aims to solve several problems that have plagued developers for many years, such as versioning conflict (also known as DLL Hell).

Common language specification

Microsoft produced the Common Language Specification (CLS), which defines how compilers can work with .NET. Microsoft made the CLS freely available to vendors producing compilers, and the vendors can use the specification to design compilers that plug in to the .NET architecture. These compilers can produce a binary piece of code adhering to a standardized format set forth in the CLS.

With several different compilers to choose from, a developer simply selects a .NET language and writes code. The code is compiled into an executable and then shared with other developers using .NET languages.

Language interoperability

Language interoperability simplifies development. With language interoperability, developers can write code in one language that easily accesses code in another language. In addition to that, the .NET Framework's built-in classes are accessible to all languages that support the CLR. This means that they are all using the same types and can access data in a consistent way.

As of this writing, the CLR supports approximately 30 different languages, including Visual Basic (called VB.NET), JScript (known as JScript.NET), and C++. If you were to look at that list of supported languages, you would probably notice the absence of Java. Instead of supporting Java, Microsoft has opted to create C#, a new language that features the power of C++, the elegance of Java, and the simplicity of Visual Basic.

Since C# is a brand-new language, it doesn't have the baggage that existing languages suffer from. There is no need for backward-compatibility in C#. Thus, it is lean, object-oriented, and Web-enabled.

 C# is under review by the European Computer Manufacturers' Association (ECMA) for standardization. After it is standardized, vendors will be able to develop C# compilers for their own platforms, such as Linux and Mac OS X. This means that if you choose to use C# as your .NET language there's a good chance you can use it on other platforms later, if you so choose.

C# is covered more in the next chapter.

How the CLR Works

Briefly, the CLR works like this: Source code is compiled to intermediate language (IL) and metadata is created using the metadata engine. The IL and metadata are optionally linked with other code compiled by different compilers and the result is an executable program or library containing the IL code, which exists as a file saved on disk.

When executed, the IL code and any functionality derived from the .NET base class library are combined using the class loader. The combined code is then tested for type safety by the verifier before just-in-time compilation. The just-in-time compiler processes the IL and produces native managed code that is passed on to the .NET runtime.

This process is represented in Figure 5-2.

Managed code

Code developed with a compiler that targets the CLR is called *managed code*. Managed code benefits from the features of the CLR, including cross-language integration, enhanced security, versioning and deployment support, cross-language exception handling, debugging and profiling services, and a simplified model for component interaction.

CLR-enabled compilers provide information that describes the types, references, and members in .NET code. This is called *metadata*. This metadata is stored along with the code. Every common language runtime application contains metadata. The CLR uses this metadata to load classes, execute methods, handle memory, generate native code, and manage security.

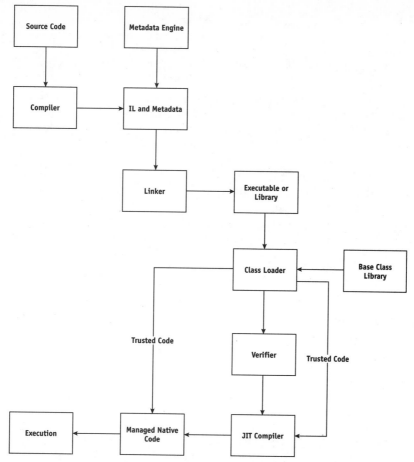

Figure 5-2 *The .NET CLR compilation process*

No dependence on individual runtimes

Visual Basic programs have always required a special runtime in order to function. This runtime existed as a DLL that contained core features needed by all Visual Basic programs. Other languages, such as Visual C++, also need special runtimes deployed with the executable program. When the executable program runs, it dynamically links to the runtime and accesses the functions it needs.

This dependence on a runtime has been a pain for developers. The biggest drawback is the added "weight" of the runtime. For example, the Visual Basic runtime is over one megabyte in size. Although 1 megabyte may not seem like a lot, it does make a difference in machines that don't have a lot of RAM.

The CLR eliminates the use of language-specific runtimes by storing programs in a common format and compiling it to machine code on an as-needed basis. As this machine code executes, the CLR monitors the execution to ensure that no unauthorized actions and memory leaks occur.

Garbage collection

The CLR also handles the allocation and de-allocation of memory resources, removing this responsibility from the individual language (and thus, the developer). This is called *garbage collection*. If no garbage collection were present, failed objects would remain in memory and cause memory leaks.

Memory leaks can grow over time and eventually use up the entire RAM on a system, causing the system to crash. Memory leaks can be difficult to tackle from a support perspective, because the crashes can easily be intermittent. Applications that run continuously, like on a server, can run for weeks or months before they use up all the server's memory, and then mysteriously crash.

The CLR's garbage collection eliminates memory leaks by managing object lifetimes. The garbage collector periodically checks the heap (a section of memory) for objects with no references and frees up the memory occupied by these objects.

The garbage collector determines whether objects in memory can be accessed by an application; if the object is out of reach by the application code, the garbage collector considers it as garbage (hence the name) and throws it out. Both Visual Basic.NET and C# implicitly use garbage collection, whereas C++ forces the developer to use the garbage-collection object.

Unmanaged and unsafe code

Managed data encompasses objects that are managed by the CLR environment. If code is managed, it can exist as managed data. Developers have the option of using unmanaged data, or managed data, or a combination of both.

Unmanaged code is native code that does not execute under the runtime, such as an application written in Visual Basic 6 or Delphi. Unmanaged code does not benefit from the features of the runtime.

In C#, all code is managed, but a developer can mark blocks of C# code as unsafe. Unsafe code is code that sidesteps the C# type-checking system and enables the developer to use some C++ activities such as pointer manipulation.

 Although C# code can be marked as unsafe, it is still managed code. C# code cannot be unmanaged, because it is a native .NET language.

The CLR acts as a middle layer between .NET programs and the operating system. This allows it to run applications in a protected environment, similar to Java's "sandbox" model. Programs cannot perform potentially hazardous actions like deleting files or accessing ports directly without a trust. A trust is defined by the system administrator. This level of protection allows the administrator to determine application capability on a case-by-case basis.

Intermediate Language

If you recall from Chapter 3, the process of compiling a program starts with feeding the source code to the compiler, which turns the source code into computer-readable machine code. The basic definition of compilation is the transformation of high-level, human-readable source code into low-level, computer-readable machine code.

Compilation can also refer to source code that is transformed from one language (the transformer) to another language (the transformed). The transformed code can even be interpreted, with the interpreted code executed by the microprocessor. This idea is the basis behind how the CLR works at compile-time. .NET code is compiled twice, and Intermediate Language (IL) is how it works. The IL is a middle step in the compilation process.

.NET compilation process

The first step of compilation occurs when the developer tells Visual Studio.NET to build the program. Whether it's managed C++, C#, or VB.NET, Visual Studio.NET takes the source code and compiles it into IL, rather than machine code. The IL code is saved to disk and accessible as a file.

After the IL is created, it "waits" until it is executed as a .NET program. When the .NET program is executed, the CLR loads the IL and dynamically transforms it into machine code understandable by the computer's processor. This is handled by the "just-in-time compiler."

This second step is what makes the .NET runtime an interpreter, and it's the backbone behind language interoperability. IL is the same regardless of which language the source code was created in, as long as the source code language is a .NET language (like C# or any of the other 30 .NET languages). The IL is not a compiler in itself; it's a piece of code formatted a certain way so it's understandable by the just-in-time compiler.

 Remember that the original compiler, the program that turns your source into IL, can be any compiler supported by .NET. It doesn't have to be Visual Studio.NET or even a Microsoft product. For example, Fujitsu has a COBOL.NET compiler product currently in the works.

Platform independence

One of the most exciting possibilities opened by IL and the CLR is the idea of platform-independence. Because all the .NET compilers create IL based on source, and the IL is compiled at runtime into machine code by a just-in-time compiler, it's possible for other operating systems to support their own just-in-time compilers. This means that operating systems like Mac OS X could support .NET, running on the PowerPC G4 processor. The same IL file could be interpreted on any operating system that has a suitable runtime.

Microsoft has announced plans for Linux.NET, a version of .NET that runs on the Linux operating system. Linux.NET will allow developers who create applications on the Linux platform to use .NET, and thus port their .NET applications between Linux and Windows. Unfortunately, there are no current plans to port ASP.NET to the Linux platform, but it's not outside the realm of possibility.

Just-In-Time compilers

A just-in-time compiler (JITter) is the program that transforms IL into machine code. Without a JITter, the program has no path to machine code; it will only exist as IL.

10 Min.
To Go

.NET ships with two JITters, Standard JIT and EconoJIT. These two JITters differ in compilation speed, execution speed, and memory management. They are designed to meet different needs.

Standard JIT

The Standard JIT is the default JITter in .NET. StandardJIT produces highly optimized machine code, as it is needed; it also caches the code in case it needs to access it again. The Standard JIT operates like a "normal" compiler; it analyzes, compiles, and caches the code as soon as an IL method or function is invoked.

 When referring to the Standard JIT, it is customary to just say JIT; people who know .NET will know what you mean.

The compilation of IL into native code by JIT tends to be slow. However, the native code produced is extremely fast. One of the ways to alleviate the slowness of the Standard JIT is by using a machine with a lot of RAM; the more RAM in the machine, the more code that can be cached. Cached code does not need to be compiled again. However, on a machine without a lot of RAM, the JIT will have to run every time the .NET program is executed.

Although it is a pain, the slowness of the JIT isn't caused by an intrinsic flaw. The JIT is slow because it is precise and exact; it never fails to create the desired or intended result of the IL code, and the resulting native code is both efficient and optimal.

EconoJIT

EconoJIT is the other JITter included with .NET. It's designed for small systems that don't have a lot of RAM. Unlike the Standard JIT, EconoJIT creates code that is efficient but not optimal. Because EconoJIT does not need to perform optimizations as it compiles IL code, the compilation process is faster. Because low-RAM machines don't have the room for cached code, EconoJIT comes to their rescue and creates code very quickly, but at the price of optimal quality.

Done!

REVIEW

This chapter covered a lot of material, and most of it was very technical. Don't worry if you didn't get it all; as you code ASP.NET pages you will gain practical experience working with the CLR and all the technical stuff will start to make sense.

In this chapter, we covered:

- What the .NET Framework is and what it offers to developers, including simplified development and ease of management.
- What the Common Language Runtime is and what advantages it offers, including language operability.
- How the Common Language Runtime works from both a high- and low-level approach. This discussion included managed and unmanaged code, unsafe code, intermediate language, and the just-in-time compilers.

The next chapter takes a hard look at two .NET languages, Visual Basic.NET and C#.

QUIZ YOURSELF

---

1. What makes up the .NET Framework? (See "The .NET Framework.")
2. What are the five main offerings of the .NET Framework? (See "The .NET Framework.")
3. What's the difference between managed and unmanaged code? (See "How the CLR Works.")
4. What is unsafe code? (See "Unmanaged and unsafe code.")
5. What is the process of compilation for a .NET program? (See ".NET compilation process.")

Choosing a .NET Language

Session Checklist

✔ Exploring different programming languages

✔ Understanding the features of some common languages

✔ Learning about the built-in .NET languages

30 Min. To Go

By now, you should have a solid understanding of what .NET is, how it works, where it came from, and why it's here. Now you're ready to get started coding, so all you have to do is pick a language. This chapter introduces you to several .NET languages and then covers in detail one brand-new language and one other language that has undergone a huge transformation.

Why Choose?

If you come from a Visual Basic/VBScript background, you may be saying to yourself, "What do you mean, choosing a .NET language? The choice is obvious!" The choice may seem patently obvious from the outside looking in, but you must remember that .NET opens up your programming model to several dozen other languages, and it may behoove you to make a switch.

As of this writing, there are somewhere in the neighborhood of 30 different languages supported by .NET. These languages range from the popular, such as C++, Visual Basic, and Perl, to the relatively unknown, including Objective CAML and Eiffel. To some people, this language support seems downright silly. Why offer so many different languages when everything you want to do can be handled by one of the four "built-in" .NET languages — C++, C#, VB.NET, or JScript.NET?

The answer becomes clear as you examine the features of these other languages. These languages offer specialized, improved support of such things as

- String parsing
- Software engineering

- Numerical processing
- Financial calculations

Compare the language choices to a toolbox in an automotive garage. A toolbox is filled with all kinds of different wrenches. Each of these wrenches comes in different sizes, and each wrench is designed for a specific set of tasks, such as removing oil filters or tightening lug nuts. Although one wrench can perform other tasks (like a lug wrench can be used to remove other bolts), it has tasks it performs better than other tools. That's just like the .NET language choices. Although you can use a "catch-all" language like Visual Basic.NET to write your programs, you can instead choose to use a specific programming language to accomplish a specific task, and use a language like VB.NET for everything else. At the same time, what one may consider specific another may consider as catch-all; it's all about choices.

Choosing a .NET language offers you the opportunity to compartmentalize your development. The best thing about being able to choose is that you can choose not to choose, opting to use what you already know — which is perfectly fine.

This book uses Visual Basic.NET in all of its examples because VB.NET is easy to use and understand, and because it will be used by a large percentage of .NET developers. However, just because the examples are in VB.NET (and this book teaches a little bit about how to program in VB.NET) doesn't mean the code couldn't have been written in one of the other languages.

20 Min.
To Go

Some .NET Languages

As previously mentioned, .NET supports over 30 different languages, and a several of these languages are designed to excel in certain areas of software development, such as financial applications and software engineering.

This section covers three of these languages. One of them started as a scripting language, one is a pure object-oriented language designed for software engineering, and one is a mainframe language that has been in use for four decades.

Python

Python is a lightweight, portable, object-oriented programming language. Its development began in Amsterdam back in the early 1990s. Python has an elegant syntax that doesn't suffer from oversimplification. One of the neatest things about Python is that it can be extended by adding new modules implemented in a compiled language such as C.

Python aficionados define their language of choice as a "totally awesome . . . language that will someday crush the $'s out of certain other so-called VHLL's ;-)"; VHLL stands for Very High Level Language. Python is often compared with Tcl, Scheme, and Perl.

Python offers enhanced memory management and a full set of string operations that make it good for string parsing and processing. Many mainstream Web sites use Python, including Yahoo! Mail. Anytime you see a URL with a .py in it, it's most likely a Python application.

Although other languages try to encapsulate all their functionality within the language or development environment, Python makes use of modules. These modules allow for interfaces to system calls and libraries, as well as windowing systems such as Macintosh, Windows (MFC), and UNIX (X11, Motif). Python is also perfect for applications that need a "built-in" programming language, similar to how AutoCAD has LISP and Microsoft Office has Visual Basic for Applications (VBA).

In the scope of .NET, it's almost as if Python has been planning for it all along. Python is modular. Large programs are built out of a collection of modules, and modules can define classes that provide further encapsulation (classes and encapsulation are covered a little later in this book). Python also has exception handling, which is important for catching and handling errors. These features allow Python to be a worthy choice as a .NET language, because it has features found in the four built-in .NET languages.

Eiffel

Eiffel is a software development environment created by Interactive Software Engineering (ISE) and based on a method that covers the entire software development lifecycle, including analysis, design, implementation, and maintenance. Eiffel is both an environment and a language; the Eiffel environment uses the Eiffel language.

Eiffel is designed for mission-critical, large-scale applications. It is especially popular in the defense industry for its ability to tackle large complex application development. Eiffel applies object technology and the concepts of Design by Contract (a software development methodology) to create highly reliable, reusable applications.

The Eiffel language was designed as a pure object-oriented language to solve the programmer problems and allow software developers to create powerful, reusable, error-free applications.

The idea behind Eiffel and .NET is primarily twofold. The first plan is to integrate Eiffel into Visual Studio.NET. This will allow developers new to Eiffel to develop applications inside a familiar environment. The ramifications of this integration are intense; up to this point, it was difficult to learn and apply an entirely new software development system with so much work already being performed in a tool like Visual Studio.NET.

The second plan is to enable ASP.NET development in Eiffel:

```
<% @Page Language="Eiffel#" %>
```

To accomplish this integration, ISE is approaching its goals in two steps. The first step is creating a subset of Eiffel, called Eiffel# (pronounced *Eiffel Sharp*). Eiffel# allows developers to target the .NET Framework and still use Design by Contract and Eiffel syntax. The second step is extending Eiffel# to encompass the full Eiffel object model.

Eiffel# will provide ambitious .NET software developers to use a tried-and-true software engineering language to create complex, mission-critical applications. Until .NET, there was not an easy way for ASP developers to create applications of that caliber.

COBOL

COBOL, which stands for *Common Business Oriented Language,* was created in 1960 to provide mainframe application programmers an easier way to create programs. COBOL uses an English-like syntax, which makes it easy to learn but occasionally very difficult to use.

As a testament to its pros and regardless of its cons, COBOL is in widespread use. In fact, new application development is still performed in COBOL on mainframes and minicomputers, like the ubiquitous AS/400. Nearly 70 percent of the world's software applications were written in COBOL.

COBOL uses a natural language syntax that is designed to be easy to read and self-documenting. COBOL is designed to perform simple computations on large sets of data. The language has undergone some major revisions in its 40-year history, and software vendors such as Fujitsu have released specialized versions of COBOL for different needs. For example, there is an object-oriented version of COBOL called O-O COBOL.

Despite COBOL's prevalence in the information technology industry, many people question its value and wonder why a .NET-friendly COBOL exists. The answer is twofold. First, consider how many COBOL applications are already written. Estimates place the number of lines of COBOL code in use at close to 2 billion. While vendors like Fujitsu have created tools to help transition COBOL applications to the Web, there has never existed an easy way for COBOL developers to create applications interoperable with other languages and tools, such as Visual Basic.

The other advantage of a .NET-friendly COBOL is the elimination of retraining of millions of COBOL developers in other Web-enabled languages. "COBOL.NET" allows developers to program directly for the Web, and this allows companies to use existing talent; in fact, since the .NET environment closely resembles the "centralized computing" model of the mainframe, COBOL developers are already one step ahead.

Like the other .NET languages, COBOL is to be ASP.NET-ready. The plan is to allow COBOL to be used at the page level, like so:

```
<script language="COBOL" runat="server">
COBOL CODE GOES HERE
</script>
```

With access to the .NET classes and the benefits of the .NET environment, a completely new era of application development in COBOL is ready to be ushered in.

10 Min.
To Go

The Built-In .NET Languages

.NET supports four built-in languages: C++, JScript.NET, C#, and Visual Basic.NET.

C++

For the longest time, C was the language of choice for software development. It was portable and fast, and compilers were available for just about every platform. Beginning in the 1980s, object-oriented technology experienced a tremendous renaissance with the introduction of a language called Smalltalk, which had been around for quite some time, but nobody really knew about it until *Byte* magazine published an article about in a 1981 issue.

Smalltalk is an object-oriented language based on the ancient language Simula 67, which is considered the very first object-oriented language. Smalltalk is a .NET-friendly language; Simula 67, however, is not.

Object-oriented programming (OOP) surged in popularity as windowing systems such as the Macintosh OS, Windows, and X11 (a UNIX windowing system) became prevalent. OOP was quickly coming to replace procedural languages. To keep up with the changes, object-oriented versions of existing languages were created. For example, from Pascal came Object Pascal and LISP spawned LISP CLOS (Common List Object System).

 Object-oriented programming is further discussed in Session 10.

Bjarne Stroustrop at Bell Labs undertook the task of creating an object-oriented version of C. He took the core language of C and created a superset of the language; he named the new language C++. C++ supports nearly every behavior of C while adding new capabilities of its own, notably object-oriented techniques like classes. In fact, it's perfectly reasonable to write code in C++ that doesn't make use of OOP at all.

C++ is now the most popular language for complex software construction, specifically for graphical user interface (GUI) applications. C++ is very powerful and very fast. The old adage is that anything you want to do on a computer you can do in C++.

Microsoft didn't want to leave C++ programmers out in the cold when. NET was created. At the same time, Microsoft didn't want to alienate C++ developers by making sweeping changes to the language to make it "fit" in the .NET Framework. So Microsoft decided to create managed extensions for C++. Managed extensions for C++, or Managed C++, helps Visual C++ developers create applications for .NET.

Using Managed C++, Visual C++ developers can create managed code (refer to Session 5 for information on managed and unmanaged code). Visual C++ developers can still create unmanaged programs; these are not .NET-enabled and thus can't take advantage of the .NET features. However, unmanaged C++ code and Managed C++ code can be mixed in the same application.

The managed extensions for C++ allow Visual C++ developers to create applications using the .NET data types directly in C++ source code. Managed C++ can also create .NET classes for use in other .NET applications. In other words, Managed C++ does all the ".NET stuff" that any of the other .NET languages can do.

 ASP.NET does not currently support C++.

JScript.NET

JScript.NET is the .NET-friendly version of Microsoft JScript, which is an implementation of the ECMA 262 language specification, commonly known as JavaScript.

JScript.NET is essentially the same as JScript, with some new features such as strong typing and object-orientation. Unlike JScript, which was confined to a host application such as ASP or an HTML page, JScript.NET can be used to create standalone .NET applications.

C#

When Microsoft created the .NET Framework, it decided to produce a new language that offered the simplicity of Visual Basic and the power of C++. Microsoft had an existing product called Visual J++ that it was discontinuing due to the lawsuits with Sun over Java, so it had the creator of Visual J++ create the new .NET language, called C# (C Sharp).

C# is easy to write, read, and maintain. The code is structured like C++, but is devoid of the confusing syntax of C++ in favor of a more user-friendly approach. C# features type safety, garbage collection, versioning, scalability, and a wealth of other features that traditionally had to be coded by the developer in C++; C++ doesn't support these features inherently.

 You may be thinking to yourself, why learn C# if I know C++ and can use Managed Extensions? The difference is, C# is a new language that natively supports .NET, while managed extensions are an addition to C++ which means things like garbage collection are still not built-in. The choice is yours, of course, and it all boils down to you doing what you think is right. C# exists to help you make that decision.

C# chooses simplicity over power, and it's slower than C++. However, C# can make your code more stable overall, so it's conceivable that a C# developer can make up for the performance decrease in reliability.

Like C++ and the other .NET-friendly languages, C# is object-oriented. You can create a class in another language like Visual Basic.NET and use it within C#. It's difficult to think about C# without thinking about Java, since C# and Java share many similarities. Although Microsoft does not officially say that C# is its answer to Java, most people have accepted that it is.

The C# compiler is part of the Visual Studio.NET installation. It's also built into the .NET Framework installation, so you can use it if you have the .NET Framework but don't have Visual Studio.NET. The compiler is available at the command line. Check your .NET Framework documentation for information on how to invoke the C# compiler.

Visual Basic.NET

In 1991, Microsoft released Visual Basic 1.0. Visual Basic 1.0 provided the first opportunity for new programmers to easily create 16-bit Windows applications. When Visual Basic 3.0 came out, client/server application development was "in" and Visual Basic quickly became a great choice for development in the client/server arena. Visual Basic already had an awesome interface designed by Alan Cooper (who is known as the Father of Visual Basic).

The Visual Basic Extension, or VBX, is credited with the early popularity of Visual Basic. A VBX allowed developers to drop in programming functionality. Using a VBX, a developer could easily add functionality to an application without writing all the code. VBXs were released that could do just about anything a Visual Basic developer wanted, including connect to databases, send and receive-mail, and talk to a mainframe.

Although Visual Basic 3.0 was very popular, it had some glaring shortcomings. It was 16-bit only, and Windows 95, a 32-bit operating system, was on the horizon. VBXs could only be created in Visual C++; a Visual Basic developer couldn't create a VBX in Visual Basic. To meet these shortcomings, Microsoft released Visual Basic 4.0. VB4 offered 32-bit development, support for creating DLLs and OCXs (the replacement for VBX), and offered substantial improvements to the language.

From VB4 to VB6, the tool underwent some changes. As client/server popularity waned and the Internet became the prevalent platform, Microsoft added on new functionality to the VB development system, like the ability to create ActiveDocuments and WebClasses, to keep up with these changes.

When Microsoft created .NET, they made radical changes to the Visual Basic language and Visual Basic developers hope that their tool will finally shed its reputation as a "toy language" not up to par with a "real language" like C++ or Java. The biggest changed to Visual Basic.NET is that it's now object-oriented and can do things its predecessors only dreamed about, like true inheritance (Visual Basic.NET is object-oriented). It supports the common type system so it can use the same data types as all the other .NET languages, and like the other .NET languages, it can inherit and use classes developed in other languages. It also supports free threading, operator overloading, and a wealth of other features only found in "real" programming languages, like structured error handling, exception handling, and type safety.

Visual Basic.NET represents a startling departure from Visual Basic 6. Getting used to all the changes will be difficult at first, and if you don't know object-oriented programming, it may be overwhelming for you. This book uses Visual Basic.NET for all its examples because Visual Basic.NET is still easy to read, use, and maintain, just as it has always been.

Done!

REVIEW

In this chapter, you learned about several languages that support .NET. The purpose of this chapter was to show you that you have choices, and to give you an overview of some of the popular languages supported by .NET. Specifically, we covered:

- The reasoning behind choosing a language
- The Python language
- The Eiffel language and how it works in .NET
- The COBOL language and how it works in .NET
- The four built-in .NET languages

The next chapter covers XML and SOAP, two technologies that are very important to .NET.

QUIZ YOURSELF

1. Approximately how many languages are supported by .NET? (See "Why Choose?")
2. What is a VHLL? (See "Python.")
3. What percentage of the world's applications is written in COBOL? (See "COBOL.")
4. What is the main difference between Visual Basic.NET and Visual Basic 6? (See "Visual Basic.NET.")

Understanding XML

Session Checklist

✔ Learning about the origin of XML

✔ Understanding the different features of XML

✔ Discovering some XML technologies

✔ Seeing how XML applies to Web applications

**30 Min.
To Go**

Extensible Markup Language, or XML, is the backbone of .NET. XML is described as the next phase in the evolution of the Internet. In this chapter, you will learn the principles, basic syntax, and implementation used in XML, and get a feel for what XML means to .NET.

What Is XML?

XML and HTML are both descendants of the complex and arcane language SGML (Standard Generalized Markup Language). For a long time, SGML was the language of choice for building other markup languages, like HTML. As the Internet became a viable place to do business, technologists realized that a new, simplified markup language was necessary, and XML was born.

Consider the humble Web page. You know that it has components called *tags* with names like <HTML> and <BODY>, but how does the browser know what to do with these tags? Somewhere, the Web browser has defined a relationship between which tags are meaningful and which instructions the program must follow to interpret them. In HTML, there is no separation between the presentation and the structure. HTML only describes how data should be presented; it doesn't describe the data itself.

XML raises the bar by describing a common way to describe any kind of data and allow it to be sent to, received by, and understood by any application that supports its protocol. XML describes data; it can be thought of as *metadata*. An example of the power of metadata is XHTML. XHTML is a description of everything that can be done within an HTML 3.2–compliant browser in terms of one XML document. XML can encompass everything that HTML does for a browser.

XML document features

XML requires very strict conventions of structure so that the meaning is available to all recipients. Here is a sample XML document:

```
<?xml version="1.0" ?>
<!--Our first XML document-->
<foo bar="Hello World">This is data
</foo>
```

You can break the document into five major pieces:

- **Processor instructions** as in `<?xml version="1.0" ?>` are only read by the parser, a component that understands XML and makes it available to other applications. In ASP.NET, the parser is MSXML.DLL but may be known by its version number as well (MSXML3.DLL, MSXML4.DLL, and so on).
- **Comments** are added to XML documents in the same style as in HTML as in the line: `<!--<!--Our first XML document-->`
- An **element** is the most fundamental component of an XML document and can contain data, other elements and another type of data called an attribute.
- An **attribute** is a compartment for storing data that is associated with a particular element. Elements can have any number of attributes, but attributes never have an element that describes them.

  Both elements and attributes are sometimes referred to collectively as a *node* in a document's hierarchy, or the strict definition of how pieces of data in the XML document relate to each other. For example, attributes are considered *child nodes* to their *parent node* of an element. An element that is a child node of another element is also called a *subelement*. Keep in mind that a node is the location and container of the data in the document and not the data itself.

- **Data** is either stored within double quotes associated with an attribute or between the opening and closing delimiters of an element.

```
<?xml version="1.0" ?>
<!--Our second XML document-->
<foo bar="Hello">This is data
<!--MS style closing element tag-->
 <foobar type="subelement" />
<!--W3C style closing element tag-->
</foo>
```

This chapter is one step on the thousand-mile journey of mastering XML. All emerging standards are based on the W3C Specification. For a more detailed introduction to all of the subtleties of XML, consult the Annotated XML Specification at `www.xml.com/axml/axml.html`.

Well-formed XML

Now that you're familiar with the terms used to describe the building blocks of an XML document, you must understand the fundamentals of how to make sure that the structure and data are assembled correctly. XML documents that can be parsed successfully and available to all standard consumption are known as *well-formed*. Closing tags are the first part of a well-formed XML document, but the rules of closing tags are not nearly as forgiving as in HTML. The following is not well-formed XML though it may be parsed correctly by a Web browser:

```
<?xml version="1.0" ?>
<HTML>
<HEAD>
<TITLE>Good HTML, Bad XML
</HEAD>
</TITLE>
</HTML>
```

Proper nesting looks like this:

```
<?xml version="1.0" ?>
<HTML>
<HEAD>
<TITLE> can be read by XML parser
</TITLE>
</HEAD>
</HTML>
```

The other components of a well-formed XML document are case sensitivity and special characters. When an XML document is parsed, an element called <TAG> is considered different form an element called <Tag>. Because XML parsers are looking for characters like <,>,&, and " to determine the structure of the document, you will have to "escape" or encode the characters out as < , > , & , and " respectively.

Valid XML

Although all these rules may seem like another walk in the new standards park, you may be wondering about the advantages of XML . What makes XML a language for metadata is its ability to define the structure and function of a document.

Structural validations

The same way that you cannot expect an elephant to fit in most doghouses, you need to qualify exactly what type of data you are going to receive in order to understand what you are getting. For the examples of validating the structure or internal consistency of an XML document, consider this sample XML document:

```
<?xml version="1.0" ?>
<Book Author="Rob Standefer">
<Title>ASP.NET Weekend Crash Course</Title>
<Chapter>Introducing.NET </Chapter>
```

```
<Chapter>The Evolution of Server-Side Scripting</Chapter>
<Chapter>Programming Basics</Chapter>
<Chapter>Setting Up ASP.NET</Chapter>
<Chapter>Working with the .NET Framework</Chapter>
<Chapter>Choosing a .NET Language</Chapter>
<Chapter>Understanding XML</Chapter>
<Chapter>Programming with VB.NET</Chapter>
</Book>
```

As humans, we can understand immediately that book, title, and chapter are related, but a machine must be told exactly what relation these information nodes have to each other. We have three different mechanisms for accomplishing this task.

Document type definitions

The original attempts in SGML to create rules for content within a particular document developed a specification for SGML parsers called *DTD*, or Document Type Definition. An example of what a DTD looks like can be found below:

```
<?xml version="1.0" ?>
<!-- DTD is not parsed as XML, but read by parser for validation -->
<!DOCTYPE Book [
<!ELEMENT Book (Title, Chapter+)>
<!ATTLIST Book Author CDATA #REQUIRED>
<!ELEMENT Title (#PCDATA)>
<!ELEMENT Chapter (#PCDATA)>
<!ATTLIST Chapter id #REQUIRED>
]>
```

We can already recognize enough vocabulary to understand this DTD as a definition of a Book document that has elements Book, Title, and Chapter and attributes Author and id. A DTD can exist inline, (inside the XML document), or it can be externally referenced using a URL.

A DTD will also include information about data types, whether values are required, default values, number of allowed occurrences, and nearly every other structural aspect you could imagine. At this stage, just be aware that your XML-based applications may require an interface with these types of information if your partners have translated documents from SGML to XML or are leveraging part of their SGML infrastructure.

XDR

Microsoft has implemented a different approach to XML document validation structure with the concept of an *XML Schema*. This schema is based on the W3C Recommendation of the XML-Data Note (www.w3.org/TR/1998/NOTE-XML-data), which defines the XML-Data Reduced Schema, sometimes referred to as an XML Schema. This document contains the same information that you could find in a DTD. The main difference is that it has the structure of a well-formed XML document. This example below shows the same constraints as the DTD above, but in an XML Schema format:

```
<?xml version="1.0" ? >
<!-- XML-Data is a standalone valid document-->
<Schema xmlns="urn:schemas-microsoft-com:xml-data">
```

```
<AttributeType name="Author"  required="yes"/>
<AttributeType name="id"  required="yes"/>
<ElementType name="Title" content="textOnly"/>
<ElementType name="Chapter" content="textOnly"/>
<ElementType name="Book" content="eltOnly">
<attribute type="Author" />
<element type="Title" />
<element type="Chapter" />
</ElementType>
</Schema>
```

There are a few things that an XML Schema can do that a DTD cannot. You can directly add data types, range checking, and external references called *namespaces,* which are discussed later.

XSD

Beginning with the release of MSXML4, Microsoft offered compatibility with a new validation standard called XSD, or the Extensible Schema Description (www.w3.org/XML/Schema), which added additional information for database and programming functions within the document's contents.

Here is a third representation of the contents allowed for the book document:

```
<?xml version="1.0" ?>
<!-- XSD is an XDR schema with more features -->
<xsd:schema xmlns:xsd="http://www.w3.org/2001/XMLSchema">
<xsd:element name="Book" type="CatalogInfo"/>
<xsd:complexType name="BookInfo">
<xsd:sequence>

<xsd:element name="Chapter" type="ChapterList" />
</xsd:sequence>
</xsd:complexType>
<xsd:complexType name="ChapterList">
<xsd:sequence>
<xsd:element name="Chapter" />
</xsd:sequence>
</xsd:complexType>
</xsd:schema>
```

Notice that an XSD Schema adds new functionality: the ability to have references of node relationships by a private name to the validating component.

Functional validation

Have you ever noticed this line in a Web page's HTML code?

```
<!DOCTYPE html PUBLIC "-//W3C//DTD HTML 4.0 Transitional//EN">
```

You may have wondered why a document would have to describe its content, in this case html. This is an example of a document type that is defined externally.

Anybody who has used the Internet by now has a good idea of that a *URL* ((Uniform Resource Locator) is a name that corresponds to data on a particular Web server accessible from the Internet. URLs point to data or the execution of a particular application. XML recognizes another Internet aware type of data.

A *URN* (Universal Resource Name) associates the functions of a type of application that is not bound to a particular location, but an expected behavior. For example, you may see an attribute like this in an XML:

```
xmlns="urn:schemas-microsoft-com:xml-data"
```

Here the attribute xmlns is a URN understood within the version of MSXML parsing the document. This resource, like any Internet resource, is designed to be unique. The example above states that the value of xmlns is as "xml-data."

Both a URN and URL belong to a collective a more general category of Internet resources called a *URI,* or Uniform Resource Identifier.

Namespaces

Now that you understand a general pointer to a program's functions and data via a URN, how can you map your own document's information to that external application? This is what puts the "X" in XML. A *namespace,* noted in the XML specification as xmlns, is a mechanism to define all nodes in an XML document in relationship to either another XML document or an XML-aware application. xmlns="urn:schemas-microsoft-com:xml-data is a flag to the XML parser that all contents of this XML document must be understood in terms of schemas-microsoft-com. But what happens if you have one URN that has a node called type and your XML document uses a type node, too? The solution is a "short name" that can be used as a prefix.

```
<?xml version="1.0" ?>
<!--Schema can validate two different type attributes as a type-->
<xsd:schema xmlns:xsd="http://www.w3.org/2001/XMLSchema"
xmlns:dt="urn:schemas-microsoft-com:datatypes">
<xsd:element name="Book" type="CatalogInfo"/>
<xsd:complexType name="BookInfo">
<xsd:sequence>
<!--One element with two type resources-->
<xsd:element name="Chapter" xsd:type="ChapterList"/>
</xsd:sequence>
</xsd:complexType>
<xsd:complexType name="ChapterList">
<xsd:sequence>
<xsd:element name="Chapter" />
</xsd:sequence>
</xsd:complexType>
</xsd:schema>
```

The prefixes dt: and xsd: allow the XML parser to differentiate the two attributes within the document, but they expose the identical name type to external components in isolation of each other. It is this support that allows an annotation or mapping of one type of schema onto another document while utilizing the same underlying structure. This is how XML has the potential to be understood in any application on any platform, any device, and any language.

Don't underestimate the subtleties of XML documents and their schemata. XML is continually updated specifications and in production encompasses advanced topics such as encoding, white space, security, and data types. Make sure you read every schema carefully and conduct extensive validation tests.

Using XML in Web Applications

20 Min.
To Go

At this point, you should be comfortable with the reading and basic writing of an XML document. This next section will show some basic examples of the toolboxes available for manipulating an XML document within your application. The .NET Framework is built around two fundamental technologies: the Common Language Runtime, as seen in Chapter 6, and XML. Because there are a wide variety of uses for this universal data format, no one method of programming XML integration is enough. Four programming interfaces can interact with XML: the Document Object Model or *DOM,* the Simple API for XML(*SAX*), *XSL*(Extensible Stylesheet Language), and some specialized functions in the .NET framework.

Document Object Model

The Document Object Model (DOM) is a way to reference and modify the entire XML document. Applications using the DOM can navigate all of a document's nodes, then modify and persist the nodes' contents. With this set of functions, you can gather and change information on all attributes, CDATA sections, comments, documents, document fragments, document types, elements, entities, entity references, namespaces, processing instructions, and text nodes within a document.

DOM programming is primarily for using an XML as a true client-centric document, as you would handle a photograph, Notepad text file, or HTML page; it is the only API that can be run on most browsers. Also, if your application will access a document at random, for example searches of small documents or hiding certain parts of a document for display, DOM is optimal. Because you have the entire document available at any given time after an XML document has been loaded into DOM, it is ideal for saving a file in a non-XML format or exposing certain nodes to another application components.

DOM can accomplish this flexibility because it loads the entire document into memory. This may be fine for client use, but it should be planned and benchmarked for server applications.

Simple API for XML

In sharp contrast to DOM, the Simple API for XML (SAX) approaches its manipulation of a document as a stream of data parts instead of their aggregation. SAX requires the programmer to decide what nodes the application will recognize in order to trigger an event. DOM uses a parallel approach to the document, meaning it can access several different level nodes with one method. SAX navigates an XML document in serial, starting at the beginning and responding to its contents once for each node and in the order they appear in the document.

Because it has a considerably smaller memory footprint, SAX can make managing large documents (usually one measured in megabytes) and retrieving small amounts from them much easier and quicker. Because a SAX application approaches a document in search of nested messages for which it generates responses, aborting a load under SAX is easier than doing so under DOM. The speed by which you can find a certain type of node data in a large document is also improved.

Extensible Stylesheet Language

Have you ever lost the afternoon trying to build a document converter? It is arguably the most tedious code and yet one of the most common aspects of an application's end user functionality. You cannot always guarantee that the final output of your XML-enabled application is destined for a digital device that "speaks" XML. So how can you get the data you have worked so hard to form well, validate, search, and modify?

The Extensible Stylesheet Language (XSL) picks up where Cascading Style Sheets (CSS) leave off. While CSS gave a repeatable presentation of underlying HTML, XSL gives a new XML representation based on an original document and an XSL document. The elegance and power of XSL is that it not only allows a translation to HTML, RTF, WAP, or any document style that is no longer XML, but the same changes can also be applied to output a different XML document.

Let's return to our XML document describing this book. If you were interested in creating a Web page that only contained the author, you could use the following XSL stylesheet:

```
<?xml version="1.0"?>
<xsl:stylesheet xmlns:xsl="http://www.w3.org/1999/XSL/Transform">
<xsl:template match="/">
<HTML>
<BODY>
<TABLE BORDER="2">
<TR>
<TD>Written By:</TD>
</TR>
<!--XPath query of Book node -->
<xsl:for-each select="Book[@Author]">
<TR>
<TD>
<xsl:value-of select="Author"/>
</TD>
</TR>
</xsl:for-each>
</TABLE>
</BODY>
</HTML>
</xsl:template>
</xsl:stylesheet>
```

XPath

XPath is another W3C recommendation (www.w3.org/TR/xpath). XPath is a language based on the navigation of an XML hierarchy tree when looking for a subset of its content. In the example above, the XPath query on Line 13 looks simple enough to understand:

```
Book[@Author]
```

This translates to a request for all Book elements that have an attribute of Author. Suppose we wanted to check for all titles of a particular book. The XPath query would look like this:

```
Book/Title
```

This translates to a request for all Title elements that are a child node of an element of Book. XPath is flexible enough that you could omit the Title element and the query would return all elements.

Keep in mind that validation of the document does not occur unless specifically requested in the transformation. You can ignore or include namespace prefixes in your transformations as well.

> **Because XPath returns all child nodes associated with each parent node selected, be very specific in the requests or use a preprocessing XSL to eliminate unnecessary data transfer.**

10 Min. To Go

XSLT

Choices and ease of use are the hallmarks of successful document translation. The xsl namespace provides a framework for the most commonly used flow control and data. These elements form the syntax described as *XSLT* (Extensible Stylesheet Language Transformation). The stylesheet element defines all parent nodes as part of the XSL stylesheet as an inline definition. The template element in this case points to the stylesheet to be used as the root of the document, but it can also be used to invoke external templates. Within an XSLT, the data returned by XPath is processed using a for-each loop where the node contents are added to the stylesheet output based on the value-of select element. Alternately, you could use more sophisticated looping to make a Web page with the chapter titles based on this example:

```
<?xml version="1.0"?>
<xsl:stylesheet xmlns:xsl="http://www.w3.org/1999/XSL/Transform">
<xsl:template match="/">
<HTML>
<BODY>
<TABLE BORDER="2">
<TR>
<TD>Written By:</TD>
</TR>
<!--XPath query of Book node -->
<xsl:for-each select="Book/">
<xsl:choose>
```

```
<xsl:when test="Chapter">
<TR>
<TD>
<xsl:value-of select="Chapter"/>
</TD>
</TR>
</xsl:when>
<xsl:otherwise/>
</xsl:choose>
</xsl:for-each>
</TABLE>
</BODY>
</HTML>
</xsl:template>
</xsl:stylesheet>
```

.NET technologies

ASP.NET has some incredible methods for accessing XML documents. These technologies will be covered in more depth in later chapters, but to whet your appetite, I will introduce the concepts of `XMLDocument` and `XMLDataDocument`. The DOM is accessible using `XMLReader` and `XMLWriter` while `XMLNavigator` provides the interface for using XSL. `XMLDataDocument` begins to blur the difference between a semi-structure, universal XML document and a tightly coupled, database specific dataset through ADO.NET. You can pick and choose whether to use the DOM or database functions to navigate the same content.

Done!

REVIEW

In this chapter, you learned about XML. You learned what XML is, and how to ensure its syntax is well formed. You learned about validating an XML document against a DTD, XML Schema, and XSD document. You then moved on to programming process, covering the basics of SAX, DOM, and XSL.

QUIZ YOURSELF

1. What is the difference between well-formed and valid XML? (See "What Is XML?")
2. What are the three ways to validate an XML document? (See "Valid XML.")
3. What are the two pieces and functions of XSL (See "Extensible Stylesheet Language.")
4. What is XPath? (See "XPath.")
5. What is the DOM? (See "Document Object Model.")

Programming with Visual Basic .NET

Session Checklist

✔ Learning about the genesis of Visual Basic .NET

✔ Understanding core concepts of Visual Basic .NET

✔ Understanding VB6 and Visual Basic .NET compatibility

**30 Min.
To Go**

When Microsoft released Visual Basic 1.0, the world of Windows development was irrevocably changed. While programming Windows applications had previously been the privilege of C++ developers, Visual Basic broke the barrier and unleashed scores of developers hungry to take advantage of the commercial success of the Windows platform.

A lot has changed since 1.0, and Visual Basic is now known as Visual Basic .NET. This chapter aims to help you learn enough about Visual Basic .NET so you can use it in your ASP.NET applications.

The Genesis of Visual Basic .NET

Microsoft was founded in 1975 to sell a BASIC compiler. For a long time, BASIC was Bill Gates's favorite programming language. He used to say that anything anyone could do in any language, he could do in BASIC.

Times have changed, and even Bill Gates would be hard-pressed to construct a large database-driven Web application in BASIC. Knowing that BASIC wouldn't be around forever in a limited capacity, Microsoft released evolutions of the product throughout the 1980s, culminating in QuickBasic and its free cousin, QBasic.

QuickBasic was a really neat development tool. It introduced subs and functions to BASIC programmers, and it actually created compiled programs. It had its own development environment, based on edit.com (a DOS application), and it even had an integrated debugger.

While QuickBasic grew in popularity among students and hobbyists, it was never considered a serious language for "true" application development. That was best left to developers using C or C++.

Finally, after Windows 3.1 came out and the Windows market share soared, Microsoft released a BASIC development tool for Windows: Visual Basic 1.0. It had an incredibly intuitive interface, designed by Alan Cooper (known as the father of Visual Basic). Visual Basic 1.0 (VB1) let developers build user interfaces with drag and drop controls. It was clunky, slow, and hard to use, but it was promising.

By the early to mid '90s, Microsoft had released Visual Basic 3 (VB3). It was VB3 that began the meteoric rise in VB's popularity. VB3 sported a component architecture that let developers use plugged-in controls. That meant that third-party development houses could create custom controls that developers could reuse in their applications. It was all drag-and-drop, of course.

VB 3's modularity, combined with soaring popularity of client/server computing, sealed its place in the application developer's toolbox. As the years went on and the world moved to 32-bit computing, VB followed. Visual Basic 4 was the first 32-bit version of VB, and it even offered a 16-bit version for those Windows 3.1 stragglers.

By the time VB5 came out, component development was the in thing and developers wanted to roll their own custom controls. Microsoft replaced the .VBX control architecture of VB3 with the .OCX in VB4. With VB5, it was possible for developers to create both COM objects and custom controls (.OCX). VB5 also offered several language enhancements and improved database support.

When Visual Basic 6 was released, it was generally regarded as the most significant change in VB since the VB4 was released. VB6 supported ADO, WebClasses, DHTML applications, IIS applications, and a robust COM development architecture. It also offered native compilation, better performance enhancements, and a wealth of other features. Some, however, considered it a tacked-on addition to the VB line, a mid-season replacement of an aging product in need of an overhaul.

In 2000, Microsoft released the first beta of Visual Basic .NET, which represents an almost complete rewrite of Visual Basic. It shares a history with its VB cousins, but it's name change — from VB to Visual Basic .NET — is fitting as this version of VB is like no other.

Visual Basic .NET Core Concepts

Visual Basic .NET is an object-oriented language (object-oriented concepts are covered in Chapter 10). It can take advantage of object-oriented features like inheritance and abstraction. At its most basic level, however, Visual Basic .NET is still a very easy language to learn and use.

While Visual Basic .NET can be used to create all kinds of different applications, including Windows applications, console applications, and Web services, this discussion focuses on how Visual Basic .NET applies to ASP.NET pages. Don't worry, though; what you learn in this chapter can be applied to other types of Visual Basic .NET projects.

Some of what you need to know in order to use Visual Basic .NET is covered in Chapter 3 like data types, conditionals, and loops. That information won't be repeated here. Instead, this chapter focuses on other key concepts of Visual Basic .NET.

Comments

Comments are very simple to write but very hard to remember to add to code. A comment in Visual Basic .NET is anything that follows the apostrophe ('):

```
'This is a Visual Basic .NET comment
```

A Visual Basic .NET comment is a single line comment, meaning each line comment line must have its own ' preceding it. For example:

```
'This is a Visual Basic .NET comment
But this is not because there is no apostrophe
```

Comments aren't compiled into an executable so don't worry about them taking up space. Try to remember to add comments to your code. They make code easier to read and maintain.

20 Min. To Go

Variables

A *variable* is a basic unit of programming, and it's extremely important. A variable lets you store a value in memory, and by definition, a variable can be changed.

In Visual Basic .NET, variables are created using the Dim statement:

```
Dim variablename As somedatatype
```

If you want to declare a variable called strUsername as a string, you would write this code:

```
Dim strUsername As String
```

A cool feature new to Visual Basic .NET is the ability to initialize a variable when it is declared. Say you want the strUsername variable to contain the value "newuser" when it is declared. This is accomplished as follows:

```
Dim strUsername As String = "newuser"
```

This applies to all data types. Whether as a data type or an object instantiation, a variable can be initialized with a default value.

Object variables

There are two ways to declare a variable as an object. Assume the object name is oSomeObject and the type is ObjectType. First, the standard way:

```
Dim oSomeObject As ObjectType
```

Using this method, you will need to initialize the object variable before you can use it:

```
Dim oSomeObject As ObjectType
oObjectType = New ObjectType
```

Alternatively, you can initialize the object variable when you declare it:

```
Dim oSomeObject As New ObjectType
```

This statement declares the variable and initializes it to its type, so it can immediately be used:

```
Dim oSomeObject As New ObjectType
oSomeObject.SomeMethod
```

Multiple variables

Visual Basic .NET supports declaring multiple variables on one line. Consider this code:

```
Dim x, y As Integer
```

What do you think this code will do? If you said that x and y are both integers, you are right. While in VB6 this wasn't the case (VB6 would make x a Variant), Visual Basic .NET handles it more intuitively. All variables in a Dim statement are of the type defined in that Dim statement.

Constants

A *constant* is essentially a variable with a value that does not (and cannot) change. Declaring constants in Visual Basic .NET is very simple:

```
Const SOME_CONSTANT As String = "Some Data"
```

All constants must be declared with a type, in this case, String. The initial value is not required.

Defining procedures

There are two types of procedures in Visual Basic .NET: the Sub and the Function. In ASP.NET, you use Subs as event handlers for form objects (Visual Basic .NET has built-in event procedures for Windows forms).

Sub

A *sub* is a routine that does not return a value. Subs are declared like this:

```
Sub RoutineName()
'Code
End Sub
```

The parentheses can contain the parameters you want your sub to support. For example:

```
Sub MyRoutine(myString As String, myInteger As Integer)
'Code
End Sub
```

This sub takes two parameters, myString and myInteger, and both are required when the sub is called. This sub could be called like so:

```
MyRoutine("someval", 4)
```

This call would execute `MyRoutine` and pass the values "someval" and 4. Say you want `myInteger` to be optional. You can do this via the Optional keyword, but you must define an initial value for the parameter:

```
Sub MyRoutine(myString As String, Optional myInteger As Integer = 4)
'Code
End Sub
```

This sub can be called two different ways, either with the `myInteger` parameter or without. If the `myInteger` parameter is left off the procedure call, the procedure will treat it as having what value you specify in the procedure's declaration.

Function

A *function* is a sub that returns a value. Functions must be declared as a type, so that the caller can know the type of the returned value. Functions are declared like so:

```
Function MyFunction() As String
'Code
Return "somevalue"
End Function
```

Notice the `Return` statement. This statement tells the function what value to return to the caller. The parameter of the `Return` statement, in this case "somevalue", must match the type declaration of the function. Because "somevalue" is a string, it matches the type declaration of `MyFunction`, which is `String`. If the code had instead returned the integer 4, an error would be raised.

This function would be called like so:

```
Dim strGetResult As String = MyFunction()
'or
Dim strGetResult As String
strGetResult = MyFunction()
```

Anytime you call a procedure, whether it's a sub or a function, you must include the parentheses in the call — even if you aren't passing a parameter.

Error handling

Error handling in VB6 was a pain. In VBScript, it was practically nonexistent. Visual Basic .NET, however, takes the plunge into serious error handling and gives you a more tried and true approach known as *exception handling*.

Exception handling has been around for a long time, existing in other languages like C++ and Java. It follows a basic model: try something and catch an error.

Exception handling in Visual Basic .NET is handled with the Try...Catch...Finally...End Try syntax. Here's an example:

```
Try
intResults = 4 \ intDivisor
Catch
```

```
intResults = 0
Finally
Response.Write intResults
End Try
```

This code tries to execute the code after the Try statement. If an error occurs, it executes the code following the Catch statement. The Finally statement is optional; it always executes after the Try statement is successful and when the Catch statement handles an error.

Think of it this way:

```
Sub MySub()
Try
 'Desired execution code goes here
Catch
 'Error handling code goes here
End Try
End Sub
```

The ideal situation is for the desired execution code to successfully execute. If something goes wrong, the Catch statement is there to handle it. This kind of error handling replaces the clunky On Error Goto and On Error Resume Next statements in VB6.

Unsupported Visual Basic Syntax

**10 Min.
To Go**

The question on every VB6 developer's mind is, "What doesn't work in Visual Basic .NET that worked in VB6?" While Microsoft tried to preserve some compatibility with VB6, it was inevitable that ancient and inefficient functionality were to die off. Microsoft offers the Microsoft.VisualBasic.Compatibility.VB6 namespace for those developers who just can't let go. For the rest of us, there are other replacements in the .NET Framework class library.

Gone forever

There are two statements that are gone forever, never to return. They are DefType and Gosub.

DefType

People who entered programming after 1989 never really understood what DefType was for. It was a carryover from Visual Basic's humble beginnings as QBasic/QuickBasic, and it really goes all the way back to the original BASIC language.

DefType allowed you to define all variables starting with certain letters to be of a certain type. It wasn't uncommon to see this code at the top of a QBasic program, like gorilla.bas:

```
DefInt A-Z
```

This code would define all variables starting with the letters A through Z to be of type Integer. DefType and all of its Def brethren are gone.

Gosub

Most people don't know what gosub is used for, which is ironic considering the importance of gosub to the original BASIC programming language and its progeny, like QBasic. Gosub was typically used like so:

```
Sub MySub()
Dim i As Integer
'Code here
Gosub MyOtherSub
'More code
Exit Sub

MyOtherSub:
'do work here using i
Return
End Sub
```

Gosub has long been regarded as the root of all evil. Gosub is widely held responsible for most of the spaghetti code that developers have produced over the years. It is officially dead in Visual Basic .NET.

Visual Basic .NET compatibility

There are some legacy functions and statements that VB6 developers just can't let go off, and Microsoft is respectful of this. To that end, Microsoft has replaced a lot of the deprecated keywords, such as DateDiff, with classes in the .NET Framework class library.

The following table contains some of the keywords that have been deprecated, along with their replacements:

Class	Keyword	Replacement
Collections	Collection	System.Collections
Constants	vbCrLf, vbLf, vbCr	Microsoft.VisualBasic.ControlChars
Date and Time	DateAdd, DateDiff, DateValue, TimeValue	System.DateTime
File System	Close, Put, FreeFile, Input, Seek, etc.	System.IO
Objects	CreateObject, GetObject	New keyword
Math	Randomize, Rnd, Round	System.Random, System.Math

Done!

REVIEW

This chapter introduced you to programming with Visual Basic .NET. By now, you should have a pretty good understanding of how the language works. Specifically, this chapter covered:

- The genesis of Visual Basic .NET
- Some core Visual Basic .NET concepts
- Error handling with Visual Basic .NET
- VB6 compatibility

The next chapter plunges you into ASP.NET programming head-first.

QUIZ YOURSELF

1. Who is the "father of Visual Basic""? (See "The Genesis of Visual Basic .NET.")
2. What kind of language is Visual Basic .NET? (See "Visual Basic .NET Core Concepts.")
3. How do you add a comment to your code? (See "Comments.")
4. What is the difference between a sub and a function? (See "Defining procedures.")
5. What two statements are forever excised from VB? (See "Gone forever.")

Building the Guts of a Program

✔ Understanding how to build functionality into ASP.NET applications

✔ Learning how to send e-mail from an ASP.NET page

✔ Figuring out how to upload a file through an ASP.NET page

✔ Knowing how to access the server's file system from an ASP.NET page

**30 Min.
To Go**

I have always believed that the best way to learn something is to see how it is done. This chapter shows you how to build the guts of a program — in other words, the code that makes your programs work. This chapter jumps ahead and uses code that you haven't seen yet. Don't worry about not really understanding what's going on. Read through the code and the explanations, and when you get to the ASP.NET chapters later in the book, you'll have a better idea of how ASP.NET works and how you can use it.

These sample ASP.NET pages may prove very useful to you in your own ASP.NET development efforts. The full source code is included on the CD-ROM.

How It's Possible

In the days of ASP, performing a task such as uploading a file was almost always handled by a COM object. In fact, a cottage industry arose where vendors specifically produced COM objects for ASP developers. These COM objects were the only choice for ASP developers who wanted to send e-mail, write event log messages, or work with the Web server's file system.

The .NET Framework provides a set of classes that simplify these tasks and provide built-in functionality for ASP.NET developers. Simply import the namespace into your ASP.NET page, and you're ready to go.

Any of the .NET Framework's hundreds of classes are available to your ASP.NET application. The classes are organized into logical namespaces, which will help you easily find the class you need to perform a specific function.

So what about those legacy COM objects and vendors? Well, some of those vendors have embraced .NET, and they're creating .NET-enabled class libraries to fill in any gaps in functionality. Others are creating *wrappers* around their COM objects, which let .NET developers easily use the components they invested time and money into.

Some of the stuff may be too advanced for you at this stage. That's alright; you don't have to learn every last bit before you go on to the next chapter. Think of this chapter as a quick reference to help you get your feet wet with ASP.NET application development, and as a taste of what you can accomplish on your own.

Sending E-Mail

Sending an e-mail from a Web page is such a simple operation and a very desirable one. Since 1997, users have been asking how to send e-mail from an ASP form. Several free and commercial COM objects were created to accomplish this basic task, including Microsoft's Collaborative Data Objects for NT Server (CDONTS).

The code

Sending e-mail from an ASP.NET page doesn't require the use of COM objects, third-party or otherwise. The .NET Framework exposes a set of classes that provides built-in e-mail functionality. Look at this code:

```
<%@Import namespace="System.Web.Mail"%>
<script language="vb" runat="server">
Sub btnSendEmail_OnClick(sender As Object, e As EventArgs)
Dim oMessage As New MailMessage

oMessage.To = txtTo.Text
oMessage.From = "question@somesite.biz"
oMessage.Headers.Add("Reply-To", "support@somesite.biz")
oMessage.Subject = txtSubject.Text
oMessage.Body = txtMessage.Text

'Send the Message
SmtpMail.Send(oMessage)

'Give feedback to the user to indicate the mail has been sent
Response.Write("<P>Your mail has been sent!</P>")
End Sub
</script>
<HTML>
<HEAD>
<title>Form To Email Sample</title>
</HEAD>
<body>
<form id="Form2Email" method="post" runat="server">
<P>
To: <asp:TextBox id="txtTo" runat="server"></asp:TextBox>
</P>
```

```
<P>
Subject: <asp:TextBox id="txtSubject" runat="server"></asp:TextBox>
</P>
<P>
Message Text:
<asp:TextBox id="txtMessage" runat="server"
TextMode="MultiLine"></asp:TextBox>
</P>
<P>
<asp:Button id="btnSendEmail" runat="server" Text="Send Email"
OnClick="btnSendEmail_OnClick"></asp:Button>
</P>
</form>
</body>
</HTML>
```

This ASP.NET page is very straightforward. The user can input information about the message, and click the Send Email button. An e-mail is then sent to the specified recipient containing the subject and message body specified in the form.

**20 Min.
To Go**

How it works

The .NET Framework exposes two classes for sending e-mail: `MailMessage` and `SmtpMail`. Both are exposed by the `System.Web.Mail` namespace (namespaces are covered in Chapter 13). `MailMessage` defines the various properties of an e-mail message, such as the recipient, the subject, and the message body. `SmtpMail` handles sending the message through its Send method.

To send e-mail from an ASP.NET page, the SMTP service must be installed on the server. It's typically installed by default, but you should check your server or ask your system administrator.

The form uses four Web controls (Web controls are covered in Chapter 18) to get the input from the user. When the user clicks the Send Email button, it fires the `OnClick` event. The `OnClick` event contains code that creates an instance of the `MailMessage` class, sets its properties, and then sends the message using `SmtpMail`. When the message is sent, text is written back to the client using `Response.Write` to let the user know the message has been successfully transmitted.

Let's examine the code that makes it all happen. This is the opening tag of the `<script>` block (`<script>` blocks are covered in Chapter 12):

```
<script language="vb" runat="server">
```

This code defines our event. `btnSendEmail` is the name of the button, and `OnClick` is its event. The stuff in the parentheses is standard:

```
Sub btnSendEmail_OnClick(sender As Object, e As EventArgs)
```

This code instantiates an object from the `MailMessage` class (objects and classes are discussed in Chapter 11). We'll use the `MailMessage` class to set the properties of our mail message:

```
Dim oMessage As New MailMessage
```

This code sets the properties of the MailMessage class (or our instance, oMessage):

```
oMessage.To = txtTo.Text
oMessage.From = "question@somesite.biz"
oMessage.Headers.Add("Reply-To", "support@somesite.biz")
oMessage.Subject = txtSubject.Text
oMessage.Body = txtMessage.Text
```

This code executes the Send method of the SmtpMail class, taking oMessage (which contains information about our message) as a parameter:

```
'Send the Message
SmtpMail.Send(oMessage)
```

This code closes out our script block:

```
'Give feedback to the user to indicate the mail has been sent
Response.Write("<P>Your mail has been sent!</P>")
End Sub
</script>
```

A message is displayed in the browser using Response.Write, the subroutine is closed with End Sub, and the script block is closed with a </script> tag.

Uploading a File

For a long time, file upload was the Holy Grail for ASP developers. Using the RFC 1867 standard, it was possible to send a file to the server, but ASP offered no easy built-in support for handling the file once it was uploaded (for example, saving it to disk).

The ability to receive and handle uploaded files is important to Web developers, because it allows for specialized functionality such as managing documents, receiving resumes, providing e-mail services (with the files as attachments), and so on. In HTML, there's a standard method for uploading a file:

```
<html>
<head>
<title>File Upload Sample</title>
<body>
<form method="post" enctype="multipart/form-data">
<input type="file" name="txtFile">
</form>
</body>
</html>
```

The important things to notice in this code are the <form> tag and the <input> tag. The <form> tag contains the enctype attribute, which tells the Web server what to expect and the browser what to display. The <input> tag is of type "file", which tells the browser to display an input box with a Browse... button so the user can select a file.

Because ASP offers no easy built-in support for file uploads, it would be necessary to use a third-party component such as SA-FileUp. ASP.NET does not have any dependency on a third-party component. The .NET Framework provides the HttpPostedFile class, which enables the developer to provide file upload capability through programmatic access to the file on the Web server's file system.

The code

Using the HTML example as a template, here's what the ASP.NET page would look like:

```
<%@Import Namespace="System.IO"%>
<script language="vb" runat="server">
Sub btnUploadFile_OnClick(sender As Object, e as EventArgs)
'Check to see if a file was selected
If Not txtFile.PostedFile Is Nothing Then
Dim strDir As String = "C:\Files"
Dim strFileName As String
strFileName = Path.GetFileName(txtFile.PostedFile.FileName)

txtFile.PostedFile.SaveAs(strDir & strFileName)
Response.Write("Your file has been saved. The location is: " & _
strdir & "\" & strFileName)
Else
Response.Write("You must select a file to upload.")
End If
End Sub
</script>
<html>
<head>
<title>File Upload Sample</title>
</head>
<body>
<form id="FileUploadSample" method="post" runat="server"
enctype="multipart/form-data">
Select the file you wish to upload:
<input type="file" id="txtFile" runat="server">
<p>
<asp:Button ID="btnUploadFile" runat="server" Text="Upload the File"
OnClick="btnUploadFile_OnClick" />
</p>
</form>
</body>
</html>
```

This code creates a page that contains an input box for selecting a file to upload and a button that, when clicked, executes the code that uploads the file. If no file is selected before the button is clicked, an indicating message is displayed to the user.

How it works

The .NET Framework exposes a namespace called `System.Web.UI.HtmlControls`, which in turn exposes programmatic access to files uploaded to the server via the `<input type="file" runat="server">` tag. This programmatic access is provided by the `HtmlInputFile` class, which exposes the `PostedFile` property. `PostedFile` is an instance of the `HttpPostedFile` class (exposed by `System.Web`), which provides the properties we use to determine the file name, content type, content length, and so on.

 `System.Web` **and** `System.Web.UI.HtmlControls` **were not explicitly imported into the file upload sample because they are automatically imported into every ASP.NET page.**

Notice that the `System.IO` namespace was imported into the page. This namespace exposes the `Path` class, which in turn exposes the `GetFileName` method. `GetFileName` is used to extract just the file name from the uploaded file.

The code itself is very simple in its implementation. The form uses two controls, an HTML control (`<input type="file" runat="server">`) and a Web control (`<asp:button>`). When the user clicks the Upload the File button, its `OnClick` event is fired. The `OnClick` event checks for the presence of a file (in other words, the user selected a file); if a file was not selected, a message is written to the client's browser indicating that a file must be selected.

If a file is present, the code gets information about the file, and then saves it to the local file system. A message is then written to the client's browser to indicate that the file has been successfully uploaded.

Let's take a closer look at the code. This imports the `System.IO` namespace, which we will need to munge (excise) the path information:

```
<%@Import Namespace="System.IO"%>
```

This code should seem familiar. It's the standard `<script>` opening tag and the `OnClick` event's declaration:

```
<script language="vb" runat="server">
Sub btnUploadFile_OnClick(sender As Object, e as EventArgs)
```

This code consists of a comment (noted by the ') and the first part of a conditional, which asks, "Does `txtFile.PostedFile` not contain nothing?"

```
'Check to see if a file was selected
If Not txtFile.PostedFile Is Nothing Then
```

This code sets the directory for the uploaded file (`strDir`) and then uses the `Path` class exposed by `System.IO` to munge the path information from `txtFile.PostedFile.FileName`, which is the complete path and file name of the uploaded file:

```
Dim strDir As String = "C:\Files"
Dim strFileName As String
strFileName = Path.GetFileName(txtFile.PostedFile.FileName)
```

At this point, `strFileName` contains only the file name of the uploaded file. The following is the meat and potatoes of this example:

```
txtFile.PostedFile.SaveAs(strDir & strFileName)
```

The SaveAs method of the PostedFile class is called, accepting the specified directory and file name as parameters. When this code executes, the uploaded file is stored on the server in the c:\files directory.

This code simply lets the user know that the specified file has been uploaded:

```
Response.Write("Your file has been saved. The location is: " & _
strdir & "\" & strFileName)
```

This code completes the conditional and lets the user know what is needed if a file is not chosen:

```
Else
Response.Write("You must select a file to upload.")
End If
End Sub
</script>
```

The code then closes the event's declaration with End Sub, and then closes the script block.

File System Access

**10 Min.
To Go**

Say you've provided file upload functionality in an ASP.NET application. After the file is on the server, how do you move it, copy it, delete it, or do whatever else you want to do? With ASP, you would use FileSystemObject, which is actually a very nice object for performing I/O (input/output) work.

Although FileSystemObject proved very useful for ASP developers, it didn't offer a lot of the features that developers were interested in, like getting file attributes. ASP.NET does not face this limitation, thanks to the .NET Framework and System.IO.

The code

System.IO is a powerful namespace that essentially gives carte blanche access to the Web server's file system. For this discussion, we'll work with code that creates a file. Take a look at the code:

```
<%@Import namespace="System.IO"%>
<script language="vb" runat="server">
Sub btnCreateFile_OnClick(sender As Object, e As EventArgs)
Dim strDir As String = "C:\files"
Dim strFileName As String = strDir & txtFileName.Text

Dim oStream As StreamWriter = File.CreateText(strFileName)
oStream.Write(txtFileContents.Text)
oStream.Close()

lblResults.Text = "Your file was successfully created at " & _
```

```
    strDir & strFileName
End Sub
</script>
<HTML>
<HEAD>
<title>Create File Sample</title>
</HEAD>
<body>
<form id="CreateFile" method="post" runat="server">
<p>
What would you like to name the file?
<BR>
<asp:TextBox id=txtFileName runat="server"/>
</p>
<p>
Enter the text you would like the file to contain.
<BR>
<asp:TextBox id=txtFileContents runat="server"/>
</p>
<p>
<asp:Button id=btnCreateFile runat="server" Text="Create the File"/>
</p>
<p>
<asp:Label ID="lblResults" runat="server"/>
</p>
</form>
</body>
</HTML>
```

This code is deceptively simple. If you look closely, it resembles the file upload sample. The user enters a file name and some file contents. When the user clicks the Create the File button, the file containing the user-specified contents is created on the server in a directory, c:\files.

How it works

The .NET Framework exposes a handy namespace for working with I/O aptly named System.IO. System.IO exposes the StreamWriter class, which is used in the Create File sample. This StreamWriter class exposes the File class. The File class contains methods for working with files such as Open, OpenRead, OpenText, OpenWrite, Create, CreateText, CopyTo, Delete, and MoveTo. These are the most basic I/O features provided by the .NET Framework.

 Although the File **class refers to a generic file (and is the first choice for creating new files),** System.IO **also exposes a** FileInfo **class that provides more specific file features provided by properties such as** Exists, LastAccessedTime, **and** CreationTime.

The code uses four Web controls: two text boxes, a button, and a label. The text boxes let the user enter the desired file name and file contents. Clicking the button fires the OnClick event, which contains the code that performs the work of creating the file server-side. Finally, the label is there to report the results back to the user. You could use Response.Write instead (as in the previous examples in this chapter).

Take a closer look at the code. This is the standard stuff that will be familiar from the previous examples:

```
<%@Import namespace="System.IO"%>
<script language="vb" runat="server">
Sub btnCreateFile_OnClick(sender As Object, e As EventArgs)
```

The code imports the System.IO namespace, opens the <script> block, and the OnClick event declaration.

These are the Dim statements that define the variables used to store information about the target directory (strDir) and the target file (strFileName):

```
Dim strDir As String = "C:\files"
Dim strFileName As String = strDir & txtFileName.Text
```

The following is the meat and potatoes of the sample:

```
Dim oStream As StreamWriter = File.CreateText(strFileName)
oStream.Write(txtFileContents.Text)
oStream.Close()
```

An instance of StreamWriter is created (oStream). oStream is populated using the CreateText() method of the File class. CreateText() takes strFileName as a parameter.

The Write() method of the oStream object (an instance of StreamWriter) is invoked, and the file is physically created. oStream is then closed with the Close() method.

This last bit of code changes the text of the label to reflect successful completion of the file, and shows the new file name:

```
lblResults.Text = "Your file was successfully created at " & _
        strDir & strFileName
End Sub
</script>
```

The event declaration is closed with End Sub, and the script block is closed with </script>.

Done!

REVIEW

This chapter demonstrated the crash course idea behind this book's title. You were exposed to real-world examples of ASP.NET in action. Specifically, you learned:

- How to send e-mail from an ASP.NET page
- How to upload a file to an ASP.NET page
- How to create files on the server file system from an ASP.NET page

You've made great progress from this chapter. You may want to consider using the examples from this chapter in your own applications, and refer back to them as you read the rest of the book to help get a better understanding of how ASP.NET applies to your own application development.

QUIZ YOURSELF

1. How did ASP developers typically send e-mail from an ASP page? (See "Sending E-Mail.")
2. What .NET Framework class handles actually sending an e-mail? (See "How it works" under "Sending E-Mail.")
3. Which namespace exposes programmatic access to uploaded files? (See "How it works" under "Uploading a File.")
4. What kind of access to the file system does System.IO provide? (See "The code" under "File System Access.")
5. What are some methods you can use to work with a file using System.IO? (See "How it works" under "File System Access.")

Working with Objects

Session Checklist

✔ Understanding the foundations of high-level programming

✔ Examining underlying object-oriented concepts

✔ Learning the anatomy of an object

✔ Exploring how object-oriented programming applies to ASP.NET

**30 Min.
To Go**

I n order to take full advantage of the benefits of the .NET Framework in your ASP.NET development, you need to understand the organization and limitation of code you will be reusing on a daily basis. This chapter explores the concepts of object-oriented development. If you have already developed applications using C++, Java, or any other object-oriented language, you can skip this chapter.

Foundations for High-Level Programming

Although the evolution of computer languages shortens the software development cycle further every couple of years, every new paradigm is built on the same basic tenets: code must find data, do something to it, and make it available someplace else. Everything experienced from a running operating system exists based on a series of offsets of essentially the same binary state in exceedingly complicated patterns.

The evolution of structures

Structures are precursors to classes, which act as the foundation of object-oriented programming. A structure is used within a program to provide a certain type of functionality.

Assembly addresses

If you are developing on any platform in any language that runs on an AMD, Cyrix, Transmeta, or Intel processor, your processor "thinks" in a language known as x86 assembly language. Here is a snippet of assembly:

```
Mov        edx,ebx
Cmp        [ebx],0
Jne        0
Mov        ah,[ebx+1]
```

Above, the code instructs the processor to move ebx register to edx, compare address of ebx to 0, jump if not equal to 0 or copy a one byte offset from the memory location for the ebx register to ah register.

Although this may be very powerful and interesting, it will not get you ready by Monday to develop Web pages. This is an example to give you perspective on what more readable code and good programming practices will do for you. Compilers and linkers will eventually translate all your code into machine language readable by the targeted executing environment.

Structures

Although this raw level of access to the processor is extremely useful for code optimization, hardware drivers, and game programming, the majority of applications use very specific data types in the same repeatable way. Moreover, certain functions will read and manipulate this data. To facilitate this interaction, programmers developed languages like C to give a more readable control to the processor's operations. Grouping linked types of data together gives a context for applying rules to the same pieces of data in fewer steps, as seen in this code example:

```
//definition of structure
    typedef struct {
                    int      my_int;
                    double   my_double;
                    }
    my_struct_def;
//reference to structure as a whole
    my_struct_def my_struct_in_memory;
    my_struct_def *my_struct_value = &my_struct_in_memory;
// reference to part of structure
    my_struct_value->my_int = "hi";
```

This code declares a structure, and then shows usage of both the structure as a whole and as its parts. Using linked lists and other advanced relations of these structures forms the foundation for database structures, message queues, and other higher level programming constructs.

 Consult the documentation on your final language of choice for the execution rules and safety in the .NET Framework. We have only scratched the surface of advanced programming technologies such as pointers, dereferencing, and address manipulation.

Limitations

Structuring data is a very natural progression, but you will also need a mechanism for dealing with functions with as much ease and scope. How will you get to use all the functions you need at once if you don't even know what they are? Are you doomed to learning every granular function just to get through your day? The short answer is no.

**20 Min.
To Go**

Third-generation languages and beyond

We began our discussion earlier in terms of assembly one level above the first generation language of the actual bit patterns routed to and from registers on the microprocessor. An assembler translates the opcodes, or human readable form, into machine code.

The second code example was a departure into a third-generation language, a level where all .NET Framework interactions occur.

What abstraction means

In C, macros were the primary way of taking functions and reusing them without recoding, but the level of complexity in building customizations and new use cases becomes very tedious very quickly. Languages like C++ and SmallTalk pioneered the ability of a programmer to aggregate functions in a similar fashion, as structure aggregates data access. This new level of indirect reference, know as *abstraction,* gave rise to new possibilities in code design and reuse.

Abstraction allows you to separate the idea from the implementation. This facilitates code reuse because the code is designed to accomplish a task without regard to the application that contains the code. Abstraction allows you to define common features of objects and procedures. Using abstraction, you can figure out that two functions that perform similar tasks can be combined into a single function, reducing complexity. (For more on abstraction, see the upcoming section, "Abstraction.")

Adding classes to software

Now that you have seen how to combine functions within other functions and data with other data, look at a simple VB.NET code fragment for data access to see where this abstraction takes place:

```
Dim D As DataService = New DataService()
Dim mD As DataSet = D.GetData()
Test_DataGrid.DataSource = MyData.Tables("Tst").DefaultView
Test_DataGrid.DataBind()
Message.InnerHtml = "Rows: " & mD.Tables("Tst").Rows.Count.ToString()
```

Let's start with the DataService() reference above. In this one line of code, you have added to memory all initial data and references to functions that will be used under the name of D. In C++ and Java terms, this is the equivalent of constructing a new class. A *class* is the generic term for a prescribed execution of functions and initial memory allocation for data.

The beauty of a class is that it takes an existing template from a program and allows your software to use it in any way that its functions and underlying data dictate. In the second line of code, you call the function D.GetData() in order to acquire data from another source. To top it off, you do not have to know what underlying functions make this D.GetData()work. You just need to know that it has a prescribed data type and context, or *interface,* available.

And Then There Was the Object

We have gone from assembly to data types, data types to structures, functions to function pointers, and their aggregation into classes. Object-oriented programming provides an environment for mapping a business process to a model of the way the world works. In other words, it allows you to approach application programming using the real-world paradigm, where you can associate concepts. This is where abstraction is useful. The world is defined in terms of specific instances of generic concepts. For example, if you say, "My car needs a new tire," the person may not know the specific model of car or tire, but he has a concept of your interaction based on his experience of those two concepts' interactions. You can look at both the car and tire as an *object,* or a concept describing specific pieces (rim, tread, and so on) and behaviors (roll, wear, flatten). In programming terms, an object is composed of classes containing all private functions and data being used by an *instance,* or a particular running copy of the application. The interface for these functions and data allows for some very powerful tools for modeling the human world in a format that ultimately translates to a computer's "thoughts."

An *object* is an instance of a class. If you have a class called Tire, you can create an instance of that class called, for example, Performance. Your Performance object is of the Tire class, so it can do whatever the Tire class provides. If the Tire class provides a Flatten() method, then the Performance object has that Flatten() method.

General OOP concepts

In a full implementation of object-oriented programming OOP, there are four behaviors that an otherwise unavailable in a language: abstraction, encapsulation, inheritance, and polymorphism.

Abstraction

In the example earlier in this chapter, we discussed this behavior. It is often said that it is better to have good documentation of an interface than the source code, because it is more important to know what is necessary. Abstraction also makes it easier for programmers to give performance boosts or interact with other new components while providing backwards compatibility by only varying the internal classes and maintaining the same interface.

Consider the Tire class and the object instance, Performance. The Tire class has two methods, Flatten and Deflate. Using abstraction, you can pinpoint that Flatten and Deflate have the same results (air is removed from the tire). You can combine Flatten and Deflate into one function that removes the air from the tire.

Encapsulation

When an object creates an instance, it already contains not only all the functions it needs to execute, but already has reserved its memory addresses for any work needed. This allows a greater level of security, because it only "publishes" an interface for other programs to invoke in its instance. A private copy of memory addresses also diminishes the chance of data corruption from shared access.

Encapsulation is the process of combining elements to create a new entity. Encapsulation goes hand-in-hand with abstraction. Encapsulation provides a mechanism for working with objects without knowing the internals of the object, or how it works.

Inheritance

Classes are the operational engine working below the logical chassis of your VB.NET programming. You can describe the relationship of classes above as our class Tire having a subclass called TractorTire and deriving from a superclass TireFactory. The derived classes, such as TractorTire, , can have their own functionality added to their own instance, while still accessing the same functions of the base class, Tire. For example, say the Tire class has the Flatten method. The derived class, TractorTire, inherits this Flatten method from the Tire class.

Polymorphism

As long as the message communicated by sending object in the interface is consistent with the receiving object, the specific behavior is completely independent of the sender. By this method, different objects can respond to the same message in different ways. Conversely, an object can be structured to support *operator overloading,* which allows the object to act with different behaviors to a message that has the same interface, but with different data types.

Polymorphism refers to the ability to process an object differently depending on its data type or class. Polymorphism allows you to redefine methods for derived classes. In our Tire example, when the Flatten method is called on an object derived from TractorTire, it's separate from any object derived from the original Tire class, and any changes made to TractorTire.Flatten are separate from Tire.Flatten.

Anatomy of an object

Now that you have a good grasp of what goes on behind the scenes of an object, you are ready to see how they are used in every day, modern object-oriented programming. Modern languages such as Java, VB.NET, and C# are highly object oriented in their structure and execution. The components of an object (referred to as *members*) you will most often use are methods, properties, collections, and events.

Properties

The core of any application is the data. Although there may be data manipulated on underlying levels of any instantiation or manipulation of an object, the object-oriented term a variable is a property.

```
Sub ShowTableName(ByVal myDataSet As DataSet)
Dim mT As DataTable
Dim Ctr As New Object
'Set Property
Ctr = 1
For Each myTable in myDataSet.Tables
'Get Property
```

```
MsgBox ("Table " & Ctr & " = " & myRow(mT.TableName))
Ctr = Ctr + 1
Next myTable
End Sub
```

The preceding code shows two different examples of properties: We cycle through the data in the `Tables` property to display the data in the `TableName` property. These are both examples of when you access variable data, or in OOP terms, get a property from an object.

Another behavior for properties is changing the value. Although we used a special base class `Object` property for storing our counter, the conventions for when we change a variable's value or set a property are similar. For example, if we had write access to the property, we could change it in this fashion:

```
myTable.TableName="NewTableName"
```

Do not assume that every property is simply a "box" for data. Any number of functions and other data manipulations may occur behind the scenes before you can access the variable you seek.

Methods

When you use a low-level language, you call functions, but when you discuss object-oriented programming, the same behavior applies when you invoke a method. Let's review the sample code from above:

```
MyData.Tables("Test").Rows.Count.ToString()
```

Here, we see in one method invocation of two methods called on the same object. The `MyData` presents the `Rows` property, and the `Count` method does the simple function of calculating how many rows are in a table. Because this is stored as an integer, we must convert it to an string for display with the `ToString()` method.

Events

Although objects are excellent for abstracting base classes and making programming with a particular object's members easier, .NET is fundamentally based on computers talking with computers. So how do we get from one method to the other?

```
' PropertyChanged event handler added
testData.PropertyChanged+= New
System.ComponentModel.PropertyChangedEventHandler(DataSetProperty_Changed)
End Sub
' PropertyChanged event handler used
Sub DataSetProperty_Changed(object sender, PropertyChangedEventArgs e){
Console.WriteLine("CHANGED " + e.PropertyName)
End Sub
```

Without going into great detail, mechanisms called *queues* deliver messages in the order that they are received. In object-oriented terms, these messages are known as *events*. Methods usually call events, and an *event handler* is a generic term for an application that can respond to an event. For example, a member of the `DataSet` object is `PropertyChanged`, which is an event that is generated by invoking a `RaisePropertyChanged` method. In this way, we can have one object monitor the activity of another object's activity.

Collections

As if we did not have enough layers to debug and manipulate, an object itself can be a member of a special type of object implementation called a *container object* that contains objects. We can modify the code from the earlier example to illustrate a collection:

```
Sub ShowTableCount(ByVal myDataSet As DataSet)
Dim mT As DataTable
Dim Counter As New Object
MsgBox ("Count: " & mT(TableCollection.Count.ToString()))
End Sub
```

This object construction saves us from looping through our set of `DataTable` objects by exposing them as an aggregate object.

You will see advanced object management issues such as the .NET Framework's assembly interfaces, type library conversion, the Component Object Model and its use in Component Services. These are every day experiences with component integration and should be examined once you have a handle on ASP.NET, regardless of your language of choice.

*10 Min.
To Go*

ASP.NET: The best of Object-Oriented Programming

We will jump to a preview of Chapter 24 for this example of object-oriented program in action. The following code is designed to show a simple Web page based on records from a database.

```
<%@ Import Namespace="System" %>
<%@ Import Namespace="System.Web" %>
<%@ Import Namespace="System.Data" %>
<%@ Import Namespace="System.Data.OleDb" %>
```

These first four lines of code show some very advanced aspects of the ASP.NET platform called *namespaces,* which is abstraction even higher than an object, grouping objects under a logical naming convention. The hierarchical structure shows that in the ASP.NET application framework, both `System.Web` and its sibling `System.Data` inherit objects from the root namespace, `System`. The concept of a namespace is related to that of an *assembly*, a binary of one or more parts that houses all internal and external references to objects, data types, and versions used by the code. Namespaces can contain many assemblies and vice versa.

```
<html>
<body>
<script LANGUAGE ="VB" runat="server">
Dim superexet As New DataSet
Dim rexet As New DataTable
Dim iLp, iNumRows As Integer
Dim SQLstm As String = "SELECT * FROM Authors where id > 10"
Dim cnxn As String = "Provider=SQLOLEDB;Server=.;"_& _
"uid=sa;pwd=;database=pubs"
```

On the surface, this part of the code hearkens back to our humble C beginnings with an evolved representation of how data is stored, or the setting of properties. But when you use Dim, you create a new copy of that object in memory, with all of its memory reservation and execution of constructors.

```
supercnxn = New OleDbDataAdapter(SQLstm, cnxn)
supercnxn.FillDataSet(superexet, "Table1")
' DataSet as many instances of a RecordSet
rexet = superexet.Tables("Table1")
iNumRows = rexet.DataRow.Count
```

The above example is difficult to understand without knowing the object member's definitions, and whether you are invoking a method or retrieving a property. As the code appears, both supercnxn.FillDataSet() and superexet.Tables() appear to be methods, but in fact the latter is a property. Object-oriented terms can be implemented with or without parameters and it makes sense to the real-life behavior. Both can resolve to functions somewhere down the call stack.

```
If iNumRows = 0 then
Response.Write("No records.")
Else
Response.Write("<p>ADO.NET Data in ASP.NET</p>")
For iLoop = 0 To iNumRows - 1
Response.Write("<br>" &__
rexet.DataRow(iLp).Item("au_fname") & " " &__
rexet.DataRow(iLp).Item("au_lname") & "</br>")
Next iLoop
End If
rexet.Close
rexet = Nothing
cnxn.Close
</script>
</body>
</html>
```

Done!

REVIEW

We have examined the underlying microprocessor behavior that occurs when writing low level code. We have built structures and classes on top of this framework to quicken development. We have described the different behaviors of an object and looked at examples using the VB.NET language in an ASP.NET page application.

QUIZ YOURSELF

1. What is the difference between a data type and a structure? (See "The evolution of structures.")

2. What programming construct aggregates functions and structures together? (See "Third-generation languages and beyond.")

3. What are the four hallmarks of object-oriented programming? (See "General OOP concepts.")

4. What is the difference between a function and a method? (See "Anatomy of an object.")

5. What is the difference between a variable and a property? (See "Anatomy of an object.")

PART

II

Saturday Morning
Part Review

1. Where does the .NET Framework run in the context of the Windows operating system?
2. What is the filename extension for ASP.NET pages?
3. The CLR takes input source code and then does what?
4. What is the point of garbage collection?
5. Name the two Just-In-Time compilers shipped with the .NET Framework.
6. What are the three languages built into .NET?
7. What is the name of the .NET implementation of Eiffel?
8. What do you need to do to use COBOL in an ASP.NET page?
9. Name one advantage of C# over C++.
10. What three features will help Visual Basic shed its reputation as a toy language?
11. What does XML stand for?
12. What parser is used by ASP.NET?
13. What is needed for an XML document to be considered valid?
14. What is the XML DOM?
15. What does the `<xsl>` tag do?
16. How do you initialize a variable when you declare it?
17. What do constant declarations require?
18. How do you return a value from a function?
19. When does the code in the `Finally` block execute in a Try..Catch..Finally block?
20. What namespace provides compatibility with VB6 for VB.NET applications?
21. What namespace do you use for working with the server's file system?
22. What tag exposed by `System.Web.UI.HtmlControls` do you use for file upload?

23. What does the `SmtpMail` class do?

24. `StreamWriter` exposes a class with methods for performing file-related actions, such as Open, Delete, and Copy To. What is the name of the class?

25. What service needs to be installed on the server in order for an ASP.NET page to send email?

26. What is the foundation of object-oriented programming?

27. What is a method?

28. What is a property?

29. Name the four tenets of object-oriented programming.

30. Name some object-oriented languages.

PART

III

Saturday
Afternoon

Session 11
ASP.NET versus ASP

Session 12
Introducing ASP.NET

Session 13
Using Namespaces and Classes

Session 14
Building ASP.NET Applications

Session 15
Managing Session State

Session 16
Building Your First ASP.NET Page

ASP.NET versus ASP

Session Checklist

✔ Grasping the core differences between ASP.NET and ASP

**30 Min.
To Go**

I t's no secret that Active Server Pages (ASP) allowed millions of Visual Basic developers and newbies alike to create Web applications. If you are an ASP developer, you may be interested in how ASP.NET is directly different from ASP. This chapter compares ASP and ASP.NET in four major areas: environment, deployment and versioning, scalability and stability, and debugging and error handling.

Environment

Environment refers to the programming environment, including the execution path, database access, programming languages, and so on. When comparing ASP and ASP.NET, environment differences can become the most obvious because they're the first you encounter when you sit down to write an ASP.NET application.

Execution

Execution refers to the environment in which an application will run, and the requirements for that application to function. In the context of ASP and ASP.NET, execution includes the Web server requirements and how ASP and ASP.NET handle application startup. ASP almost requires Internet Information Server (IIS) and isn't extensible, while ASP.NET can run outside of IIS and is fully extensible.

ASP

ASP is tightly integrated with and tied to IIS. Unless you purchase a third-party program such as Chili!ASP, you must run IIS to run ASP. ASP runs within IIS as an ISAPI filter, asp.dll. The ASP engine is undocumented, which prevents extension of the runtime. Instead, ISAPI filters must be created to accomplish tasks that ASP does not support. ISAPI filters are low-level programs typically written in C, which leaves Visual Basic developers out in the cold.

ASP compiles a script the first time it is accessed by a user. If the script cache fills up, ASP starts to empty it without any control by the developer. If the machine crashes or IIS restarts for whatever reason, the compilation process starts all over again.

ASP.NET

ASP.NET is designed to run on any Web server without requiring IIS infrastructure. The ASP.NET environment is extensible via httphandlers, high-level programs that can extend ASP.NET independent of the ASP.NET infrastructure. Httphandlers can be written in VB.NET, so you don't need to know a low-level language like C.

ASP.NET compiles a script and writes it to disk. This is called *compilation persistence*. This disk cache is configurable by the developer and has several settings that can be manipulated depending on the application's needs.

Languages

A programmer chooses a language based on several criteria, including elegance, ease of use, what platforms it supports, and performance. Whereas ASP didn't offer much in language selection, ASP.NET supports over 30 different languages.

ASP

ASP supports two built-in, interpreted (not compiled) scripting languages, VBScript and JScript. Through third-party plug-ins, ASP can support a few other languages including PerlScript and C. Language plug-ins are infamous for crashing IIS and the general opinion has been, "If you're going to write it in Perl, why bother trying to force it into ASP?"

ASP.NET

ASP.NET supports three built-in, compiled languages: Visual Basic.NET, JScript.NET, and C#. These languages are full languages, not scaled down scripting languages like VBScript. Because the languages directly support the Common Language Runtime, there's no forcing of the language into the ASP.NET context. Building an ASP.NET application with one of these languages should be as seamless as developing an application outside of the ASP.NET environment.

Database support

Database support is a very important part of ASP and ASP.NET. Data access with ASP is clunky and different depending on the data source. ASP.NET simplifies data access and eliminates recordset loops.

ASP

ASP supports database access using ActiveX Data Objects (ADO). ADO communicates with databases via ODBC and OLE DB; ODBC provides a standard connection to a database and OLE DB is a layer between ADO and ODBC to simplify data access and retrieval.

ASP and ADO require database-specific code. For example, some databases do not support the `RecordCount` property of the `Recordset` object; if you use the `RecordCount` in a Microsoft Access–based ASP page, and then move the database to Oracle, your code is instantly broken.

ASP developers must use recordsets to get data from a database, and loop through the recordset to get the values. The recordset looping is accomplished through code like this:

```
<% Do Until MyRS.EOF
Response.Write MyRS("field")
MyRS.MoveNext
Loop %>
```

This code can be painful. In fact, that little `MoveNext` statement has caused many a nervous breakdown, because if you forget it, you'll have an endless loop.

ASP.NET

ASP.NET offers database support via ADO.NET, the evolution of ADO. ADO.NET can communicate with ODBC and OLE DB databases, binary streams, and XML streams. Unlike ADO, ADO.NET is not tied to database specifics so differences between back-end databases do not affect your programming.

ASP.NET and ADO.NET eliminate the recordset looping plague. In its place, use:

```
SqlDataReader.Read()
```

or:

```
OleDbDataReader.Read()
```

It offers groups of data controls, such as the DataGrid, that bind to your data and display it in tables or however you want. ASP.NET also supports data binding directly to controls, and there are several other choices for retrieving and working with data.

Objects

Object support is important in ASP and ASP.NET to encapsulate certain functionality and make it easier for developers to create applications. ASP has limited object support with six built-in objects and access to COM and COM+ components. ASP.NET features that and a whole lot more.

ASP

Every ASP developer probably knows the six built-in objects by heart: `Server`, `Application`, `Session`, `Response`, `Request`, and `ObjectContext`. These objects expose key functionality to ASP applications. For example, `Request` exposes the `Forms` collection, which provides access to submitted form values. This is in place of reading in the http headers and manually retrieving the data.

ASP also supports COM and COM+ objects, via the `CreateObject` method on the `Server` object. ASP only supports the default interface for COM/COM+ objects, and does not feature support for multiple interfaces. Creating COM components requires a tool such as Visual C++ or Visual Basic.

ASP.NET

ASP.NET supports COM and COM+ objects, and it supports multiple interfaces and inheritance. (Inheritance is discussed in Session 10.) ASP.NET can inherit methods of objects created in different languages, with those objects created using a text editor.

ASP.NET supports industrial-grade programming. The same tools used to build complex Windows applications are accessible to ASP.NET. This includes all the classes in the .NET Framework. You can do socket programming, complex graphics programming, and anything else you can do in a Windows application.

Browser support

Although not as much a concern as it was just a few years ago, support of the different browsers is still a consideration when developing a Web application. ASP has remained browser-independent, whereas ASP.NET requires the developer to be more conscious of browser differences.

ASP

ASP is browser-independent. This means that the code you write in ASP does not care which browser is being used to access the page.

ASP.NET

ASP.NET supports server-side controls, which are rendered as DHTML on the client browser if the browser supports it, and HTML on other browsers. The controls use detection to figure out how to behave consistently among the different browsers. ASP.NET does not require you to write browser-detection code; it has several built-in facilities to help the controls decide how to render the GUI.

Deployment and Versioning

**20 Min.
To Go**

Deployment and versioning encompass the process of configuring and deploying an application to production, and maintaining it by writing new code. ASP and ASP.NET differ fundamentally in deployment and versioning.

Configuration

Before an application can be deployed, the developer must configure the application to work on the server and be aware of the requirements placed upon it. ASP does not offer a simple way to do this, but ASP.NET offers a very simple text file to handle application configuration.

ASP

Configuring an application is not a cut-and-dried task. It really depends on what you mean by *configuring*. Because ASP runs under IIS, you must use IIS to configure your ASP application. Using the IIS management console, you specify custom error pages, memory usages, users, and so on. This requires access to the server either as a role allowed to configure Web sites remotely or through the server console.

ASP.NET

ASP.NET encapsulates its entire configuration into a single XML-based text file, config.web. Config.web has sections for each configuration option, such as security, httphandlers, browser capabilities, and Web services (Web services are discussed in Chapter 29). This config.web file is programmatically accessible to your applications and can be modified using a simple text editor. All you need to do is edit the file and save it in the root of your application's folder on the server.

Deployment

I once had a client who used a script file in Windows Script Host to deploy his ASP application. When it ran, it would display a message saying, "Avert your eyes, it may take on other forms!" There is not one simple way to deploy an ASP application. ASP.NET, however, allows you to deploy an entire application with one command.

ASP

The process of deploying an application requires configuring IIS, registering components, setting up MTS, and ensuring the registry settings are correct. Transferring an application from one server to another is a complex job with few tools to automate the process.

ASP.NET

ASP.NET applications store their settings and components in text files. It is possible to copy an entire ASP.NET application, which exists solely as text files, via an XCOPY command. It's not necessary to register components, because they do not make registry entries and they don't need to be compiled before they are copied. All configuration is in the config.web file, which is a basic text file as well.

Versioning

Versioning is a touchy subject for many people. It has caused numerous problems and forced system restarts. ASP does not have graceful versioning of components. ASP.NET, however, has a great approach.

ASP

Any time you deploy a new version of a component (that is, COM object) on your server, you must stop and start the IIS service, or reboot the system. When the new version of the component is deployed, the old version is simply replaced, although very often it lingers in the registry.

ASP.NET

ASP.NET approaches versioning in a different way. When a new component is deployed, a new thread is spawned when the page using the new component is first accessed by a user. The old component coexists with the new component in memory because they are on separate threads. When the old component is no longer used, the ASP.NET worker process releases memory dedicated to the old component.

Scalability and Stability

Scalability and stability are the cornerstones of any successful application. Nobody wants to use an application that crashes all the time, and nobody wants to foot the bill to create a new application when the old one won't support an influx of new users or data. ASP and ASP.NET approach scalability and stability in their own separate ways, and when the creators of ASP.NET sat down to design the product, they had these two key areas in mind.

Scalability

Scalability refers to an application's ability to grow as its use grows. Its *use* can be defined as the number of users who use the application, the amount of data in the database, and other criteria. ASP supports limited scalability, and it's not simple at all. ASP.NET, on the other hand, was designed with scalability in mind from the beginning, so it offers an easy way to introduce scalability into applications.

ASP

Scalability with ASP has been severely limited thanks to the `Application` and `Session` objects. These objects don't scale on Web farms. The objects are tied to the computer that created them. If you want to put an ASP application in a Web farm, you must eliminate the Application and Session objects and replace them with a custom design or a third-party solution.

ASP.NET

ASP.NET approaches scalability with Web farms and Web gardens in mind. Session state can be configured to run in a web farm, or it can be persisted in SQL Server. ASP.NET supports several different types of caching, so database access code does not need to be put into an application variable using the `Application` object.

A *Web garden* is a Web server with multiple CPUs.

Stability

Stability is paramount to a successful application. ASP is not known for its crash protection, but ASP.NET takes an approach opposite of ASP and has crash protection built in.

ASP

ASP operates under the assumption that all code has been thoroughly tested. Infinite loops go unchecked, memory leaks run rampant (ultimately requiring a reboot), and the session timeout is the only recourse.

ASP.NET

ASP.NET takes an opposite approach. It assumes it has been fed the worst code imaginable. The ASP.NET process makes a note of this bad code and isolates the bad code's thread; it disallows any other code from running on the thread, then destroys the thread with bad code.

If a memory leak occurs, the ASP.NET process can spawn a new instance of itself, and then the new instance quietly kill its evil twin, all without rebooting.

**10 Min.
To Go**

Debugging and Error Handling

Application debugging is an essential part of the software development lifecycle. Nobody writes perfect code from the get-go. I once witnessed a student introduce a bug into a two-line BASIC program when he first wrote it:

```
10 PRINT "I'm learning BASIC."
20 GOTO 20
```

None of us is safe from mistakes like this. ASP and ASP.NET have completely different approaches to debugging and error handling, and ASP.NET offers a whole set of new functionality that ASP developers have been dreaming about for years.

Debugging

The process of debugging can be simultaneously rewarding and enraging. Developers spend countless hours debugging their programs. ASP pretty much doesn't offer debugging outside of Visual Interdev, and ASP.NET features powerful debugging tools that don't require an IDE.

ASP

Unless you're using Visual Interdev, you're on your own when it comes to debugging ASP. Most ASP developers use a bunch of `Response.Write` statements to output variable values and error messages. Even Visual Interdev's debugger can be a pain to work with.

ASP.NET

ASP.NET offers code profiling independent of any IDE. ASP.NET also offers the powerful trace facility, which is discussed in detail in Chapter 28. Trace allows a developer to determine when and where errors are occurring, and it can occur at the page level or the application level. Visual Studio.NET offers a very powerful debugger as well.

Error handling

Sometimes, despite vigorous debugging, errors still occur. Without error handling code, your application will most likely drop dead when an error occurs. Graceful error handling is the pinnacle of careful software development. ASP essentially offers zilch in the error handling department, but ASP.NET offers some glorious new tools.

ASP

Error handling in ASP exposes a few choices. You can use custom error pages defined in IIS, but these only apply to generic http errors like 404 and 500. VBScript offers `On Error Resume Next`, but no `On Error GoTo`. Many ASP developers plan for errors in their code and redirect the user to a special errors page or output a message in red.

JavaScript offers a `Try...Catch`, which helps trap errors, but VBScript doesn't offer anything remotely similar.

ASP.NET

Most of the .NET languages support `Try...Catch`. Using a `Try...Catch` block allows for exception handling (think of exceptions as errors). The code in VB.NET looks something like this:

```
Try
  x = 0
  z = 4/x
Catch e As DivideByZeroException
  Response.Write "You can't divide by zero."
Finally
  Response.Write z
End Try
```

ASP.NET supports several types of error handling, and each language offers its own error-handling style.

Done!

REVIEW

In this chapter, you learned about how ASP.NET differs from ASP. Each topic was covered the same way, with ASP presented first and ASP.NET compared and contrasted. Specifically, we covered:

- Environmental differences, including programming and execution
- Differences in deployment and versioning
- How ASP.NET differs from ASP in scalability and stability
- Methods of error handling and debugging in ASP and ASP.NET

The next chapter presents the beginning of our in-depth discussion of ASP.NET.

QUIZ YOURSELF

1. Do you need IIS to run ASP.NET? (See "Environment.")
2. How is ASP.NET configured? (See "Deployment and Versioning.")
3. What is a Web garden? (See "Scalability and Stability.")
4. How does ASP.NET handle a memory leak? (See "Scalability and Stability.")
5. Does ASP.NET require an IDE for debugging? (See "Debugging and Error Handling.")

SESSION

Introducing ASP.NET

Session Checklist

✔ Explaining what ASP.NET is

✔ Gaining exposure to the features of ASP.NET

✔ Learning how ASP.NET works

✔ Understanding ASP.NET syntax

**30 Min.
To Go**

You are now ready to explore ASP.NET, learn about all it has to offer, and see how to use its features. This chapter starts your exploration into what ASP.NET is, how it works, and what is needed to get your ASP.NET development started.

What Is ASP.NET?

ASP.NET is an environment for building and delivering Web server-based applications. It offers features for simplified Web application development, deployment, and maintenance. Many developers historically used ASP to build dynamic, Web-based client/server applications. ASP.NET takes the dynamic Web application to the next level, offering Windows-like functionality and ease-of-use in the most complex applications.

ASP.NET can be broken down into a set of eight core features. These core features offer a high-level understanding of what ASP.NET is and what it has to offer.

Full .NET support

ASP.NET is based on the Common Language Runtime, so the power and flexibility of the entire CLR is made available to Web application developers. This provides features such as language independence and garbage collection. With ASP.NET, it's possible to port applications written in legacy languages such as COBOL to the Web with ease. ASP.NET also supports the full class libraries, including the messaging and XML classes, so you don't have to know one set of libraries for Web development and one set of libraries for Windows development.

Simplicity

ASP.NET simplifies the normal operations of Web application development, such as form processing, authentication, and configuration. ASP.NET lets you separate presentation code (such as HTML) from application logic at the file level. This aids in code reuse and debugging.

Manageability

All configuring of ASP.NET applications is performed in XML-based text files. Any time you make a change to the configuration file (called Web.config) and save it, the setting is instantly made to the application without a need for restarting services or disconnecting users. When it's time to deploy an ASP.NET application, you simply copy the application's files to the server.

Tool support

Visual Studio.NET fully supports application development in ASP.NET. Visual Studio.NET allows you to drag and drop controls and edit your code directly, as well as quickly deploy your applications.

Performance

ASP.NET uses compiled CLR code on the server; ASP.NET is not interpreted. ASP.NET is a modern environment and it takes advantage of just-in-time compiling, early binding of objects, and caching services to provide the best performance possible.

Customizability

The ASP.NET architecture is designed to allow developers to plug in their code at any level. The ASP.NET classes can be inherited by custom components and extended to provide special functionality, such as custom authentication schemes.

Security

ASP.NET can use Windows authentication, cookies, and Microsoft Passport for security. Instead of across-the-board security settings for a whole server, ASP.NET supports per-application security configuration.

Scalability

ASP.NET was designed from the beginning to perform in clustered environments and on multiprocessor CPUs. The ASP.NET process closely monitors memory and processor usage, and it automatically regulates itself when things get out of hand.

How ASP.NET Works

**20 Min.
To Go**

The first thing you need to know before you start creating ASP.NET pages is how the process of requesting and delivering an ASP.NET page works.

Client perspective

From the client's perspective (where *client* reflects the system requesting pages from the server, driven by a user), the ASP.NET interaction process is straightforward. The user browses to an ASP.NET page by some standard means of browsing Web pages (clicking links, typing in URLs, and so on). The page loads in the browser. The user interacts with the page through form elements such as text boxes and buttons. The user submits the request via the page's user interface and the results are returned to the browser.

It doesn't get any more straightforward than that. All the user has to do is click around on the page and use the interface elements defined on that page. The server, however, has to do a lot more to make things happen.

Server perspective

From the server perspective, the process begins when a user requests a page and seemingly ends when the output is returned to the server. However, ASP.NET is not confined to repeatedly performing this cycle as a user clicks around on the user interface. ASP.NET is capable of interaction that is more dynamic.

The server process can be broken down into these steps:

1. The user requests an ASP.NET page from their browser.
2. The browser sends an HTTP request to Internet Information Server.
3. An ISAPI filter running in IIS intercepts the request and passes it on to the XSP worker process.
4. The worker process hands the request to the HTTPModules and the HTTPHandlers defined in the configuration files.

An HTTPModule is a class that can participate in every HTTP request, such as a class for state management or authentication. An HTTPHandler is the equivalent to ISAPI extensions; they provide an endpoint for processing of an HTTP request. The handler invoked is determined by the settings of the <httpHandlers> setting in Web.config.

5. The ASP.NET page is read from disk or cache and loaded into memory; it is then executed.

   This step includes whatever compilation is necessary.

6. The ASP.NET code outputs plain HTML and pipes it through a chain of defined modules down to IIS, which in turn delivers it to the browser.

   It would appear that the process is complete. However, the HTML returned to the browser can contain interface elements that perform server-side actions when manipulated. This is dynamic interaction. The process continues:

7. If the user interacts with the an HTML element that has a server-side event handler, the form is posted back to the server along with some hidden form fields that contain information about what element was clicked and what event was fired.

8. The ASP.NET page is loaded into memory in the same manner as before.

   This time, however, the page contains the hidden form fields and ASP.NET reads in the data and fires the appropriate event handlers.

9. The resulting HTML is sent to the browser and the process continues in a post-back cycle.

   This post-back cycle maintains the dynamic nature of an ASP.NET page.

Because ASP.NET takes advantage of the .NET Framework, including the Common Language Runtime, there are .NET "things" going on behind the scenes as an ASP.NET page is accessed and rendered. For example, the code within the ASP.NET page must be compiled, and the CLR performs this task. The .NET Framework also provides classes used by the page.

Page Structure

An ASP.NET page is a text-file containing code (for server-side execution and dynamic output) and markup (for content). ASP.NET pages have the default file extension of .aspx; it is possible to map any extension you want to ASP.NET pages in IIS.

ASP.NET supports ten distinct elements. Not all of these elements are required in an ASP.NET page in order for it to function. Depending on what you want to do, you simply decide which elements apply to your application and use them appropriately.

The ten elements are: code declaration blocks, code render blocks, directives, HTML control syntax, custom control syntax, data binding expressions, server-side object tags, server-side include directives, and server-side comments. Let's examine each element in detail.

Code declaration blocks

Code declaration blocks are used for code defining methods and variables. These methods and variables will be compiled in the dynamically generated Page class that represents the entire ASP.NET page.

A code declaration block can take two forms, with both forms using the <script> tag. The first form is:

```
<script runat="server">
'Code goes here
</script>
```

This code block expects code written in the default language specified at the Page level, and if no default language is specified at the Page level, it defaults to Visual Basic.NET.

The second form of the code declaration block is:

```
<script runat="server" src="filename" />
```

This code declaration block simply uses code that exists in an external file. Like the other form of `<script>`, it expects code written in the default language specified at the Page level, or in Visual Basic.NET.

Alternatively, you can specify a language attribute on the `<script>` tag:

```
<script language="VB">
'Code goes here
</script>
```

The same goes for the external `<script>`:

```
<script language="VB" src="externalfile.vb" runat="server"/>
```

In ASP.NET, in order for the code to run server-side, the `runat="server"` attribute of `<script>` is *required*. This attribute tells ASP.NET to run the code on the server. Otherwise, it will try to run the code on the client, and the entire code block will be visible to the client as well, via View Source in the browser. So you're facing a double-whammy if you leave off the `runat="server"` attribute: First, the user will encounter an error because he can't run client-side C# or VB.NET, and second, your code will be accessible to anyone who views the source.

How do you decide when to insert the code inside the `<script>` tag and when to use an external file? It all depends on style and needs. Some developers like to have external script files because it makes it easier to reuse code. Other developers feel that embedded code is better because it is more self-documenting. Still others find it more secure to put the code in an external file. Define your style and the answer will be clear to you.

Code render blocks

Code render blocks allow developers to define inline code that executes when the page is rendered, rather than when the page is compiled. There are two styles of code render blocks: inline code and inline expressions. Use the inline code when it is necessary to define self-contained code blocks or control flow blocks. Use inline expressions as a shortcut for `Response.Write`.

All code render blocks start with `<%` and end with `%>`. This is an example of inline code:

```
<%
Dim strText As String = = "Message for user
Response.Write(strText)
%>
```

Imagining the code snippet above is on a page, we could use an inline expression later in the same page like so:

```
<%=strText %>
```

A good way to remember when to use code declaration blocks and when to use code render blocks is to think of code declaration blocks as the foundation of your page, and code render blocks as code that uses the foundation as the page is built (rendered).

**10 Min.
To Go**

Directives

Directives specify optional settings for an ASP.NET page. Some of these settings include session state, ASP backward compatibility, namespace usage, and the default language for the page. ASP.NET supports six directives, with each directive providing a set of attributes that you can set depending on your needs.

@Page

The @Page directive sets page-specific attributes. The syntax for the @Page directive is:

```
<%@Page attribute=value %>
```

You can only use on @Page directive per .aspx file, so if you want to specify more than one attribute, you separate them with spaces on the same @Page directive:

```
<%@Page attribute1=value1 attribute2=value2 %>
```

The @Page directive supports more than a dozen attributes. Don't worry if you don't understand some of the attributes. You won't use many of them when you start developing ASP.NET applications for the first time. Some of these attributes are discussed more in later chapters. These attributes include:

- AspCompat: This determines whether the page is backward compatible with ASP. If this is set to False, ActiveX DLLs called by ASP applications will not function. The default setting is False.
- Buffer: This turns on HTTP response buffering. Set it to True to turn it on, False to turn it off. The default is True.
- CodePage: This sets the code page value for the response.
- ContentType: This sets the HTTP content type of the response. This can be set to any standard MIME type, such as "text/html."
- Culture: This indicates the culture setting for the page, and it supports any valid culture string.
- Description: Use this attribute to provide a description of the page. It supports any string value.
- EnableSessionState: Set this attribute to True to turn on session state management, False to turn it off, and ReadOnly if session state should be read but not changed. The default is True.
- EnableViewState: Set this to True to indicate that view state should be maintained across page requests. The default is True.
- ErrorPage: This defines a target URL for redirection if an unhandled page exception occurs.

- Inherits: This attribute is used in code-behind development. Code-behind development is discussed in Chapter 17.
- Language: This is probably the most used attribute. It specifies the default language for the ASP.NET page.
- LCID: This defines the local identifier for code in the page.
- ResponseEncoding: This defines the response encoding of page content, and accepts values from Encoding.GetEncoding.
- SRC: This indicates the code-behind class to compile. Code-behind is discussed in Chapter 17.
- Trace: Setting this to True turns on tracing, which is discussed in Chapter 28. The default is False.
- TraceMode: This indicates how trace messages should be displayed when tracing is enabled. It supports SortByTime, the default, and SortByCategory
- Transaction: Transaction support is used by setting this attribute to one of these values: NotSupported, Supported, Required, and RequiresNew.

@Control

The @Control directive sets user control–specific attributes. User controls are discussed in detail in Chapter 18.

@Import

The @Import directive explicitly imports a single namespace into a page. Importing a namespace into a page makes all of that namespace's classes and interfaces available to the page. The imported namespace can be part of the .NET Framework or a user-defined namespace. @Import has one attribute, namespace, which is a string value indicating the namespace to import:

```
<%@Import namespace="value" %>
```

The @Import directive accepts only one namespace value. To use more than one namespace in an ASP.NET page, you must specify additional @Import directives.

Namespaces are covered in more detail in Chapter 13.

@Register

The @Register directive associates aliases with namespaces and class names. This is used when creating custom server control syntax. Custom server controls are covered in Chapter 18.

@Assembly

An assembly is a collection of resources that are built to work together to provide a specific functionality. The @Assembly directive is used to link an assembly to the current page. Linking an assembly to the page exposes all the assembly's classes and interfaces.

@OutputCache

This page directive handles the output caching policies of a page. Output caching is discussed in further detail in Chapter 29.

HTML control syntax

HTML control syntax allows a developer to use standard HTML tags as server controls. It's done by simply adding a `runat="server"` attribute to the HTML tag. For example:

```
<INPUT TYPE="text" ID="txtExample" runat="server" />
```

The `runat="server"` attribute makes the control accessible to the server side code when the form is submitted, and it allows the server code to assign event handlers to the control. We'll talk more about controls in Chapters 17 and 18.

Custom server control syntax

Custom server controls are the controls included with the .NET Framework or controls you author. An example of these controls is:

```
<asp:TextBox ID="txtExample" runat="server" />
```

Like HTML controls and the @Control directive, custom server controls are discussed in Chapters 17 and 18.

Data binding expressions

Data binding expression syntax creates data binding relationships between controls and data sources. Data binding expressions can be written anywhere in the page, including in the value side of an attribute and the opening tag of a control.

Data binding expressions are discussed in detail in Chapter 23.

Server-side object tags

Server-side object tags allow you to declare and instantiate objects, including COM and .NET objects. The tag takes the form of `<object />`, and takes two required attributes, and one attribute that you pick depending on your needs. The syntax of the `<object>` tag is:

```
<object id="id" runat="server" />
```

You must specify one of three object types on the tag: .NET Framework class name as `class`, ProgID of a COM object as `progid`, or ClassID of a COM object as `classid`.

```
<object id="id" runat="server" class=".NET class name" />
<object id="id" runat="server" progid="COM object ProgID" />
<object id="id" runat="server" classid="COM object ClassID" />
```

When the compiler encounters a server-side object, it instantiates the object and assigns it to a read/write property on the page named whatever is in the `id` attribute of the object. This property exposes the object to the page as a non-UI variable, and the object is not in the page's server control tree. The `class`, `progid`, and `classid` attributes are mutually exclusive. Using more than one of these attributes on a single `<object>` tag will generate an error.

Server-side include directives

A server-side include directive simply instructs the page to include the raw contents of an external file. This directive can exist anywhere inside the page. The include directive has this syntax:

```
<!-- #include pathtype="filename" -->
```

Pathtype can be either `file` or `virtual`, where `file` points to a relative path and `virtual` points to a virtual path. `Filename` is simply the path (if necessary) and filename of the file being included. The `<!--` and `-->` tags are HTML comment tags, and they are required so HTML does not treat the include as literal text. This is an example of includes at work:

```
<html>
<body>
<!-- #include file="navigation.inc" -->
Pick from the navigation and then click one of the five items below:
<% Dim n As Integer
For n = 1 to 5 %>
<!-- #include virtual="/lottery/items.inc" -->
<% Next n %>
</body>
</html>
```

Many developers use includes to encapsulate often-used HTML code, like headers and footers.

Server-side comments

A server-side comment is used any time you want to prevent server code from executing. This includes server controls. The server-side comment has a syntax like so:

```
<%-- this is commented --%>
```

You can't use this comment syntax within `<% %>` code render blocks. When you use `<script ruant="server">` or `<% %>`, you should use the language's comment syntax (for example, ' for VB and // for C#). Server-side comments can be nested, and they can be used on different lines.

This code prevent the text box control from being displayed.

Done!

REVIEW

This chapter introduced you to ASP.NET and the concepts to get you started in coding ASP.NET pages. You are now halfway there! Specifically, this chapter covered:

- What ASP.NET is
- ASP.NET's core features
- How ASP.NET works
- ASP.NET page structure

The next chapter covers some of the .NET classes that will help you get your ASP.NET application development going.

QUIZ YOURSELF

1. In one sentence, what is ASP.NET? (See "What Is ASP.NET?")
2. From a server perspective, what is the first thing that happens when an ASP.NET page executes? (See "How ASP.NET Works.")
3. What is an HTTPModule? (See "How ASP.NET Works.")
4. What is the AspCompat attribute used for? (See "Page Structure.")
5. When can you not use a server-side comment? (See "Page Structure.")

Using Namespaces and Classes

Session Checklist

✔ Learning how to use namespaces

✔ Understanding some of the default namespaces

30 Min. To Go

All of the .NET Framework namespaces are exposed to ASP.NET. A namespace exposes classes and interfaces that provide functionality, so you don't have to write code that provides that functionality. For example, one namespace exposes a set of classes for connecting to databases and working with data, while another exposes classes for working with the file system (creating text files and such). The .NET Framework namespaces replace most of the COM objects that ASP developers used in their applications.

How to Use Namespaces

A namespace is a hierarchically organized set of objects. These objects include predefined types such as classes and interfaces. Namespaces are grouped by functionality; for example, all the data access classes are organized into the Data namespace under the System namespace. Specific data access classes, such as those that use ADO.NET, are grouped into the OleDb namespace under the Data namespace under the System namespace, so you get System.Data.OleDb.

Namespaces are stored in portable executable (PE) files. These files typically exist as DLLs or EXEs. Several namespaces, including nested namespaces, can exist in one PE file. One or more PE files are combined to form an assembly, which can be deployed, versioned, and reused. An assembly can be thought of as the equivalent of a COM object. Assemblies are used to deploy your custom classes, which are grouped into namespaces.

Namespaces are imported into ASP.NET applications using the @Import directive. ASP.NET automatically imports several commonly used namespaces into all pages. They are as follows:

- System
- System.Collections,
- System.Collections.Specialized
- System.Configuration

- `System.IO, System.Text`
- `System.Text.RegularExpressions`
- `System.Web`
- `System.Web.Caching`
- `System.Web.Security`
- `System.Web.SessionState`
- `System.Web.UI`
- `System.Web.UI.HtmlControls`
- `System.Web.UI.WebControls`

After the namespace is imported into your ASP.NET page, you simply use the objects it exposes. Consider this code snippet (this code may not execute; it's just an example):

```
<%@Import namespace="System" %>
<script language="vb" runat="server">
Console.Write "Console is an object exposed by the System namespace."
</script>
```

In this example, we've imported the `System` namespace and used the `Console` object it exposed. Some developers choose to write out the entire path to the object, such as `System.Console.Write`. This is only important when you are using two objects with the same name. So let's say you define a namespace called `MyNamespace` and it has one class, `Console`. The `Console` class has one member method, `Write`. In your code, you would have to differentiate between the two namespaces and objects they expose:

```
<%@Import namespace="System"  %>
<%@Import namespace="MyNamespace" %>
<script language="vb" runat="server">
System.Console.Write "System namespace"
MyNamespace.Console.Write "Custom namespace"
</script>
```

Notice the two separate @Import directives. Remember that each namespace must be imported on its own line.

 When creating your own namespaces, try not to mimic too much of the .NET built-in namespaces until you get more experience. You'll save yourself a lot of confusion.

The Namespaces

*20 Min.
To Go*
There are over 80 namespaces included in the .NET Framework. Many of them are out of the scope of this book, such as the namespaces devoted to creating WinForms (Windows applications) and the namespaces devoted to threading. To get you started in ASP.NET development, I'll cover seven of the namespaces automatically imported into all ASP.NET pages in this chapter, and then cover other namespaces, such as `System.Data.OleDb`, in the chapters where they are pertinent.

Each namespace has one or more objects, with some namespaces (such as `System`) sporting a few dozen. To save both space and your sanity, only a certain subset of objects under each namespace will be discussed. Like the namespaces themselves, these objects were selected to help you get your ASP.NET development jumpstarted.

System

`System` contains the fundamental classes that define commonly used events and event handlers, interfaces, attributes, value and reference data types, and processing exceptions.

Exceptions

Exceptions are thrown when your code performs an action that is forbidden, or results in an error. For example, `DivideByZeroException` is thrown when you try to divide a value by zero.

Most of the exceptions that aren't specialized exist in the `System` namespace. Data-specific exceptions, by comparison, are stored in the `System.Data` namespace. These are some of the exceptions found in the `System` namespace:

- `ArithmeticException`: The `ArithmeticException` is thrown when the value of an arithmetic operation is infinite or can't be represented in the result type. For example, multiplying decimals and trying to put the results in an integer will throw this exception.

- `DivideByZeroException`: This exception is thrown when a function tries to divide a value by 0.

- `FormatException`: This exception is thrown when the format of an argument doesn't match the format of its method. For example, if you have a method that accepts two arguments but you pass three, the `FormatException` will be thrown.

- `MissingMethodException`: This exception is thrown when you try to call a method that does not exist. For example, if you call the `GetTime()` method on `System.Decimal`, the `MissingMethodException` will be thrown because there is no `GetTime()` method on `System.Decimal`.

- `OutOfMemoryException`: This exception does exactly what it looks like. It's thrown when there's not enough memory to run the program.

- `OverflowException`: An `OverflowException` will be thrown when an arithmetic operation results in an overflow. For example, multiplying an integer containing 65,000 by itself 1,000,000 times will result in an overflow ($65{,}000^{1000000}$).

Classes

`System` exposes several dozen classes. Some useful classes exposed by `System` include

- `Array`: This is the base class for all arrays in the Common Language Runtime. It provides methods for creating, searching, sorting, and manipulating arrays.

- `Console`: The `Console` class provides access to the standard input, standard output, and standard error streams.

- `Convert`: The `Convert` class is used to simply convert base data types to other base data types.
- `EventArgs`: `EventArgs` is the base class for event data. The `EventArgs` class provides access to events fired by controls.
- `Math`: `Math` exposes methods for mathematical operations, including trigonometric and logarithmic functions.
- `Uri`: This class provides an object representation of the URI to facilitate easy access to its parts.

Structures

The structures include the data types supported by `System`. The structures include `Boolean`, `Byte`, `Char`, `DateTime`, `Decimal`, `Single`, `String`, `Double`, `Int16`, `Int32`, `Int64`, `UInt16`, `UInt32`, and `UInt64`. Each structure, such as `System.Decimal`, contains methods that can be performed on variables of that type (`Decimal`). The `System.Decimal` structure supports member methods such as `Add` and `Subtract`.

System.Collections

The `System.Collections` namespace contains classes and interfaces that define various collections of objects, including lists, arrays, queues, and dictionaries.

These are some of the classes exposed the by the `System.Collections` namespace:

- `Comparer`: This class provides methods for comparing two objects for equivalence.
- `Queue`: This class represents a first-in, first-out collection of objects.
- `SortedList`: `SortedList` represents a collection of associated keys and values that are sorted by the key, and accessible by key and by index.

System.IO

`System.IO` provides a set of classes for working with files. The `System.IO` namespace could be considered a replacement for the `Scripting.FileSystemObject` used in ASP. `System.IO` provides functionality such as creation and deletion of files and directories and random access to files.

Exceptions

System.IO exposes a set of exceptions that pertain to its operations. Some of these include

- `DirectoryNotFoundException`: This exception is thrown when an attempt is made to access a directory that doesn't exist.
- `FileNotFoundException`: This exception is thrown when a specified file is not found on the disk.
- `IOException`: This exception is thrown when an I/O error occurs.

Classes

These are some of the classes included in the System.IO namespace:

- `Directory`: This class exposes methods for creating directories and moving through them.
- `File`: The `File` class exposes methods that allow you to create, copy, delete, move, and open files.
- `StringReader`: The `StringReader` class implements a `TextReader` object that reads from a string.
- `StringWriter`: The `StringWriter` class implements a `TextWriter` object that writes to a string.
- `TextReader`: This class is an abstract class that represents a reader that can read a sequential stream of characters.
- `TextWriter`: `TextWriter` is an abstract class that represents a writer that can write a sequential stream of characters.

System.Web

**10 Min.
To Go**

`System.Web` provides classes and interfaces that enable server/browser communication. It includes classes for working with http requests, http output to the client, cookie manipulation, file transfer, and a lot more.

The `System.Web` namespace exposes a lot of the functionality found in ASP's six intrinsic objects. `System.Web` can easily become your most used namespace.

These are some of the classes exposed by System.Web:

- `HttpApplicationState`: `HttpApplicationState` enables developers to share information across sessions and multiple requests within an ASP.NET application.
- `HttpBrowserCapabilities`: The `HttpBrowserCapabilities` exposes methods that allow the server to gather information about the client browser.
- `HttpCookie`: `HttpCookie` provides a way to access manipulate http cookies.
- `HttpCookieCollection`: `HttpCookieCollection` is a collection of cookies; the class allows for accessing multiple cookies.
- `HttpPostedFile`: The `HttpPostedFile` class exposes methods to simplify access to files uploaded by a client.
- `HttpRequest`: The `HttpRequest` class could be considered a replacement for the Request object in ASP. `HttpRequest` enables browser to server communication. Specifically, `HttpRequest` provides access to the http request sent by the client, which can include things such as form values and cookies.
- `HttpResponse`: `HttpResponse` is a logical evolution of the Response object in ASP. `HttpResponse` enables server to browser communication. It sends http output to the client. This can be things like HTML and cookie information.
- `HttpServerUtility`: The `HttpServerUtility` class exposes several helper methods that can be used in the processing of Web requests.

- `TraceContext`: The `TraceContext` class captures and presents information about a Web request. `TraceContext` is used in tracing, a way to simplify finding and fixing errors. Tracing is discussed in detail in Chapter 28.

System.Web.UI

The `System.Web.UI` namespace exposes classes for working with user interface elements. For example, it exposes a Control class that defines the properties, methods, and events shared by all server controls. You can then create a class that inherits the properties, methods, and events of the Control class.

Some of the classes exposed by `System.Web.UI` include:

- `Control`: This class defines the properties, methods, and events for all server controls. Server controls are discussed in Chapters 17 and 18.
- `ControlCollection`: The `ControlCollection` class exposes a container that enables a control to keep track of its child controls.
- `Page`: The `Page` class defines the properties, methods, and events of all pages that are processed on the server. `Page` objects are compiled and cached into memory when they are requested.
- `StateBag`: The `StateBag` class manages the state of control properties. This is useful when you build a form and you want it to retain its values if for some reason the user clicks the Back button or an error is encountered.
- `UserControl`: The `UserControl` class exposes the properties, methods, and events of all the `UserControls` in an application. `UserControls` are discussed in Chapters 17 and 18.

System.Web.UI.HtmlControls

`System.Web.UI.HtmlControls` exposes objects that you can use to programmatically access properties, methods, and events of HTML controls. Any time you create an HTML control with the runat="server" attribute in its tag, that control is exposed to the server through `System.Web.UI.HtmlControls`.

The controls in `System.Web.UI.HtmlControls` are discussed in detail in Chapters 17 and 18.

System.Web.UI.WebControls

The `System.Web.UI.WebControls` namespace exposes the instrinsic ASP.NET server controls, which are used via the `<asp:ControlName>` tag. These controls include the validation controls, the ad rotator, the calendar, the datagrid, and many more.

The controls in `System.Web.UI.WebControls` are discussed through Part IV of this book.

Done!

REVIEW

This chapter covered seven of the mandatory namespaces that are imported into every ASP.NET page. The chapter took a to-the-point approach, presenting a synopsis of each namespace and a discussion of several of the member classes. Specifically, we covered:

- What a namespace is
- How to use namespaces
- The seven automatically imported namespaces
- Classes and exceptions found in the namespaces

The next chapter takes everything you've learned and leads you on the path of building an ASP.NET application.

QUIZ YOURSELF

1. What is a namespace? (See "How to Use Namespaces.")
2. What are the seven automatically imported namespaces? (See "How to Use Namespaces.")
3. What is an exception? (See "The Namespaces.")
4. How many namespaces can you import on a single @Import directive? (See "How to Use Namespaces.")
5. What are the classes in System.Web used for? (See "The Namespaces.")

Building ASP.NET Applications

Session Checklist

✔ Going through the process of creating an ASP.NET application

✔ Learning how to develop application logic

✔ Understanding Application and Session events

✔ Implementing security for an ASP.NET application

**30 Min.
To Go**

Now that you know what ASP.NET is and how to use it, you're ready to explore the process of building ASP.NET applications. This chapter covers that process, which encompasses concepts that exist outside of code, such as deployment and security, and inside code, such as the global.asax file.

What Is an ASP.NET Application?

An ASP.NET application is defined as a collection of files, pages, modules, handlers, and executable code stored in and invoked from a virtual directory on a Web server. For instance, if you have an ASP.NET employee time management system called TimeTrack, you could publish the application in the "/timetrack" virtual directory. All subdirectories of this virtual directory are exposed to the "TimeTrack" application.

Each ASP.NET application on a Web server is executed in its own space, called an Application Domain. This guarantees against version conflicts and autonomy of your application; in other words, the classes in one application won't interfere with the classes in another. This also improves security and preserves the concept of state for a single application.

Creating an ASP.NET application

All you have to do to create an ASP.NET application is create the file and find (or make) a place to put it. All a page needs to be considered an ASP.NET page is the .aspx extension, and it helps to actually have ASP.NET code in the page, but it's not required.

The first thing you do when creating an ASP.NET application is writing the pages. All you need is some code:

```
<%@ Page Language="VB" %>
<html>
<head>
<title>My Start Page</title>
</head>
<body>
<B><% Response.Write("This is my start page.") %></B>
<BR>
<B><% Response.Write("It was created on " & DateTime.Now.ToString())
%></B>
</body>
</html>
```

The second step in creating an ASP.NET application is figuring out where to put it. You can use the IIS console to create a virtual directory, or you can put your files in an existing virtual directory.

You can save this page as mypage.aspx and drop it into your virtual directory. Then point your browser to it. The URL will be something like:

```
http://yourserver/yourvirtualdir/mypage.aspx
```

For this book, all of my code is in a virtual directory under IIS named /wccaspx. My server is named Klaven, which is what the Professor Frink character on *The Simpsons* exclaims when he's excited:

```
http://klaven/wccaspx/mypage.aspx
```

Deployment

Realistically, you wouldn't put your newly created pages in a production virtual directory for the entire world to see. You first need to test them by putting them in a virtual directory that isn't published.

When you're ready for the outside world to see your application and wonder at its marvels, all you have to do is again figure out where you want it to go and put it there. I want to deploy mypage.aspx to my public Web server in a virtual directory called /wccbook. I could do it like so:

```
http://www.Standefer.com/wccbook/mypage.aspx
```

All you have to do to deploy the file is copy it to the virtual directory. If you have a bunch of files and directories, you just copy them all. Because ASP.NET applications are specific to virtual directories, you need only copy the files and directories that are in the virtual directory that contains your application. Let's say I have another virtual directory on my server called /timetrack. Since all my virtual directories are under the default webroot of IIS for Klaven, c:\inetpub\wwwroot, I see a directory structure like this:

```
c:\inetpub\wwwroot\wccbook
c:\inetpub\wwwroot\timetrack
```

Now I want only /wccbook copied to my Standefer.com server. All I have to do is run this command at the DOS prompt:

```
xcopy c:\inetpub\wwwroot\wccbook \\standefer\c$\inetpub\wwwroot
```

This will copy the wccbook directory and all its files and subdirectories to the wwwroot directory on my web server.

Creating Application Level Logic

**20 Min.
To Go**

Using a special file called global.asax, it's possible to store application logic and event handling code that is accessible across the entire application. The code in global.asax does not handle user interface generation and is not involved in individual page requests.

The global.asax file in ASP.NET is a natural evolution of the global.asa file in ASP. It has a lot of the same concepts but offers many more advantages.

The global.asax exposes high-level application events, such as `Application_OnStart`, `Session_OnStart`, `Application_OnEnd`, and `Session_OnEnd`. The global.asax file is stored in the root of the application's directory. For example, the global.asax file for the wccbook application would be stored as /wccbook/global.asax.

When the application is first accessed, ASP.NET automatically compiles global.asax into a dynamic class. This class extends the `HttpApplication` base class. The global.asax file is configured so that any requests for the file itself are rejected. This prevents users from downloading your global.asax and peeking at its internals.

The global.asax file is compatible with global.asa files from ASP. You can basically reuse any global.asa file by simply renaming it global.asax and putting it in your ASP.NET application directory.

The global.asax file is not required for an application. If you don't create one, ASP.NET assumes your application doesn't have any application or session event handlers defined. When you do create a global.asax file, simply define the event handlers in a server-side script block:

```
<script runat="server" language="vb">
Sub Application_OnStart(Sender As Object, e As EventArgs)
'Application start code here
End Sub
Sub Application_OnEnd(Sender As Object, e As EventArgs)
'Application cleanup code
End Sub
Sub Session_OnStart(Sender As Object, e As EventArgs)
'Session startup code
```

```
End Sub
Sub Session_OnEnd(Sender As Object, e As EventArgs)
'Session cleanup code
End Sub
</script>
```

Events defined in the global.asax must conform to the "Application_EventName" or "Session_EventName" pattern. Let's examine the application and session events separately.

Application events

Application events fire the first time an application is requested and when the application ends. The application events are Application_OnStart and Application_OnEnd. As their names imply, Application_OnStart executes when the application is first started, and Application_OnEnd runs when the application is ended.

The Application_OnStart **event fires the first time an application is accessed by any user. The Application is exposed to all users, not just the one user who first visited the application. This differs from Session, which is user to user.**

Anything you want to happen when the application is first requested goes in the Application_OnStart event:

```
<script language="vb" runat="server">
Sub Application_OnStart(Sender As Object, e As EventArgs)
'Application is started, so give the date and time
'Put the date and time in a variable
Dim strDateTime As String
strDateTime = DateTime.Now.ToString()
End Sub
</script>
```

This code populates a variable with the date and time the first time the application is started. We could write some extra code that writes this information to a log, or we could write some entirely different code that just issues a welcome message.

You can also declare variables in the global.asax file that are accessible at the application level. These are accessed using the Application("variablename") syntax. This can be a very useful tool for sharing information across an entire application.

Session events

A session event, unlike an application event, fires every time a new user "enters" and "leaves" the application. A session is defined at the user level; whatever occurs in the Session_OnStart and Session_OnEnd affects each discrete user. Consider this code:

```
<script language="vb" runat="server">
Sub Session_OnStart()
Response.Write("Your session has started.")
End Sub
</script>
```

When User A starts a session, the `Session_OnStart` event is fired and the message is displayed. When User B starts a session, the `Session_OnStart` event is fired and the message is displayed, but only to User B and not to User A. This differs from the `Application_OnStart` event, which would fire when User A starts the application and thus only User A would see the message.

A session variable is a variable that exists during the lifetime of a session. It's an easy way to share information across pages. For example, you can store a value in a session variable that says a user is logged in, and set the timeout for the session. When the timeout is reached, the login is no longer valid and the user is redirected to a login page. Here's a simple example:

```vb
<script language="vb" runat="server">
Sub Page_Load()
If Session("loggedin") = 0 Then
Response.Redirect("login.aspx")
End If
End Sub
</script>
```

The above code would run at the page level. Session variables do not need to be defined in the global.asax, but many developers do choose to initialize them there. In the global.asax:

```vb
<script language="vb" runat="server">
Sub Session_OnStart()
Session("loggedin") = 0 'initialize the session variable
End Sub
</script>
```

Maintaining session state in ASP.NET applications is further discussed in the next chapter.

When changes are made to an active global.asax file and the file is saved, ASP.NET detects that a change has occurred and effectively restarts the application after it completes the current requests for the application. This sends the `Application_OnEnd` event to any listeners, flushes the state information, closes all browser sessions, and restarts the application. The application then waits for the first request from a browser and when one is received, it recompiles the global.asax file and fires the `Application_OnStart` event. This can end up taxing your server when traffic is high, so plan your changes to occur during low-traffic times. Just be sure to not drink too much coffee.

Securing Your Application

10 Min. To Go

Security is one of the most important things to consider when you develop an application, and it's also one of the most overlooked. Security encompasses everything from logging user access to granting and denying user privileges.

ASP.NET offers many improvements in security over ASP. In fact, ASP.NET was designed with enhanced security in mind. Security in ASP.NET involves three functions: authentication, authorization, and impersonation. The security level is defined in the Web.config file (Web.config is covered in Chapter 27).

Authentication

Authentication is the process of accepting credentials from a user and validating those credentials against some authority, such as a database, Windows access control list, or XML file. Authentication simply makes sure the user is who the user claims to be. When the credentials are tested against the authority, there are two possible outcomes: authenticated or not authenticated.

ASP.NET relies on authentication providers for authenticating users. Authentication Providers are modules that contain the code (or functionality) necessary to authenticate the user's credentials.

ASP.NET supports three authentication providers: Windows, Passport, and Cookie.

Windows authentication

Windows authentication is used in conjunction with IIS authentication to validate user credentials. The actual authentication is performed by IIS. ASP.NET uses the authenticated identity to authorize access.

To set the security level to Windows authentication in Web.config, use this structure:

```
<security>
<authentication mode="Windows" />
</security>
```

Passport authentication

If you've ever used Hotmail, you've used Passport. Passport is Microsoft's single sign-on authentication service. It offers services such as the single sign-on and profile services. It can retain user information as well as credit card numbers. The benefit of using Passport is that is secure and already developed; all you have to do is integrate it into your site.

The entry in Web.config for the Passport authentication mode is:

```
<security>
<authentication mode="Passport" />
</security>
```

Cookie authentication

The cookie authentication mode allows the ASP.NET developer the flexibility of creating a custom authentication scheme. With this scheme, the developer creates a form that requests user credentials; when the form is submitted, the credentials are sent to the server and checked against a database. If the credentials are authenticated, the server creates a cookie on the client that contains the credentials. When the user requests the application again, the cookie is sent in the http headers and the ASP.NET application authenticates the user.

Cookie authentication is set up in Web.config as such:

```
<security>
<authentication mode="Cookie" />
</security>
```

The cookie authentication mode has some other elements you can define to further configure the cookie authentication scheme.

The other configuration scheme is simply "none":

```
<security>
<authentication mode="none" />
</security>
```

The default mode is Windows.

Authorization

After a user has been authenticated, the user must be authorized. Authorization determines what part of an application a user may access or use. There are two ways to authorize a user: file authorization and URL authorization.

File authorization

When Windows authentication is used, file authentication is active. The file authorization module handles file authorization (big shocker there). The file authorization module does a check against the access control list (ACL) to determine if a user should have access to a given resource.

URL authorization

URL authorization maps users and roles to pieces of the URI (Uniform Resource Identifier) namespace. URL authorization is performed by URLAuthorizationModule, which handles allowing or denying access to arbitrary parts of the application.

URL authorization is specified in the Web.config file:

```
<security>
<authorization>
</authorization>
</security>
```

Under the <authorization> element, the developer must specify one or both of the elements accepted by URL authorization, allow and deny.

```
<security>
<authorization>
<allow users="Robert" verb="POST" />
<deny users="Jim" verb="*" />
</authorization>
</security>
```

This block of code shows the two elements <allow> and <deny>, and the two attributes most commonly used, users and verb. Users defines the users that are granted or denied access to the application's resources, and verb specifies the http actions (GET, POST, HEAD) to which the action applies. The example above grants access to Robert, and denies it to Jim.

There are two special characters that you can specify in the users attribute:

```
<security>
<authorization>
<allow users="*" verb="*" />
<deny users="?" verb="*" />
</authorization>
</security>
```

Specifying * in the users attribute of <allow> grants access to all users, while specifying ? in the users attribute of deny will deny access to anonymous users. The process is a trickle-down one; while all users are granted access in the <allow> element, there follows a <deny> element, which revokes access for anonymous users. If it were the other way around, anonymous user access would be restored in the <allow users="*" /> element.

At the same time, specifying * in the verb attribute applies the authorization to all http verbs.

Impersonation

Impersonation allows you to run an application with the identity of the user on whose behalf the application is executing. This may be a little hard to understand at first. The idea behind impersonation is so you don't have to deal with authentication and authorization within your ASP.NET code.

With Impersonation enabled, ASP.NET defers to IIS to authenticate the user and IIS passes a token back to ASP.NET to let it know that a user has been authenticated or unauthenticated. The ASP.NET application impersonates the user regardless of which token is received; the application then relies on NTFS permissions to allow the application, which is impersonating a client, access to the files.

Impersonation is disabled at the server level by default and all application domains will inherit the setting. You can enable impersonation at the application level by editing the application's Web.config file. This would look something like this:

```
<security>
 <identity>
  <impersonation enable="true"
                 name="userid"
                 password="password />
 </identity>
</security>
```

You would simply replace "userid" with the client login you want to impersonate, and put the client's password in the password attribute.

Only application code is impersonated. The process token handles compilation and configuration. Because impersonation is disabled by default, applications that do not require impersonation can simply be left alone to run with their original process token.

Done!

REVIEW

In this chapter we took a high-level approach to building ASP.NET applications. Specifically, we covered:

- What an ASP.NET application really is
- Creating an ASP.NET application
- Deploying an ASP.NET application
- Using global.asax to manage application-level logic
- Setting application security

In the next chapter, we look at how ASP.NET handles session state management.

QUIZ YOURSELF

1. What are some parts of an ASP.NET application? (See "Creating an ASP.NET application.")
2. What does the concept of Application Domains guarantee? (See "Creating an ASP.NET application.")
3. Is the global.asax file required for an application? (See "Creating Application Level Logic.")
4. What are the three authentication providers? (See "Securing Your Application.")
5. What are the two types of authorization? (See "Securing Your Application.")

SESSION

15

Managing Session State

Session Checklist

✔ Seeing how session state works

✔ Comparing and contrasting ASP and ASP.NET session management

✔ Learning about ASP.NET session state modes

✔ Understanding the performance implications of session management

**30 Min.
To Go**

I f you come from an ASP background, you are almost certainly familiar with session state, along with its advantages and disadvantages. A session is the period of time during which a unique user is interacting with a Web application. Retaining data during a session requires managing the session state. ASP.NET approaches session state from a different perspective than that of ASP, and this chapter will show you how.

How Session State Works

Use session state to persist data during a user session. But before we jump into how ASP.NET handles session state, let's look at how session state currently works.

Session state is really nothing more than a section of memory similar to a dictionary or collection. Data is stored in value pairs; the first value is the key, which identifies your data, and the second value is the data itself. Managing session state is commonly referred to as *using session variables*. ASP uses session variables in this manner:

```
Session("username") = "rstandefer"
```

In this example, "username" is the key and "rstandefer" is the value. Session() is the ASP function that tells the server that you want to persist a value through a unique user session.

By putting the value in a session variable, any page can access the value without the user reentering the data:

```
'Get the username
```

```
Dim szUserName
szUserName = Session("username")
'szUserName will contain rstandefer in this example
```

ASP maintains session state by issuing an HTTP cookie to the client that stores a key unique to that client when the session begins. Each time the client makes a request to the server, it sends the HTTP cookie and the server can read the key from the cookie and subsequently "restore" the server session state.

Problems with ASP Session State

Although the idea behind session state is very sound, ASP's implementation of session variables is limited. Most ASP developers will agree using session variables is a hit-or-miss proposition. I once had a painful bug where my page would not read the value of a session variable when the page was opened in Netscape. It turned out that I had to cast all of my session variables as strings in order for Netscape to extract the correct information from the header. I don't have a good explanation for this, and that's the problem.

This particular problem was specific to my application, but ASP session variables inherently have certain limitations. These limitations are process dependence, cookie dependence, and server farm limitations.

Process dependence

ASP session state exists within the process that hosts ASP (typically, Internet Information Server, or IIS). Whatever actions affect the process also affect session state. So if IIS crashes or is restarted for any reason, session state is lost.

Cookie dependence

In order for session state to work properly, the client application, such as a browser, must be able to accept http cookies. Some clients treat cookies as security risks and thus disable them, which in turn disables session state on the server. Remember that session state on the server is dependent upon a unique key stored in a cookie on the client; if the cookie can't be written, the unique key can't be assigned.

Server farm limitations

ASP session state is machine specific, which means that a user's session state does not follow the user from server to server in a Web server farm. Because each ASP server manages its own session state, and the ASP server does not transfer its session state to any other server (nor does the client transfer its session state), session state is inaccessible on any server other than the one that issued the http cookie to begin with.

When ASP.NET was designed, the creators took these three major issues into consideration.

ASP.NET to the Rescue

Thankfully, ASP.NET does not suffer from the limitations that affected session state in ASP.

Process independence

ASP.NET is capable of running in a separate process, independent of the ASP.NET host process. The ASP.NET process can be restarted as much as you want and session state won't be lost. I compare this to ActiveX servers. ActiveX EXEs run in their own processes, whereas ActiveX DLLs must be hosted in something like MTS. If MTS crashes, all of the DLLs are inaccessible, whereas if one ActiveX EXE crashes, the others aren't affected. It's not the exact same thing by any means, but it should give you a better idea of process independence.

Cookie independence

ASP.NET handles cookieless session state by providing a simple configuration setting. Simply set the `cookieless` property to `true` in Web.config.

Server farm support

By process independence, ASP.NET allows all servers in the farm to share a session state process. Through the magic of the Web.config, it's simple to set the ASP.NET configuration to point session state to a common server. Beyond this, ASP.NET session can also be stored in SQL Server.

Using ASP.NET Session State

Like just about everything else in ASP.NET, session state settings are configured through the XML configuration file Web.config (Web.config is covered in detail in Chapter 27). Web.configFor this discussion, we'll touch on the Web.config file and how it works with ASP.NET session state.

What is Web.config?

Web.config is an XML file that stores settings for an application and a machine. It is actually two different files. One is a machine configuration file and the other is an application configuration file. Both are named Web.config, and they're both identical. The catch is that the machine configuration file applies settings to all applications, whereas the application configuration file applies settings to a specific application. Further, the machine configuration file is required, whereas the application configuration file is optional; if an application configuration file is absent, the application defaults to the settings in machine configuration file.

The machine configuration Web.config is in the root Web server directory, and the application's Web.config exists in the application's directory. While the application configuration file is optional, session state settings made in the machine configuration file can be overridden by settings in the application configuration file.

A particularly good thing about Web.config is the immediate activation of settings. No reboot or restart of services is necessary after you make a change to the Web.config; changes are immediate.

Configuring the session

Now that you have a better idea about Web.config, it will be easy to understand how to configure an application to use session state the way you want it to.

Look at the following Web.config file:

```
<configuration>
 <sessionstate
mode="inproc"
cookieless="false"
timeout="30"
sqlconnectionstring="data source=sqlsrv01;user
    id=sa;password="
server="127.0.0.1"
port="4004"
 />
</configuration>
```

Remember that the Web.config file is an XML file. XML was designed to help people define data; the Web.config file makes good use of XML. You should be able to look at the sample and get a pretty good idea of what the Web.config file is doing.

The settings in this example are used to set the ASP.NET session state. Specifically:

- Mode: This setting supports three options: inproc, stateserver, and sqlserver.
- Cookieless: This one is pretty self-explanatory. Setting this to true or false tells ASP.NET whether or not to use cookieless session state.
- Timeout: This controls the length of time a session is valid. It is configured as the current time plus the timeout value on each request.
- Sqlconnectionstring: Session state can be stored in SQL Server. This setting gives ASP.NET a database connection string for the SQL Server to store session state.
- Server: When mode is set to stateserver, server tells ASP.NET which server is running ASPState, the required Windows NT service.
- Port: This setting accompanies the server setting. It points to the port number that corresponds with the server setting for the stateserver mode.

ASP.NET Session State Modes

**20 Min.
To Go**

The mode setting in Web.config accepts one of three choices: inproc, stateserver, and sqlserver. Each of these modes has its own advantages

In-process mode

This mode is virtually the same as the classic ASP session state. In other words, the host process manages session state, and if the host process crashes or otherwise restarts, the session state is lost. In-process mode is the default setting for ASP.NET. When it is used, all the other settings are ignored except for `cookieless` and `timeout`.

You may be thinking, "Why would I want to use in-process mode if I'm trying to get past the limitations of ASP?" The reason is profound: The time it takes to read and write session state is much faster when the memory manipulated is in the same process as the manipulator. This is because cross-process calls and SQL Server calls add overhead.

Out-of-process mode

The .NET Framework installation includes a Windows NT service called ASPState. Using the example of the ActiveX EXE earlier in this session, ASPState is the equivalent of an ActiveX EXE. It's a service running on Windows NT Server or Windows 2000 Server that provides the out-of-process session state management for ASP.NET.

To use ASPState, you must first start the service. To do this, open a command prompt and type

```
net start aspstate
```

You'll then see a message stating that the service was started successfully. The Windows NT service is started and available to ASP.NET.

For ASP.NET to work with ASPState, you must configure the Web.config file:

```
<configuration>
 <sessionstate
mode="stateserver"
cookieless="false"
timeout="20"
server="127.0.0.1"
port="4004"
 />
</configuration>
```

The only difference between this Web.config and the previous is the mode. It's now set to `stateserver`. This tells ASP.NET to look for ASPState on the server specified in `server` and `port`. In this case, it's the local server because the value is the loopback IP address.

SQL Server mode

SQL Server mode is very similar to the out-of-process mode, except the session persists in SQL Server rather than being stored in memory. If you are already running SQL Server as your database, SQL Server mode has the advantage of not requiring the extra overhead on your server that the ASPState service would use.

To use SQL Server mode you must first set up your database by creating the necessary tables and stored procedures that ASP.NET needs on the identified SQL Server (in our example, `sqlsrv01`). The current version of the .NET SDK provides a SQL script, state.sql, that will perform these tasks.

The state.sql file contains the script to create two tables and several stored procedures in the ASPState database. ASP.NET uses the tables and stored procedures to store the session data in SQL Server.

You have two options when it comes to running state.sql. You can open the Query Analyzer in SQL Server and load the state.sql file there and run it, or you can run it from a command line.

To execute the InstallSqlState.sql script, use this syntax:

```
osql -S sqlsrv01 -U aspstate -P statemgr <InstallSqlState.sql
```

In this example, sqlsrv01 is the database server, aspstate is the sa-equivalent username, and statemgr is the password.

SQL Server will output a lot of text that essentially tells you that your tables and stored procedures have been created. All you need to do is configure your Web.config and everything will be set:

```
<configuration>
 <sessionstate
 mode="sqlserver"
cookieless="false"
timeout="30"
sqlconnectionstring="data source=sqlsrv01;
   userid=aspstate;password=statemgr"
server="127.0.0.1"
port="40404"
/>
</configuration>
```

Your database server is now ready to manage session state.

Cookieless Session State

Configuring a site's session management as cookieless essentially allows a site whose clients prefer to not use cookies to use ASP.NET session state. This is accomplished by modifying the URL with an ID. This ID uniquely identifies the session. For example:

```
http://localhost/(3sp4gy28d02g4p53c4n33p56)/sapp/nocookie.aspx
```

ASP.NET automatically embeds this ID in all relative URLs. As long as the user doesn't modify the URL, the session state will be preserved.

Configuring an ASP.NET site to use cookieless session state is as simple as you can imagine. Just set cookieless in Web.config to true:

```
<configuration>
 <sessionstate
mode="inproc"
cookieless="true"
timeout="30"
```

```
server="127.0.0.1"
port="4004"
 />
</configuration>
```

In-process, out-of-process, and SQL Server modes all support cookieless session state.

Are There Any Other Options?

There is one other option for session state management in ASP.NET. It's called *factorability*, and it allows one to extend or replace ASP.NET features. A third party may create a session statement management system that uses Active Directory or LDAP, along with some extended features. The default session management system in ASP.NET can be replaced by some third party tool such as this.

What About Performance and Reliability?

**10 Min.
To Go**

In terms of performance from best to worst, it's in-process, then out-of-process, then SQL Server. In terms of reliability, it's the opposite: SQL Server, then out-of-process, then in-process. The following sections break this down.

In-process

In-process is the fastest mode and will perform the best because the session state memory is kept within the ASP.NET host process. This is the best mode to choose in single-server setups, or where you don't care about session information being lost (or you provide code to restart the session).

Out-of-process

When performance is important but you have a server farm, use this mode. It gives the performance of reading from memory and the reliability of a separate process that will work in a farm environment. This is also good for proxy server environments.

SQL server

Sometimes the reliability of the data is fundamental to the stability of an application, as in certain electronic commerce applications or online banking. Often these applications run in a clustered environment. SQL Server is best for these situations as it can be clustered for fault tolerance. It doesn't have the performance of out-of-process, but it is much more reliable.

How Is Session Used in Code?

At this point, you should have a good understanding of the different session state management options. Because all configuration is done in the Web.config, the actual ASP.NET code is very simple, as you can see in this example written in Visual Basic.NET:

```
<Script runat=server>
Sub putSession(sender As Object, e As EventArgs)
Session("SampleSession") = txtSession.Value
spnSession.InnerHTML = "Session has been updated.<P>
  The session variable contains the following value: " +
    Session("SampleSession").ToString()
End Sub

Sub GetSession(sender As Object, e As EventArgs)
If (Session("SampleSession") = IsNull) Then
spnSession.InnerHTML = "Session data was lost."
Else
spnSession.InnerHTML = "The session variable contains the
  following value:" + Session("SampleSession").ToString()
End If
End Sub
</Script>

<form runat="server">
<input id="txtSession" type="text" runat="server">
<input type="submit" runat="server"
OnServerClick="putSession" value="Add to Session">
<input type="submit" runat="server"
OnServerClick="getSession" value="View Session Variable Value">
</form>
<span id="spnSession runat"="server"/>
```

This is a pretty simple snippet of code. The `putSession` subroutine takes the value of a text box and stuffs it into a session variable. It then prints out a message containing the value stuffed. The `getSession` subroutine references the session variable and prints out its value, or a message indicating an error.

Notice that there is no reference to cookies, or SQL Server, or ASPState in this code. The code doesn't care about how you have configured session state management. It just does its job, and counts on Web.config to do its job.

REVIEW

Done!

In this session, we covered how ASP.NET handles session state from both a machine-wide and application-specific standpoint. We looked at how session state management works, and then at how previous versions of ASP were limited in their implementation of session state. We then moved on to how ASP.NET handles session state management, specifically identifying how it addresses the limitations of ASP. We then covered the specifics of using ASP.NET session state management, including the ins and outs of Web.config. Each mode of session state management was covered, culminating in a discussion of the performance and reliability of each. Finally, a code sample of using sessions in Visual Basic.NET was provided to demonstrate the simplicity of session state management in ASP.NET.

Quiz Yourself

1. What is session management designed for? (See "How Session State Works.")
2. What are the three main limitations in ASP session state management? (See "Problems with ASP Session State.")
3. What is another term for session management? (See "How Session State Works.")
4. How does ASP.NET store the session configuration? (See "Using ASP.NET Session State.")
5. What are the two types of ASP.NET configurations? (See "Using ASP.NET Session State.")

Building Your First ASP.NET Page

You've come a long way since you started this book, and it all culminates in this chapter. We're going to build an ASP.NET page that performs a specific task.

*30 Min.
To Go*

What Do We Want to Do?

Before we can write any code, we need to decide what we want our page to do. ASP.NET can solve all kinds of different business problems, so all we need to do is pick one and make certain we can solve the problem with what we already know.

We don't want to get too far ahead of ourselves, but at the same time, we want to create a page that actually does something. Let's create a page that performs multiplication, division, addition, or subtraction of data entered via the querystring. The page will read in the data, perform a calculation on the data, and output the result.

This basic requirement allows us to determine our substantial requirements. These are

- The page must be able to perform four different mathematical operations: multiplication, division, addition, and subtraction.
- The page must use values submitted on a querystring.
- The page must accept an instruction.
- The instruction must indicate to the page what mathematical operation to perform.
- The page requires two values.
- The page must perform the mathematical operation on the two values.
- The page must output the result of the mathematical operation.

Using these requirements, we can start the construction of our ASP.NET page, which we'll name math.aspx. First, we need a simple HTML page that will submit the data to the ASP.NET page. Because we are using the querystring, we know we need to pass the data via GET:

```
<html>
<head>
<title>
ASP.NET Mathematical Sample
</title>
</head>
<body>
<form method="GET" action="math.aspx">
    <input type="text" name="value1">
<select name="operator">
    <option value="add">+
    <option value="subtract">-
    <option value="multiply">x
    <option value="divide">/
    </select>
    <input type="text" name="value2">
    <input type="submit" value="Get Result">
</form>
</body>
</html>
```

This page provides two input boxes (text boxes), a select box with our mathematical operators, and a submit button to send the values to the server via GET.

HTTP GET means the values of the form will be sent on the querystring. http POST means the values will be submitted to the ASP.NET page via the http headers.

Name this file Math.htm and save it in the wwwroot directory on your Web server.

Build the Page Skeleton

With the HTML page created, we can go on to our ASP.NET page. The first thing to do is build the ASP.NET page skeleton. This is accomplished by adding in all the code you'll need for the page to function, and define the preliminary properties of your page.

The page we build here will serve as the basis for the application we'll build in the last session. It will also be the basis for the discussions on Web Forms and ADO.NET.

The very first part of the ASP.NET page is the @Import directive. The @Import directive tells our page which namespaces to use. We need access to mathematical operators, so which namespace do we want? Looking at the documentation for System.Math, we can see that it's designed to perform trigonometric and logarithmic calculations. We don't want to do that. The correct namespace for our needs is System.Decimal. System.Decimal exposes four methods that are important to us, Add, Subtract, Divide, and Multiply. System. Decimal also exposes a lot of other methods and properties, but we don't need them for this example.

The code to using the correct namespace is

```
<%@Import Namespace="System.Decimal" %>
```

This directive will expose the System.Decimal structure and allow us to call its methods. Open a text file in EditPlus or your favorite text editor and enter the above line. Save the file with the filename math.aspx in a virtual directory on your Web server.

The Page_Load function should contain all the code to perform our operations. This means it needs to read in the querystring, populate variables with the incoming values, and call the appropriate function to perform the mathematical operation.

Because we are using the System.Decimal namespace we have to declare any variables that will contain the incoming numeric values as Decimals. In other words, they must be of the Decimal data type. This will allow the user to input a value containing a decimal point. The System.Decimal namespace is capable of converting a numeric data type to Decimal, but for this example, we'll explicitly declare relevant variables as Decimals.

Add the Page_Load function to our ASP.NET page and we have

```
<%@Import Namespace="System.Decimal" %>
<script language="VB" runat="server">
Sub Page_Load(Source as Object, E As EventArgs)
Dim decValue1      As Decimal
Dim decValue2      As Decimal
Dim strOperator    As String
decValue1 = Request.QueryString("value1")
decValue2 = Request.QueryString("value2")
strOperator = Request.QueryString("operator")
End Sub
</script>
```

Right now, our ASP.NET page doesn't do much more than read in the values from the querystring and populate variables with the values. To perform our operations, we need to call methods on the System.Decimal namespace; we'll do that using functions.

Write Your Functions

20 Min.
To Go

Separating core functionality into functions is always a good idea. This allows for code reuse, simple maintenance, and sometimes, performance increases. Because we are using four mathematical operators, we'll write four functions, one for each operator.

We shouldn't use a Sub here because we need the function to return a value, the result of the calculation. Each function should accept two parameters, which are the values that are pertinent to the calculation. The operator does not need to be passed because the function already assumes the operator; in other words, you'll call MultiplyValues if you want to multiply two values. The great thing about writing these functions is that they are very similar so you can copy and paste code from one to another.

Remember that the underscore(_) indicates the continuation of a line.

Each of these functions will exist in math.aspx so we don't need to import the System.Decimal namespace into the functions. The function for multiplication is

```
<script language="VB" runat="server">
Function MultiplyValues(decValue1 As Decimal, decValue2 As _
Decimal)

Dim decResult As Decimal
decResult = Multiply(decValue1, decValue2)
Return decResult

End Function
</script>
```

The function for division is very similar:

```
<script language="VB" runat="server">
Function DivideValues(decValue1 As Decimal, decValue2 As _
Decimal)

Dim decResult As Decimal
decResult = Divide(decValue1, decValue2)
Return decResult

End Function
</script>
```

The function for addition is

```
<script language="VB" runat="server">
Function AddValues(decValue1 As Decimal, decValue2 As _
Decimal)

Dim decResult As Decimal
decResult = Add(decValue1, decValue2)
Return decResult

End Function
</script>
```

Finally, the function for subtraction:

```
<script language="VB" runat="server">
Function SubtractValues(decValue1 As Decimal, decValue2 As _
Decimal)
```

```
Dim decResult As Decimal
decResult = Subtract(decValue1, decValue2)
Return decResult

End Function
</script>
```

If you look at the four functions, you'll notice they're nearly identical. The only difference is the name of the operator in the function name and in the `System.Decimal` method call.

Integrating the Code

The functions could stand alone on an ASP.NET page if each page had the correct `@Import` directive for the `System.Decimal` namespace, but separating the functions into separate pages is both tedious and inefficient. The functions need to be integrated into math.aspx. This is a simple process; just copy and paste the functions, minus the `<script></script>` tags, to the math.aspx text file:

```
<%@Import Namespace="System.Decimal" %>
<script language="VB" runat="server">
Sub Page_Load(Source as Object, E As EventArgs)
Dim decValue1      As Decimal
Dim decValue2      As Decimal
Dim strOperator    As String
decValue1 = Request.QueryString("value1")
decValue2 = Request.QueryString("value2")
strOperator = Request.QueryString("operator")
End Sub

Function MultiplyValues(decValue1 As Decimal, decValue2 As _
Decimal)

Dim decResult As Decimal
decResult = Multiply(decValue1, decValue2)
Return decResult

End Function

Function DivideValues(decValue1 As Decimal, decValue2 As _
Decimal)

Dim decResult As Decimal
decResult = Divide(decValue1, decValue2)
Return decResult

End Function

Function AddValues(decValue1 As Decimal, decValue2 As _
Decimal)
```

```
Dim decResult As Decimal
decResult = Add(decValue1, decValue2)
Return decResult

End Function

Function SubtractValues(decValue1 As Decimal, decValue2 As _
Decimal)

Dim decResult As Decimal
decResult = Subtract(decValue1, decValue2)
Return decResult

End Function

</script>
```

Our functions are now integrated into the math.aspx page. We can call them directly from Page_Load, which we'll do next.

Calling the Functions

To call the functions, we simply add the function calls to the Page_Load function and pass the appropriate values. How do we know which method to call? Since we have the operator in a variable, we can use a Select...Case conditional to determine which function to call:

```
<% ...
Select Case strOperator
Case "multiply"
'Call multiply function
Case "divide"
'Call divide function
Case "add"
'Call addition function
Case "subtract"
'Call subtraction function
Case Else
'Error?
End Select
%>
```

The Select...Case conditional is perfect for our needs. Let's add it to our math.aspx page:

```
<%@Import Namespace="System.Decimal" %>
<script language="VB" runat="server">
Sub Page_Load(Source as Object, E As EventArgs)
Dim decValue1      As Decimal
Dim decValue2      As Decimal
Dim strOperator    As String
Dim decResult      As Decimal
```

```
decValue1 = Request.QueryString("value1")
decValue2 = Request.QueryString("value2")
strOperator = Request.QueryString("operator")

Select Case strOperator
Case "multiply"
decResult = MultiplyValues(decValue1, decValue2)
Case "divide"
decResult = DivideValues(decValue1, decValue2)
Case "add"
decResult = AddValues(decValue1, decValue2)
Case "subtract"
decResult = SubtractValues(decValue1, decValue2)
End Select

Response.Write("The result of your calculation is: " & _
decResult)
End Sub

Function MultiplyValues(decValue1 As Decimal, decValue2 As _
Decimal)

Dim decResult As Decimal
decResult = Multiply(decValue1, decValue2)
Return decResult

End Function

Function DivideValues(decValue1 As Decimal, decValue2 As _
Decimal)

Dim decResult As Decimal
decResult = Divide(decValue1, decValue2)
Return decResult

End Function

Function AddValues(decValue1 As Decimal, decValue2 As _
Decimal)

Dim decResult As Decimal
decResult = Add(decValue1, decValue2)
Return decResult

End Function

Function SubtractValues(decValue1 As Decimal, decValue2 As _
Decimal)

Dim decResult As Decimal
decResult = Subtract(decValue1, decValue2)
Return decResult
```

```
End Function
</script>
```

This is the complete code for the math.aspx page. It will read in the values from the querystring, perform the specified mathematical operation, and output the result with Response.Write.

Now, open Math.htm on your Web server in Internet Explorer. In the first box, type 8. Choose divide (/) as the operator, and type 0 in the second box. Click the "Get Result" button. What happened? ASP.NET threw an exception because it tried to divide by zero. To handle this, we need exception handling.

Exception Handling

10 Min. To Go

Each of the four mathematical functions in System.Decimal will throw an exception, OverflowException. System.Decimal.Divide will throw two exceptions, OverflowException and DivideByZeroException. An OverflowException occurs if the result is too large to represent as a Decimal. A DivideByZeroException is thrown if the Divide function takes zero as a divisor.

Your ASP.NET page needs to handle these exceptions using Try...Catch...Finally:

```
<%@Import Namespace="System.Decimal" %>
<script language="VB" runat="server">
Sub Page_Load(Source as Object, e As EventArgs)
Dim decValue1      As Decimal
Dim decValue2      As Decimal
Dim strOperator    As String
Dim decResult      As Decimal
decValue1 = Request.QueryString("value1")
decValue2 = Request.QueryString("value2")
strOperator = Request.QueryString("operator")

Try
Select Case strOperator
Case "multiply"
decResult = MultiplyValues(decValue1, decValue2)
Case "divide"
decResult = DivideValues(decValue1, decValue2)
Case "add"
decResult = AddValues(decValue1, decValue2)
Case "subtract"
decResult = SubtractValues(decValue1, decValue2)
End Select
Catch e As OverflowException
Response.Write("The result was too large to represent" & _
              "as a decimal.")
Catch e As DivideByZeroException
Response.Write("You cannot divide by zero.")
```

```
            Finally
            Response.Write("The result of your calculation is: " & _
                        decResult)

            End Try
            End Sub

            Function MultiplyValues(decValue1 As Decimal, decValue2 As _
            Decimal)

            Dim decResult As Decimal
            decResult = Multiply(decValue1, decValue2)
            Return decResult

            End Function

            Function DivideValues(decValue1 As Decimal, decValue2 As _
            Decimal)

            Dim decResult As Decimal
            decResult = Divide(decValue1, decValue2)
            Return decResult

            End Function

            Function AddValues(decValue1 As Decimal, decValue2 As _
            Decimal)

            Dim decResult As Decimal
            decResult = Add(decValue1, decValue2)
            Return decResult

            End Function

            Function SubtractValues(decValue1 As Decimal, decValue2 As _
            Decimal)

            Dim decResult As Decimal
            decResult = Subtract(decValue1, decValue2)
            Return decResult
            End Function
            </script>
```

This is the complete math.aspx page. It meets all the requirements, and it has exception handling. Congratulations! You built your first complete ASP.NET application. Later in this book, we'll convert it to use Web forms, and then we'll add database connectivity. Finally, we'll build a configuration file and deploy the application.

Done!

REVIEW

In this chapter, we built an ASP.NET page from the ground up. Specifically, we covered

- Defining our problem
- Creating a list of requirements
- Writing a `Page_Load` function
- Using the `System.Decimal` namespace
- Writing functions to perform our operations
- Calling the functions from `Page_Load`
- Using exception handling

From here, we're headed into Web forms.

QUIZ YOURSELF

1. What's the first thing you do before writing code? (See "What Do We Want to Do?")
2. How do you load a namespace? (See "Build the Page Skeleton.")
3. What is the `Page_Load` function? (See "Build the Page Skeleton.")
4. What is the advantage of separating our operations into functions? (See "Write Your Functions.")
5. Why do we need exception handling? (See "Exception Handling.")

PART

III

Saturday Afternoon Part Review

1. ASP is only extendable through ISAPI. Name one way you can extend ASP.NET.
2. Does ASP.NET support multiple COM/COM+ interfaces?
3. How does ASP.NET simplify configuration?
4. What must you do when you deploy a new component for your ASP.NET application?
5. What is a Web garden?
6. Give an example of a code declaration block.
7. How do you delimit a code render block?
8. What does the Language attribute of the @Page directive do?
9. What is the syntax of a server-side object tag that instantiates the `System.Data.SqlClient` class?
10. How do you include a file in a relative path?
11. How are namespaces grouped?
12. Where are namespaces stored?
13. Approximately how many namespaces are included in the .NET Framework?
14. What does the `HttpApplicationState` class of the `System.Web` namespace do?
15. What does the `Directory` class of `System.IO` do?
16. What are some features of an application domain?
17. What does a text file need to be considered an ASP.NET page?
18. How do you deploy an ASP.NET application?
19. When do application events fire?
20. When do session events fire?
21. What are the three main problems inherent in ASP session state management?

22. What tag is used to configure session state management in Web.config?

23. What are the three acceptable values for the Mode attribute?

24. What is the `sqlserver` mode good for?

25. How do you reference session variables in code?

PART

IV

*Saturday
Evening*

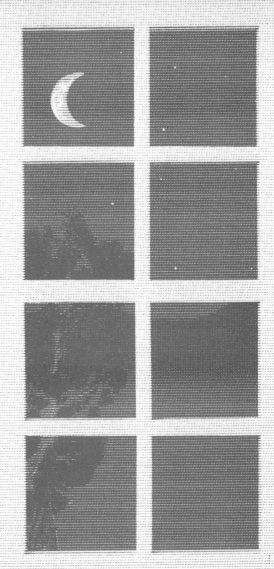

Session 17
Introducing Web Forms

Session 18
Working with Controls

Session 19
Validating User Input

Session 20
Building a Web Form

Introducing Web Forms

Session Checklist

✔ Understanding the concept of a Web form

✔ Seeing how Web forms work

✔ Finding out about some of the server controls

✔ Understanding code-behind programming

**30 Min.
To Go**

A SP.NET introduces a new way of building the graphical user interface (GUI) of a Web application. Instead of building clunky HTML forms and trying to make them work with your server-side script, ASP.NET allows you to use Web Forms. This chapter tells you about Web forms and what you can expect when you use them.

What Is a Web Form?

For all intents and purposes, a Web form is an ASP.NET page that contains visual components. It's not a special file format or anything like that, and it doesn't require anything special to make an ASP.NET a Web form (except, of course, for interface elements).

Web forms provide an event-based programming model for ASP.NET applications. They're similar to the form-based development environment of Microsoft Visual Basic.

A rich set of controls

ASP.NET Web forms take advantage of a rich set of controls exposed by the .NET Framework namespaces. These controls include HTML controls, special Web controls, and data controls designed to simplify working with databases.

Each control on a Web form has a set of properties, methods, and events that can be manipulated server-side. Because the controls have events, you can write event-driven code, like for a Click event of a button.

Web forms also support custom controls, which you can easily create by inheriting features from other controls.

The HTML controls are discussed briefly in this chapter; server controls, which include the HTML controls and Web controls, are discussed more in-depth in Chapter 18.

Browser independent

Web forms produces browser-independent code. That means you can use Web forms in all your applications and not worry about the different browser implementations. If you choose to do so, you can design your Web form to run on a specific browser, such as Internet Explorer 5, and take advantage of that browser's client features.

Separation of interface and logic

Web forms divide the Web application's user interface into two parts: the visual and the logic. The *visual* refers to the controls themselves, while the *logic* refers to the code you write to work with the controls, such as code to get the Text property of a control.

The user interface for pages that use Web forms consists of a file containing markup and Web forms–specific elements. This is your page, the file that ends in .aspx. The page is a container for the controls and any other content you want to display.

The logic for the Web form is code written to interact with the form. This can exist in the same page as the form itself or in another file, which is written in Visual Basic or C#. This separate file facilitates code behind, which can greatly simplify application development in ASP.NET using Web forms.

Web Forms and Visual Studio.NET

Visual Studio.NET includes a feature-rich environment for building Web forms, including a drag-and-drop interface very similar to Visual Basic. ASP never had anything that was this seamless; most of the interface-building tools for ASP were simply HTML builders with the capability of generating ASP code.

The Visual Studio.NET environment will facilitate easy Web forms creation. It is capable of generating both VB.NET and C# code. The toolbox will allow you to drag and drop visual controls as well as non-visual elements, such as DataSets.

The Visual Studio.NET environments will also simply code behind development.

Web Forms Page Processing

**20 Min.
To Go**

A Web form is just like any other ASP.NET page in that it is processed on the server, relies on Web.config, and so on. Web forms also provide a number of special services, such as maintaining the state of the controls and providing object access to controls.

The three stages of processing

During the processing of a Web form, it goes through three stages. These three stages form a high-level abstraction of how the Web form works.

Page_Load

This stage restores page and control view state, and the page's `OnLoad` event is fired. The `Page_Load` event runs each time the page is requested or posted. Using `IsPostBack`, you can determine whether the page is being processed for the first time. Things such as data binding and restoring state occur in `Page_Load`.

Event handling

If the page was called in correspondence with a form event, such as a Click, then the corresponding event handling code is called in this stage.

Page_Unload

When the `Page_Unload` event occurs, the page has finished rendering and is ready to be sent to the garbage collector. This is where you put cleanup work, such as removing files, closing database connections, and destroying objects.

View state and state management

Web pages are stateless. As soon as the server processes a Web form and sends it to the browser, the page information is thrown away. The next time the page is posted, the server starts the process over again. The pages are *stateless*; they don't preserve variable values and control information on the server.

A *round trip* is the process of a Web form being posted to the server, processed, and returned to the browser.

ASP.NET Web forms preserve state in several ways. A Web form saves page and control properties between round trips to the server. This is called *view state*. The Web form knows the difference between when a form is first visited and when it is processed by placing a hidden form field in the form. Additionally, the Web form is capable of storing other information between round trips, and sharing that information from page to page.

The HTML Controls

The .NET Framework exposes a namespace for working with server-side HTML control. A server-side HTML control is simply an HTML element with a `runat="server"` attribute, like so:

```
<INPUT TYPE="text" ID="txtName" runat="server" />
```

Using this control will make it accessible to server-side code through its ID. The server-side control that equates to `<INPUT TYPE="text">` is exposed by the `System.Web.UI.HtmlControls` namespace.

Each of these classes exposed by `System.Web.UI.HtmlControls` evaluates to an HTML tag.

- `HtmlAnchor`: This corresponds to the `<A>` tag.
- `HtmlButton`: This corresponds to the `<button>` tag.
- `HtmlForm`: This corresponds to the `<form>` tag.
- `HtmlGenericControl`: This corresponds to the unmapped tags, such as `<span>` and `<div>`.
- `HtmlInputButton`: This corresponds to the `<input type="button">`, `<input type="submit">`, and `<imput type="reset">` tags.
- `HtmlInputCheckBox`: This corresponds to the `<input type="checkbox">` tag.
- `HtmlInputFile`: This corresponds to the `<input type="file">` tag.
- `HtmlInputHidden`: This corresponds to the `<input type="hidden">` tag.
- `HtmlInputImage`: This corresponds to the `<input type="image">` tag.
- `HtmlInputRadioButton`: This corresponds to the `<input type="radio">` tag.
- `HtmlInputText`: This corresponds to the `<input type="text">` and `<input type="password">` tags.
- `HtmlSelect`: This corresponds to the `<select>` tag.
- `HtmlTable`: This corresponds to the `<table>` tag.
- `HtmlTableCell`: This corresponds to the `<td>` tag.
- `HtmlTableRow`: This corresponds to the `<tr>` tag.
- `HtmlTextArea`: This corresponds to the `<textarea>` tag.

Remember that all it takes to make an HTML control server-side is the `runat="server"` attribute.

Building a Web Form

10 Min. To Go

Building a Web form in ASP.NET is a simple process, especially when you use the HTML controls. Let's look at building a form in ASP and ASP.NET, and compare the results. The form will expect you to enter your name and age. When submitted, the form will write your name and age to the page.

An ASP form

This is a form implemented in ASP:

```
<%@ Language="VBScript"  %>
<html>
<head>
<title>aspsample.asp</title>
```

```
</head>
<body>
<form method="post" action="aspsample.asp" id="SampleForm">
<table>
  <tr>
   <td>Enter your name:</td>
   <td><input type="text" id="txtName"
value="<%=Request.Form("txtName")%>">
  </tr>
  <tr>
   <td>Enter your age:</td>
   <td><input type="text" id="txtAge"
value="<%=Request.Form("txtAge")%>"></td>
  </tr>
  <tr>
   <td><input type="submit" value="Submit"></td>
  </tr>
  <% If Request.Form.Count <> 0 Then %>
  <tr>
   <td>Your name is: <%=Request.Form("txtName")%></td>
   <td>Your age is: <%=Request.Form("txtAge")%></td>
  </tr>
  <% End If %>
 </table>
</form>
</body>
</html>
```

This form uses inline ASP tags (<% %>) to output the value of the form elements in `Request.Form`. This can make the code really hard to read when the form gets large. `Request.Form.Count` was used to detect form submission; if `Count` evaluates to zero, the page knows that the Submit button was not pressed.

To preserve state on the form, I had to put `<%=Request.Form()%>` code in the VALUE attribute of the text boxes. ASP doesn't support state management intrinsically.

An ASP.NET form

This is the same form as in the preceding section, but as an ASP.NET Web form using the HTML controls:

```
<html>
<head>
<title>aspsample.aspx</title>
<script language="vb" runat="server">
Sub Page_Load(Source As Object, e As EventArgs)
If Page.IsPostBack Then
   divName.innerText = "Your name is: " & txtName.Value
   divAge.innerText = "Your age is: " & txtAge.Value
End If
End Sub
</script>
```

```
</head>
<body>
<form method="post" id="SampleForm" runat="server">
<table>
<tr>
 <td>Enter your name:</td>
 <td><input type="text" id="txtName" value="" runat="server" />
</tr>
<tr>
 <td>Enter your age:</td>
 <td>
 <input type="text" id="txtAge" value="" runat="server" /></td>
</tr>
<tr>
 <td>
 <input type="submit" id="submit" value="Submit" runat="server" />
 </td>
</tr>
<tr>
 <td><div id="divName" runat="server" /></td>
 <td><div id="divAge"  runat="server" /></td>
</tr>
</table>
</form>
</body>
</html>
```

This code is much simpler. All of the ASP.NET code is in the `<script>` tag at the top of the page. It checks for `IsPostBack` to determine if the page has been posted; if it has, it sets the `innerText` property of the `<div>` control to the values submitted on the form.

Each form element is made server side by the addition of a simple `runat="server"` attribute. Because server-side HTML controls were used, we were able to reference the `Value` property of the `<input type="text">` tag.

Finally, because we're using server-side HTML controls, form state is automatically preserved, which means we don't have to write it ourselves with clunky inline code.

Code Behind Development

Code behind development refers to the concept of separating ASP.NET Web forms into two files, one for the presentation and one for the logic. The presentation file is the .aspx page, and the code behind file is a Visual Basic (or C#) file with an extension of .vb, for Visual Basic, or .cs, for C#.

Separating the logic from the presentation makes the logic independent of whatever page uses it. This means you can use one logic file for several presentation files, which simplifies maintenance and provides a way to protect your code from prying eyes.

Using code behind

Using code behind requires a few modifications to your .aspx page. Look at this @ Page directive, modified to use code behind:

```
<%@ Page Language="VB" Inherits="SamplePage" Src="sample.vb" %>
```

This directive has two extra attributes, Inherits and Src. Inherits identifies the class from which the page will inherit, and Src identifies the file storing that class. Let's put the @ Page directive into the Web form we've already built:

```
<%@ Page Language="VB" Inherits="SamplePage" Src="sample.vb" %>
<html>
<head>
<title>aspsample.aspx</title>
</head>
<body>
<form method="post" id="SampleForm" runat="server">
<table>
<tr>
 <td>Enter your name:</td>
 <td><input type="text" id="txtName" value="" runat="server" />
</tr>
<tr>
 <td>Enter your age:</td>
 <td>
 <input type="text" id="txtAge" value="" runat="server" /></td>
</tr>
<tr>
 <td>
 <input type="submit" id="submit" value="Submit" runat="server" />
 </td>
</tr>
<tr>
 <td><div id="divName" runat="server" /></td>
 <td><div id="divAge"  runat="server" /></td>
</tr>
</table>
</form>
</body>
</html>
```

Notice there is no ASP.NET code in this form. Instead, it will all be in a Visual Basic code behind file, called Sample.vb:

```
Imports System
Imports System.Web.UI
Imports System.Web.UI.HtmlControls
Public Class SamplePage : Inherits Page
  Public txtName As HtmlInputText
  Public txtAge As HtmlInputText
```

```
Public Sub Page_Load(Source As Object, e As EventArgs)
   If Page.IsPostBack Then
     divName.innerText = "Your name is: " & txtName.Value
     divAge.innerText = "Your age is: " & txtAge.Value
   End If
 End Sub
End Class
```

This code behind Visual Basic file imports the necessary namespaces, then declares a class called `SamplePage`, which inherits the Page class. We then declare our two form elements so we can programmatically access them. The `Page_Load` sub appears next, with the code we want to execute contained within it.

Deploying code behind

When you deploy a page that uses a code behind file, it's crucial that you deploy the code behind file with the page. The .NET Framework assembles and compiles the code behind file and the page on demand, based on the `Src` property of the `@ Page` directive.

If you want to "hide" the code behind file when you deploy the ASP.NET application, you can compile the class file into the application's DLL and leave the `Src` attribute empty; with the `Src` attribute empty, the .NET Framework assumes the class is already compiled. Then all you have to do is ensure that the full namespace for the class is present in the `Inherits` attribute.

Done!

REVIEW

This chapter introduced you to Web forms and how they work. Specifically, we covered

- What a Web form is and what it offers
- The Web form page processing model
- The HTML controls exposed by `System.Web.UI.HtmlControls`
- A comparison between an HTML form and a Web form
- Code behind development using Visual Basic

Web forms are a powerful part of ASP.NET and one chapter isn't enough to cover it all. Chapter 18 covers the server controls and how to use them in your applications.

QUIZ YOURSELF

1. What are the three stages of Web forms processing? (See "Web Forms Page Processing.")
2. What is a round trip? (See "Web Forms Page Processing.")
3. How do you make an HTML control run server-side? (See "The HTML Controls.")
4. What is required in the `@ Page` directive for code behind? (See "Code Behind Development.")
5. How many files make up a code behind solution? (See "Code Behind Development.")

Working with Controls

Session Checklist

✔ Understanding Web controls and what they're good for

✔ Learning about the System.Web.UI.WebControls namespace

✔ Gaining exposure to Web control usage

**30 Min.
To Go**

I n Chapter 17, you learned about Web forms and how to build one using the HTML controls, which enable server-side processing and event handling for HTML tags. In this chapter, we'll go over the Web controls, which are special controls exposed by the .NET Framework for building Web forms.

What Is a Web Control?

Web controls are user interface elements exposed by the System.Web.UI.WebControls namespace. They derive from the WebControl base class, which is contained the System. Web.UI.WebControls namespace. The WebControl defines the properties, methods, and events common to all controls in System.Web.UI.WebControls.

Web controls are classes instantiated in your ASP.NET Web forms. They aren't client-side HTML tags; rather, they are defined by inline ASP.NET code. The Web controls are natively exposed on the server and they offer a rich programming model. The Web controls could best be compared to ActiveX controls, such as the ones used in Visual Basic 6 or on a Web page.

Web controls include the basic form controls such as text boxes and radio buttons. They also include a set of complex controls such as a calendar control and an ad rotator as well as a set of data controls that includes a data grid. One of the neatest controls is a table control that allows you to easily build a table based on data from a database. In the days of ASP, dynamic tables had to be built using inline code and the MoveNext method of the Recordset object.

When the ASP.NET Web form runs, the Web control is rendered on the page, using HTML. This rendering depends on the browser type and on settings made for the control. Although

HTML is used to render the control visually in the browser, Web controls don't map to specific HTML tags, and the actual HTML rendered can vary. For example, a TextBox control may be rendered in the browser as a `<input type="text">`, `<input type="password">`, or even `<input type="textarea">`, all based on what properties are set.

Web controls offer all the features of HTML controls except for the one-to-one mapping (meaning you can't map a Web control to a specific HTML tag). Web controls offer additional functionality over the HTML controls.

Rich, consistent object model

The `WebControl` base class provides a number of properties, such as `Height`, `Width`, and `Enabled`. These properties are common to all Web controls and reduce programming errors and provides a common environment for using controls, instead of forcing the developer to implement her custom properties to perform common tasks.

Automatic browser detection

Web controls are capable of determining the level of support a browser offers for HTML. If it only supports up to HTML 3.2, the control knows to generate HTML 3.2 code. If the browser supports HTML 4.0, the control knows to generate HTML 4.0 code. The controls make the best use of the browser's abilities.

Event passing

Web controls are capable of passing events from a nested control to a container control. A nested control could be something like a button, whereas the container control could be a table. The table would be able to receive events from the button control.

Data binding

Any property of a Web control can be data bound. (Data binding is discussed in Chapter 23.)

The Web Controls

There are around 20 controls to choose from (to start!), covering everything from allowing user input to displaying a calendar. Each control has the properties of the `WebControl` base class, as well as some properties specific to the control.

Common properties

These properties are common to all the Web controls. They can be specified in the control's tag (`<asp:ControlName>`) and in ASP.NET code using `ControlName.PropertyName`.

AccessKey

`AccessKey` allows for specifying a control's keyboard accelerator key using a single letter while pressing ALT. Access keys are not supported by some browsers.

Attributes

This property contains the complete set of attributes for a control's persistence format. It is design-time only, which means it can only be used when programming.

BackColor

The BackColor property specifies the color behind the control. This property accepts standard HTML color identifiers, like "blue" or "yellow," or an RGB value, like "#CC00CC."

BorderWidth

This property lets you set the size of the control's border in pixels. This property may not work in some browsers.

BorderStyle

This property allows you to configure the control's border style. The possible values are: Dashed, Dotted, Double, Groove, Inset, None, NotSet, Outset, Ridge, and Solid.

CssClass

This property specifies the Cascading Style Sheet (CSS) class to assign to the control.

Enabled

Setting Enabled to True enables the control. Setting it to False disables it. Enabled denotes a controls active state on a form.

Font

This property gets the control's font information.

ForeColor

This property sets the color of a control's text. This property may not work in some browsers.

Height

The Height property simply sets a control's height in pixels. This property may not work in some browsers.

TabIndex

The TabIndex for a control sets its order of focus as you press the tab button. For example, if the TabIndex is set to 5, the control will be the sixth control to get focus when you press the tab key. This property works only in Internet Explorer 4.0 and later.

ToolTip

Define the text in the ToolTip with this property. A ToolTip appears when the user hovers the mouse pointer over a control. This property doesn't work in some browsers.

Width

The Width property simply sets the width of a control in pixels. It may not work in some browsers.

**20 Min.
To Go**

Displaying text

Displaying text on a page in ASP was typically done through Response.Write. After the text was written out, there was nothing you could do to change it (in ASP, anyway). ASP.NET exposes a control to let you control the text you display.

The <asp:Label> control is used to display static, read-only text on a page:

```
<asp:Label runat="server" Text="Text goes here." ID="lblText">
</asp:Label>
```

Inputting information

The whole point of a form is to get information from the users. Using the input controls does this. The user enters values into the controls, submits the form, and the server processes the values. Because the form is meant to get choices from the user, there are several controls that allow information input.

<asp:TextBox>

This control is used to accept text entry from the user. It supports different modes, like single-line, multi-line, and password:

```
<asp:TextBox runat="server" Text="Text goes here."
ID="txtText"></asp:TextBox>

<asp:TextBox runat="server" Text="Multiline text." ID="txtMultiText"
Mode="password">txtMultiText</asp:TextBox>
```

<asp:CheckBox>

A checkbox has two values, on and off (checked or not checked):

```
<asp:CheckBox runat="server" Text="Text goes here." ID="chkChoice"
Checked="False">
</asp:CheckBox>
```

<asp:RadioButton>

The radio button is like the checkbox control, but is used in a group of radio buttons to allow a single choice:

```
<asp:RadioButton runat="server" Text="Text goes here." ID="rdbText1"
GroupName="RDBGroup" Checked="False">
</asp:RadioButton>
<asp:RadioButton runat="server" Text="Text goes here." ID="rdbText2"
GroupName="RDBGroup" Checked="False">
</asp:RadioButton>
```

<asp:ListBox>

The list box is good for showing a selectable list of items. It allows for single item selection and multiple item selection. Items are entered into the control using <asp:ListItem>:

```
<asp:ListBox runat="server" SelectionMode="multiple"
ID="lstNET">
<asp:ListItem Text="ASP.NET" Value="1" Selected="True" />
<asp:ListItem Text="VB.NET" Value="2" />
<asp:ListItem Text="C#" Value="3" />
</asp:ListBox>
```

<asp:DropDownList>

The drop down list (called a *combobox* by some) allows a single selection from a list of items. Like the ListBox control, it uses the ListItem object for the list of items:

```
<asp:DropDownList runat="server" ID="drpNET">
<asp:ListItem Text="ASP.NET" Value="1" Selected="True" />
<asp:ListItem Text="VB.NET" Value="2" />
<asp:ListItem Text="C#" Value="3" />
</asp:DropDownList>
```

<asp:CheckBoxList>

When you need a group of checkboxes spanned across one or more columns, use the CheckBoxList control. It uses the ListItem control for the choices:

```
<asp:CheckBoxList runat="server" ID="cblNET">
<asp:ListItem Text="ASP.NET" Value="1" Selected="True" />
<asp:ListItem Text="VB.NET" Value="2" />
<asp:ListItem Text="C#" Value="3" />
</asp:CheckBoxList>
```

<asp:RadioButtonList>

The RadioButtonList control is similar to the CheckBoxList control but uses a group of radio buttons to create a mutually exclusive set of choices. It also uses the ListItem control for the choices:

```
<asp:RadioButtonList runat="server" ID="rblNET">
<asp:ListItem Text="ASP.NET" Value="1" Selected="True" />
<asp:ListItem Text="VB.NET" Value="2" />
<asp:ListItem Text="C#" Value="3" />
</asp:RadioButtonList>
```

Performing actions

After the user has entered values into the input controls, there needs to be a way for the user to perform an action based on those values (like submitting the form) or navigate out of the page (like clicking a link). These controls all perform an action.

<asp:Button>

The Button control creates a button on the form for submitting a page back to the server:

```
<asp:Button runat="server" Text="Click Here." ID="btnText">
</asp:Button>
```

<asp:LinkButton>

The LinkButton is the same as the Button control except it renders as a link instead of a button:

```
<asp:LinkButton runat="server" Text="Click Here." ID="lbtnText">
</asp:LinkButton>
```

<asp:ImageButton>

The ImageButton control also has the same behavior as a Button control. It renders as an image and provides the coordinates of a user-click:

```
<asp:ImageButton runat="server" ImageURL="action.gif" ID="imgText">
</asp:ImageButton>
```

<asp:HyperLink>

The HyperLink control displays a hyperlink that allows navigation to other URLs:

```
<asp:HyperLink runat="server" Text="Text goes here."
NavigateUrl="Go2Page.aspx" ID="hlText">
</asp:Hyperlink>
```

Displaying images

You may be thinking to yourself, Why would I use an ASP.NET control to display an image when I can just use `<img src>`? It's possible to use the `<img src>` tag server side, but it won't expose all the properties and methods that a Web control would. Consider a Web site that allows a user to change the look and feel. This could be done using dynamic images with the ASP.NET Image control.

The `<asp:Image>` control displays an image on the page:

```
<asp:Image runat="server" ImageURL="image.gif" ID="imgText">
</asp:Image>
```

Layout and interface

The layout and interface controls allow you to customize the look and feel, and auxiliary functionality of your pages. The controls are flexible alternatives to hardcoded HTML elements.

<asp:Panel>

The Panel control does not have an interface. It's used for grouping controls:

```
<asp:Panel runat="server" ID="pnlText">
</asp:Panel>
```

<asp:Table>

Use the Table control to create tables and tabular layouts programmatically. This saves you from trying to structure your tables with the `<tr>` and `<td>` tags. I can never remember how those are supposed to work. The Table control uses the `TableRow` and `TableCell` controls to define the structure:

```
<asp:Table runat="server" GridLines="none" BorderWidth="2px" ID="tblText">
<asp:TableRow>
  <asp:TableCell>Upper Left</asp:TableCell>
  <asp:TableCell>Upper Right</asp:TableCell>
</asp:TableRow>
<asp:TableRow>
  <asp:TableCell>Lower Left</asp:TableCell>
  <asp:TableCell>Lower Right</asp:TableCell>
</asp:TableRow>
</asp:Table>
```

<asp:Calendar>

The Calendar control displays an interactive calendar on a Web page. Scott Guthrie, one of the designers of ASP.NET, coded this on a plane trip. It allows the user to page through months and select individual days:

```
<asp:Calendar runat="server" DayNameFormat="FirstLetter" ID="MyCalendar"
SelectionMode="DayWeekMonth">
</asp:Calendar>
```

<asp:AdRotator>

The AdRotator control is a neat alternative to the JavaScript-based and Flash-based advertising banners you see on Web sites. The information about the ads is stored in an XML file:

```
<asp:AdRotator runat="server" AdvertisementFile="myAds.xml" ID="adMyAds">
</asp:AdRotator>
```

The AdRotator advertisement file, myAds.xml, would look something like this:

```
<Advertisements>
    <Ad>
        <ImageUrl>Preamp.gif</ImageUrl>
        <NavigateUrl>http://ads.myurl.com</NavigateUrl>
        <AlternateText>High End Audio</AlternateText>
        <Impressions>60</Impressions>
        <Keyword>Preamplifiers</Keyword>
    </Ad>
    <Ad>
        <ImageUrl>Amplifier.jpg</ImageUrl>
        <NavigateUrl>http://ads.myurl.com</NavigateUrl>
        <AlternateText>High End Audio</AlternateText>
        <Impressions>60</Impressions>
        <Keyword>Amplifiers</Keyword>
    </Ad>
</Advertisements>
```

Using the Web Controls

Remember that Web controls are specified in ASP.NET Web forms using the `<asp:ControlName>` syntax. For example:

```
<asp:TextBox id="txtName" text="My name is " runat="server"></asp:TextBox>
```

The attributes of the `<asp:ControlName>` tag are not attributes of an HTML element. They are properties of the control. In your ASP.NET code, you reference the properties like with any other object (this code is a snippet and may not work on its own):

```
<script runat="server" language="vb">
txtName.Text = txtName.Text & "35"
</script>
```

All you really have to know to use a WebControl is its properties and methods. If you use Visual Studio.NET, its Intellisense technology will give you a dropdown list containing the properties and methods of whatever control you are using.

Done!

REVIEW

In this chapter, you learned about Web controls. Web controls are a powerful tool for building Web forms, and they offer several advantages over HTML controls. Specifically, we discussed:

- What Web controls are
- Features of Web controls
- The common properties of Web controls
- Several of the Web controls exposed by .NET
- How to use the Web controls

Chapter 19 covers another set of controls not discussed in this chapter: the validation controls.

QUIZ YOURSELF

1. Do Web controls map one-to-one with HTML tags? (See "What Is a Web Control?")
2. What are some features of Web controls? (See "What is a Web Control?")
3. What is the TabIndex property used for? (See "The Web Controls.")
4. What property controls the active state of a Web control? (See "The Web Controls.")
5. How do you reference a property of a control on the server? (See "Using the Web Controls.")

Validating User Input

✔ Understanding the importance of input validation

✔ Learning about the validation Web controls

✔ Choosing a validation control

✔ Implementing validation controls in code

I n this chapter, you'll learn about user input validation with ASP.NET and Web forms. User input validation is a very important part of a Web application, and ASP.NET greatly simplifies this formerly daunting task.

**30 Min.
To Go**

Input Validation

Consider this scenario: A customer visits your site, which sells telescopes and accessories. The user decides to get everything he needs to do astrophotography. While navigating through your site, he adds all kinds of equipment to his shopping cart. When the user is ready to checkout, he puts a special character, such as "/", in the form field for State. The user clicks the Submit button, and because your site does not have any kind of form valida-tion, the database returns an error that the user sees. Frustrated, he closes his browser and you've lost the sale.

Of course, this story can be reversed with you as the customer, and it's equally frustrat-ing. Input validation solves this kind of problem and ensures the integrity of data on the server. So why haven't more sites employed input validation?

The problem with input validation is that it's clunky and very time-consuming. There isn't a standard way to employ input validation on a Web site. Some browsers, such as Internet Explorer, provide DHTML capabilities for client-side validation techniques. The problem with this is that it's not easy to do and it's platform-specific.

Input validation can occur on the client and on the server; client-side input validation is done using a client-side language such as JavaScript, and the server-side input validation is handled by ASP code. You're faced with a choice: Employ client-side validation and risk locking out other platforms, or perform server-side validation and cause extra round-trips each time.

The ideal situation is to validate at both ends so that the initial validation is performed at the client and further validation is performed at the server. However, this forces the developer to write more code and take up more time. Fortunately, ASP.NET does away with this pain and suffering and offers a set of controls for input validation.

ASP.NET Validation Controls

ASP.NET is designed to make validation much easier by automatically performing all the painful tasks involved in validation. ASP.NET offers six controls for this functionality:

- CompareValidator
- CustomValidator
- RangeValidator
- RegularExpressionValidator
- RequiredFieldValidator
- ValidationSummary

Each of these controls can be linked to other ASP.NET controls and HTML controls, such as text boxes, password boxes, list boxes, and so on. More than one validation control can be linked to each control on the form.

All the ASP.NET validation controls share a core set of features, described in the following sections.

Multiple validation criteria

Each validation control can be linked to an HTML form element. At the same time, more than one validation control can be linked to an HTML form element. For example, you can specify that a value in a text box contains a non-numeric value, such as a name, and then specify that a second text box must contain a value if the first box contains a value.

Automatic implementation

The validation controls are smart. They know when to generate client-side code and when to generate server-side code. Since the generated client-side code is DHTML, it's specific to Internet Explorer 4 and higher. When the control detects that the browser is not an Internet Explorer browser, it handles the validation on the server side. The control determines which model to use through the UserAgent string in the http header.

The term *http header* refers to the text returned in all documents served from an http server, such as Internet Information Server (IIS). The UserAgent is just one of many values stored in the http header.

The validation controls supplied with ASP.NET automatically perform validation on the server, even when the validation has been done on the client. This prevents users from posting invalid values to a server from a client that does not have client-side validation, such as Netscape.

You may wish to bypass the browser check altogether. This is possible through the @Page directive in ASP.NET:

```
<%@Page ClientTarget="SomeUserAgentString" %>
```

Specifying a UserAgent string in the ClientTarget attribute will tell ASP.NET what client to render content for. This string can be any valid UserAgent value or alias.

Separation of reporting

A validation control is not required to write out error messages in any specific place. In fact, you can have one HTML table containing your controls and another HTML table containing your validation messages. This separation of reporting from control location simplifies things for both the programmer and the page designer. With separation of reporting, page designers are not forced to design around a control, and programmers are not forced to code around a design.

20 Min.
To Go

The Six Validation Controls

Each of the six controls has specific capabilities and functionality. Which one you elect to use depends upon your needs.

CompareValidator

CompareValidator compares an input control to another input control, or a fixed value. The CompareValidator control is good for password fields, and typed date and number comparisons.

CustomValidator

CustomValidator allows the developer to write custom code to execute on validation. This has endless possibilities, which we'll discuss later in this chapter.

RangeValidator

RangeValidator is similar to CompareValidator, but instead of just comparing one value against another, RangeValidator can check that a value exists between two other values (fixed or in a control).

RegularExpressionValidator

RegularExpressionValidator checks the input against a regular expression. Regular expressions are good for parsing strings; the RegularExpressionValidator would thus be good for validating against a regular expression to determine ZIP code validity and making sure passwords are alphanumeric only.

RequiredFieldValidator

The `RequiredFieldValidator` control checks the input to see if the user has entered or selected anything. This control is perfect for forms that require data such as a name and address. These forms are in use all over the Web.

ValidationSummary

The `ValidationSummary` control is different from the other controls. Instead of providing validation directly, it contains the error messages from the other validation controls. The `ValidationSummary` control can be used to provide a list of errors at the bottom of the page, for example.

Using the Validation Controls

Using the validation controls within your ASP.NET pages is very easy. There's a standard way of inserting a validation control:

```
<asp:ValidatorType id="ValidatorID" runat="server"
ControlToValidate="ControlID"
ErrorMessage="Your custom error message"
Display="static">
Whatever text you wish to display inline
</asp:ValidatorType>
```

In this code, `ValidatorType` would be replaced with the type of the validator you wanted to use, such as `RequiredFieldValidator`. The `id` attribute is defined by you. The `ControlToValidate` attribute should resolve to the ID of a control on your form. `ErrorMessage` should contain the text you want to deliver to your users when validation fails.

The `Display` attribute allows you to specify how you would like your control displayed. None means validation contents are never displayed inline; this is used so the error message is only displayed in a `ValidationSummary` control. `Dynamic` displays validation contents inline if validation fails; it only takes up space on the page when it is visible. `Dynamic` also allows multiple validators to occupy the same physical space on the page when they are visible. Finally, `Static` displays validator contents inline and is part of the page layout even when it is hidden. Multiple validators of type `Static` for the same input control must occupy different physical locations on the page.

Each control has its own specific property settings. We'll cover each control and its specific properties, and then see how they work.

CompareValidator

The `CompareValidator` control can be used to compare the value in one control with the value in another control or fixed value. The `CompareValidator` control has two properties, `operator` and `type`. `Operator` is just that: The operator used to compare the two values. `Type` is the data type of the values. This code instantiates the `CompareValidator` control to compare values from two text boxes:

```
<input type="text" id="FirstValue" runat="server"/>
<input type="text" id="SecondValue" runat="server"/>
<asp:CompareValidator id="CV" runat="server"
ControlToValidate="SecondValue"
ErrorMessage="The Second Value is not greater than the first."
ControlToCompare="FirstValue"
Type="Integer"
Operator="GreaterThan"
Display="Static">
Error encountered
</asp:CompareValidator>
```

This code takes input from two text boxes and checks the second value against the first. If the second value is not greater than the first, then the text in `ErrorMessage` is returned. If we wanted to compare the text box against a fixed value, the code would be slightly different:

```
<input type="text" id="FirstValue" runat="server"/>
<asp:CompareValidator id="CompareValidator1" runat="server">
ControlToValidate="FirstValue"
ErrorMessage="First Value is not greater than 88."
ValueToCompare="88"
Type="Integer"
Operator="GreaterThan"
Display="Static">
Error encountered
</asp:CompareValidator>
```

In this code, `ControlToCompare` has been replaced by `ValueToCompare`. The `ValueToCompare` property contains a value, 88. When the validation executes, it will check to see if the value in the text box "First Value" is greater than 88. If it's not, then the error message will be displayed. If you specify both `ControlToCompare` and `ValueToCompare` in the same validator, `ControlToCompare` will always take precedence.

CustomValidator

The `CustomValidator` is a catch-all control that allows you to define your own validation needs. Sometimes the other validation controls just don't do what is necessary; the `CustomValidator` is the control to save the proverbial day.

The `CustomValidator` requires the developer to write a custom server-side or client-side function in any supported .NET language. This function must perform the validation and return a Boolean value (True or False).

```
<input type="text" id="txtMoneyType" runat="server"/>
<asp:CustomValidator id="ValidMoneyType" runat="server"
ControlToValidate="txtMoneyType"
OnServerValidate="ValidateMoneyType"
ErrorMessage="The currency type is not supported."
Display="Dynamic">
Error encountered
</asp:CustomValidator>
<!--other html stuff here, perhaps-->
```

```
<script language="VB" runat="server">
Function ValidateMoneyType()
'Do some stuff
If (..some condition..) Then
     args.IsValid = True
Else
     args.IsValid = False
End If
End Function
Author: Sub ValidateMoneyType(sender As Object, args As EventArgs)
'Do some stuff
If (..some condition..) Then
              args.IsValid = True
Else
              args.IsValid = False
End If
End Sub
</script>
```

This validation control uses a server side function to determine if the currency type chosen is valid. The function name is specified in the `OnServerValidate` property of the control. If this control were using a client-side function, we would have used `ClientValidationFunction` instead of `OnServerValidate`. The client-side function would probably be written in JavaScript to support the different browsers.

RangeValidator

**10 Min.
To Go**

Let's say you have a form on your Web site in which you want users to input a value within a range, for an IQ. You choose not to use a combo box, because the range of values is very large. You instead decide to let the user type in a value, and you want to ensure the value is between 68 and 205. The `RangeValidator` control will do precisely that:

```
<input type="text" id="txtIQ" runat="server"/>
<asp:RangeValidator id="ValidIQRange" runat="server"
ControlToValidate="txtIQ"
Type="Integer"
MinimumValue="68"
MaximumValue="205"
ErrorMessage="You entered an IQ outside the acceptable range."
Display="Dynamic">
Error encountered
</asp:RangeValidator>
```

This control makes sure the value entered in txtIQ is between 68 and 205. Like the `CompareValidator` control, the type property tells our control to compare against integers. In some cases, you may want to check the value of the control against the value of another control. To do this, you would use code like this:

```
<input type="text" id="txtIQ" runat="server"/>
<input type="text" id="txtIQMin" runat="server"/>
<input type="text" id="txtIQMax" runat="server"/>
<asp:RangeValidator id="ValidIQRange" runat="server"
```

```
ControlToValidate="txtIQ"
MinimumControl="txtIQMin"
MaximumControl="txtIQMax"
ErrorMessage="You entered an IQ outside the acceptable range."
Display="Dynamic">
Error encountered
</asp:RangeValidator>
```

Do you see the difference? In this code, we're using two other controls to determine the minimum value and the maximum value. We could use a control for minimum value and specify a maximum value, and vice versa. It's very flexible.

RegularExpressionValidator

A regular expression is a standard way to parse strings using special characters. In other words, regular expressions allow you to search on patterns rather than just strings. There are entire books devoted to regular expressions so we won't get into them here. Regular expressions are very powerful, so if you are able to master them, you will find the RegularExpressionValidator to be the most powerful validation control.

The RegularExpressionValidator compares a value against the result of a regular expression that you specify. In this example, we have a text box and we want to make sure it either contains a number from 0 to 9, a lowercase letter, or an uppercase letter.

```
<input type="text" id="txtRegExp" runat="server"/>
<asp:RegularExpressionValidator id="ValidateRegExp" runat="server"
ControlToValidate="txtRegExp"
ValidationExpression=".*[0-9].*|.*[a-z].*|.*[A-Z].*"
ErrorMessage="Your text must contain either a number, a lowercase letter,
or an uppercase letter."
Display="none">
</asp:RegularExpressionValidator>
```

The RegularExpressionValidator evaluates the regular expression in ValidationExpression. If it doesn't jibe with the text in txtRegExp, the error message is returned.

RequiredFieldValidator

The RequiredFieldValidator control is probably the most commonly used control. It is used in situations in which a value must be supplied. Anyone who has ever bought something online should be familiar with required fields.

In this example, we want to ensure that a value is entered into the text box:

```
<input type="text" id="txtUsername" runat="server"/>
<asp:RequiredFieldValidator id="ValidateReqField" runat="server"
ControlToValidate="txtUsername"
ErrorMessage="You must enter a username."
Display="static">
Error encountered
</asp:RequiredFieldValidator>
```

If no value is entered into txtUsername, then the error message is returned. This control is very simple to use.

ValidationSummary

The ValidationSummary control simply displays error messages on the page. The ValidationSummary control collects ErrorMessage values from all of the controls with failed validations and presents the messages to the user within the page.

The ValidationSummary control can present its data directly on the page or via a message box. Create the ValidationSummary control like this:

```
<asp:ValidationSummary id="ValidSummary" runat="server"
HeaderText="Validation failed with these errors:"
ShowSummary="True"
isplayMode="List">
</asp:ValidationSummary>
```

The ShowSummary property tells the control to display the error messages; setting it to false will force the control to only display the HeaderText. DisplayMode can be one of three choices: BulletList (the default), List, and SingleParagraph.

Alternatively, you can use a message box instead of a table to show the error messages:

```
<asp:ValidationSummary id="ValidSummary" runat="server"
ShowSummary="True"
ShowMessageBox="True">
</asp:ValidationSummary>
```

The ShowMessageBox property is great for those applications where you want to draw attention to the error messages.

The ShowMessageBox **property only works with Internet Explorer 4 and above. Consider this carefully if your users might be using a different browser.**

The ValidationSummary control can be very useful for fine-tuning the user experience. Sometimes you may wish to catalog errors but not display them to the user, instead choosing to just let the user know an error occurred.

Done!

REVIEW

This chapter covered input validation techniques in ASP.NET. Specific topics covered were:

- Input validation before ASP.NET
- An overview of the six validation controls in ASP.NET
- Features common to the validation controls
- Working with the six validation controls in code

The next chapter allows you to take what you have learned about Web forms and controls and build your very own Web form in ASP.NET.

QUIZ YOURSELF

1. Why don't developers like to implement input validation? (See "Input Validation.")
2. Where can input validation take place? (See "Input Validation.")
3. What are the six validation controls in ASP.NET? (See "ASP.NET Validation Controls.")
4. Name the core set of features common among the six controls (See "ASP.NET Validation Controls.")
5. What control do you use to validate a range? (See "The Six Validation Controls.")

SESSION

20

Building a Web Form

Session Checklist

✔ Constructing a Web form

✔ Simplifying the code

✔ Adding validation controls

**30 Min.
To Go**

We have covered a lot of material in the previous 19 chapters. The goal of this chapter is to guide you to applying what you have learned to the existing application that we built in Chapter 16.

A Quick Recap

In Chapter 16, we wrote an application that takes two values from an HTML page and performs a specified mathematical operation. This is the code for the HTML page we built, math.htm:

```
<html>
<head>
<title>
ASP.NET Mathematical Sample
</title>
</head>
<body>
<form method="GET" action="math.aspx">
     <input type="text" name="value1">
<select name="MathOperator">
     <option value="add">+
     <option value="subtract">-
     <option value="multiply">x
     <option value="divide">/
</select>
     <input type="text" name="value2">
     <input type="submit" value="Get Result">
```

```
</form>
</body>
</html>
```

This is the code for the ASP.NET page we built, math.aspx:

```
<%@Import Namespace="System.Decimal" %>
<script language="VB" runat="server">
Sub Page_Load(Source as Object, e As EventArgs)
Dim decValue1      As Decimal
Dim decValue2      As Decimal
Dim strOperator    As String
Dim decResult      As Decimal
decValue1 = Request.QueryString("value1")
decValue2 = Request.QueryString("value2")
strOperator = Request.QueryString("MathOperator")

Try
Select Case strOperator
Case "multiply"
decResult = MultiplyValues(decValue1, decValue2)
Case "divide"
decResult = DivideValues(decValue1, decValue2)
Case "add"
decResult = AddValues(decValue1, decValue2)
Case "subtract"
decResult = SubtractValues(decValue1, decValue2)
End Select
Catch e As OverflowException
Response.Write("The result was too large to represent" & _
                   as a decimal.")
Catch e As DivideByZeroException
Response.Write("You cannot divide by zero.")

Finally
Response.Write("The result of your calculation is: " & _
          decResult)

End Try
End Sub

Function MultiplyValues(decValue1 As Decimal, decValue2 As _
Decimal)

Dim decResult As Decimal
decResult = Multiply(decValue1, decValue2)
Return decResult
End Function

Function DivideValues(decValue1 As Decimal, decValue2 As _
Decimal)
```

```
Dim decResult As Decimal
decResult = Divide(decValue1, decValue2)
Return decResult
End Function

Function AddValues(decValue1 As Decimal, decValue2 As _
Decimal)

Dim decResult As Decimal
decResult = Add(decValue1, decValue2)
Return decResult
End Function

Function SubtractValues(decValue1 As Decimal, decValue2 As _
Decimal)

Dim decResult As Decimal
decResult = Subtract(decValue1, decValue2)
Return decResult
End Function
</script>
```

Our mission in this chapter is to eliminate the HTML page and convert our application to use Web forms. The advantage to using Web forms is the added benefit that ASP.NET provides when using server-side controls. For example, by using server-side controls we can capture an event, such as a button click, with absolute ease. We'll also be able to use validation controls easily. Using Web forms allows for a more cohesive page design and is more like Visual Basic than ASP. That's a good thing.

Redefining the Requirements

**20 Min.
To Go**

The original requirements for this application were:

- The page must be able to perform four different mathematical operations: multiplication, division, addition, and subtraction.
- The page must use values submitted on a querystring.
- The page must accept an instruction.
- The instruction must indicate to the page what mathematical operation to perform.
- The page requires two values.
- The page must perform the mathematical operation on the two values.
- The page must output the result of the mathematical operation.

Most of these original requirements will apply to version 2.0 of our application. For instance, the page will still require two values. However, it will not require that values be submitted on a query string. Rewriting our requirements to take advantage of Web forms, we have this:

- The page must be able to perform four different mathematical operations: multiplication, division, addition, and subtraction.
- The page must be complete; only one page shall be used for the application.
- The page must use server-side controls.
- The instruction must indicate to the page what mathematical operation to perform.
- The form must allow for entry of two values.
- The form must allow for the selection of an operator.
- The form must offer validation.
- The page must perform the mathematical operation on the two values.
- The page must output the result of the mathematical operation.

The new requirements state that the application must exist as a single page, use server-side controls, and offer validation. With the new requirements intact, we're ready to lead the assault on version 2.0 of math.aspx.

Designing the Form

The first step is designing the form. In other words, we need to decide what user controls we want displayed on the form.

Text boxes

The requirements state that the page must allow for entry of two values. This gives us two choices. We can use the HTML control and specify runat="server",

```
<INPUT type="text" id="txtBox" runat="server"/>
```

or we can use the ASP.NET intrinsic textbox control:

```
<asp:TextBox id="txtBox" runat="server"/>
```

Both of these methods render almost the same HTML code, but the ASP.NET control gives us the added functionality provided by ASP.NET, such as a consistent programming model. We'll use the ASP.NET controls.

Based on our requirement we can come up with code like this:

```
<form runat="server">
Please enter your values and click Get Results.
<br/>
<asp:TextBox id="txtValue1" runat="server"></asp:TextBox>
<asp:TextBox id="txtValue2" runat="server" ></asp:TextBox>
</form>
```

Dropdown list

We now have the shell of the form: Two text boxes, ready for input. The next step is adding the select box for the operators. We'll use this code:

```
<asp:DropDownList id="MathOperator" runat="server">
<asp:ListItem>x</asp:ListItem>
<asp:ListItem>/</asp:ListItem>
<asp:ListItem>+</asp:ListItem>
<asp:ListItem>-</asp:ListItem>
</asp:DropDownList>
```

This control works very much like the <SELECT> tag in HTML.

Submit button

With the text boxes added and the dropdown list control ready to accept values, we just need a control to actually submit the form. You have two choices: You can create an image for the button and use it, or you can use the button control. Due to time constraints, we'll use a standard button:

```
<asp:Button id="btnGetResult" Text="Get Result" runat="server"
OnClickOnClick="btnGetResult_Click"></asp:Button>
```

Nothing will happen when we click the button without the OnClick event specified. Because we're specifying an OnClick event, we'll have to write code for it in our page, which we'll do in the next section.

Now that we have our text boxes, our dropdown list, and our submit button, we can get a good idea of what our form will look like with this code:

```
<html>
<head>
<title>ASP.NET Math Program</title>
</head>
<body>
<form runat="server">
Please enter your values and click Get Results.
<br/>
<asp:TextBox id="txtValue1" runat="server"></asp:TextBox>
<asp:DropDownList id="MathOperator" runat="server">
<asp:ListItem>x</asp:ListItem>
<asp:ListItem>/</asp:ListItem>
<asp:ListItem>+</asp:ListItem>
<asp:ListItem>-</asp:ListItem>
</asp:DropDownList>
<asp:TextBox id="txtValue2" runat="server" ></asp:TextBox>
<asp:Button id="btnGetResult" Text="Get Result" runat="server"
OnClick="btnGetResult_Click"></asp:Button>
</form>
</body>
</html>
```

Save this program under the filename mathform_prototype.aspx and view it in Internet Explorer 5.5. If the form design suits you, move on to the next section. If not, tweak it a little, but be aware that it won't match the code in the rest of this chapter.

Writing the Code

10 Min. To Go

With the form design complete, it's time to write code to make it all work. The first thing to do is integrate the form code into our original code, math.aspx.

Refer to the Chapter 20 folder on the CD-ROM for the code listing. Reprinting it here would simply take up too much room!

With the form code integrated into the existing page, we're ready to write the code for the submit button click event and the code to add items to the dropdown list. The submit button click event will populate two variables with the values from the form, then use the Select...Case conditional to determine which function to call:

```
<script language="VB" runat="server">
Sub btnGetResult_Click(Source As Object, e As EventArgs)
Dim decValue1 As Decimal = txtValue1.Text
Dim decValue2 As Decimal = txtValue2.Text
Dim strOperator As String = MathOperator.SelectedItem.Text
Dim decResult As Decimal

Try

Select Case strOperator
Case "multiply"
decResult = MultiplyValues(decValue1, decValue2)
Case "divide"
decResult = DivideValues(decValue1, decValue2)
Case "add"
decResult = AddValues(decValue1, decValue2)
Case "subtract"
decResult = SubtractValues(decValue1, decValue2)
End Select

Catch e As OverflowException
Response.Write("The result was too large to represent" & _
          as a decimal.")

Catch e As DivideByZeroException
Response.Write("You cannot divide by zero.")

Finally
Response.Write("The result of your calculation is: " & _
      decResult)

End Try

End Sub
</script>
```

As you can see, we've moved the core functionality of the program into the OnClick event of the submit button. The OnClick event uses page-level variables (decValue1, decValue2, and decResult) and performs the exception handling. Once the OnClick event code is integrated into the existing math.aspx page, it's ready for the validation controls.

 You may have already noticed ways we could improve our math application. In the last chapter of this book, we'll revisit the entire application and make changes for performance increases, usability, and ease of maintenance.

Form Validation

The validation requirement for our application is somewhat vague; it doesn't state which form elements must have validation. Because all three values (first value, second value, and operator) are required, it's safe to assume that we should apply validation to the controls representing these values.

For this form, we'll use the ValidatorSummary control to output the results of a validation in a separate table. This will simplify usability.

The first value

When deciding on validation for the first value, you must figure out what you do and do not want in the field. What we know about the first value is that it must have an entry, and the entry must be a number.

To ensure that it has an entry, we'll use the RequiredFieldValidator control:

```
<asp:RequiredFieldValidator id="Value1HasValue" runat="server"
ControlToValidate="txtValue1"
ErrorMessage="You must enter value in the first box."
Display="none">
</asp:RequiredFieldValidator>
```

This control will ensure that the user enters a value for txtValue1. For usability purposes, we'll add a line of text to our form that states all fields are required.

The next task is ensuring that only a number is entered into the txtValue1 text box. For this we will use a CustomValidator:

```
<asp:CustomValidator id="Value1IsNumber" runat="server"
ControlToValidate="txtValue1"
OnServerValidate="CheckValue(" & txtValue1.Text & _ ")"
ErrorMessage="The first value does not contain a number."
Display="None">
</asp:CustomValidator>
<script language="VB" runat="server">
Function CheckValue(objValue As Object, e As EventArgs) As Boolean
If IsNumeric(objValue) Then
Return True
Else
    Return False
End If
End Function
</script>
```

This control uses the Visual Basic.NET function IsNumeric to determine if the value entered is evaluated as a number. We wrote a custom function, CheckValue, which accepts an object (such as txtValue1.Text) as a parameter. This function will be in our ASP.NET page and thus available to other validation controls.

 Every programmer has her own style. We could have easily substituted a RegularExpressionValidator **control, or called** IsNumeric **directly in the** OnServerValidate **property. This book has adopted a style that demonstrates verbosely how to do things in ASP.NET, which will help you learn how to use the different functions and eventually grow your own style. As you read each of the examples throughout this book, think about how you want to write your own ASP.NET code, and feel free to even change the sample code to suit you.**

With this control in place, validation for the first text box is complete.

The second value

The validation for the second value is identical to the validation for the first value, with a few simple changes:

```
<asp:RequiredFieldValidator id="Value2HasValue" runat="server"
ControlToValidate="txtValue2"
ErrorMessage="You must enter value in the second box."
Display="none">
</asp:RequiredFieldValidator>
```

Likewise, the CustomValidator for txtValue2 is the same as txtValue1 with a few simple changes:

```
<asp:CustomValidator id="Value1IsNumber" runat="server"
ControlToValidate="txtValue1"
OnServerValidate="CheckValue(" & txtValue2.Text & _ ")"
ErrorMessage="The second value does not contain a number."
Display="None">
</asp:CustomValidator>
```

You'll notice that the CheckValue function is not included in this control. That's because the function named in OnServerValidate is not necessarily tied to a particular control, and is not part of the control directly. So you can write one function that is accessible to all of your CustomValidator controls, which is precisely what we did here.

The operator

The MathOperator control, a dropdown list, needs only one validation control, a RequiredFieldValidator. The MathOperator control cannot accept user-defined values; the values are preset and the user simply chooses one.

The code for the `RequiredFieldValidator` control for `MathOperator` is:

```
<asp:RequiredFieldValidator id="MathOperatorHasValue"
runat="server"
ControlToValidate="MathOperator"
ErrorMessage="You must choose an operator."
Display="none">
</asp:RequiredFieldValidator>
```

With this control added to the page, all of the fields will be validated. The only task left is creating the `ValidationSummary` control.

The ValidationSummary

The `ValidationSummary` control will display a list of validation errors in a table at the bottom of the math.aspx page. In this case, we want to display a bulleted list of validation errors:

```
<asp:ValidationSummary id="MathSummary" runat="server"
HeaderText="The following errors were encountered:"
ShowSummary="True"
DisplayMode="BulletList">
</asp:ValidationSummary>
```

The validation requirement is met, and our math.aspx page is completed.

 You can find the complete file, math.aspx, in the Chapter 20 folder on the CD-ROM. This folder also contains all of the code in this chapter broken up into the different sections (that is, before and after validation).

Done!

REVIEW

In this chapter, you converted your existing two-page application to a single-page Web form application using ASP.NET controls. Specifically, you:

- Analyzed and redefined your requirements.
- Designed the new form.
- Wrote code to make the new form meet the requirements.
- Added validation controls for each control on the form.
- Added a `ValidationSummary` control to help our users fix their errors.

The next chapter takes you into ADO.NET and working with databases. You'll see more of math.aspx later.

QUIZ YOURSELF

1. Why did we convert the application to use Web forms? (See "A Quick Recap.")
2. Why use an ASP.NET text box control instead of an HTML text box? (See "Designing the Form.")
3. What choices do you have when creating a submit button? (See "Designing the Form.")
4. What validation control do you use to require a value? (See "Form Validation.")
5. Why use a `ValidationSummary` control? (See "Form Validation.")

PART

IV

Saturday Evening
Part Review

1. Web forms provide what kind of model for ASP.NET application development?
2. What does the `Page_Load` event do?
3. What kind of HTML controls can be derived from `HtmlGenericControl`?
4. What are some advantages of code-behind?
5. How do you hide a code-behind file when you deploy an ASP.NET application?
6. What namespace exposes Web controls?
7. How do you define a text box Web control?
8. Which Web control is intended for grouping other controls?
9. Where does the `AdRotator` get information about ads?
10. What is the syntax for declaring a Web control?
11. Name the six validating Web controls.
12. Can more than one validation control be linked to a control on a form?
13. How do you tell the ASP.NET page to perform validation only on the server?
14. What is the `ValidationSummary` control used for?
15. How can you check a page's validity?

☑ Friday

☑ Saturday

☑ **Sunday**

Part V — Sunday Morning

Session 21
Understanding Databases

Session 22
Setting Up Your Databases

Session 23
Using the Data Controls

Session 24
Understanding ADO.NET

Session 25
Working with Data

Session 26
Building a Data Aware ASP.NET Page

Part VI — Sunday Afternoon

Session 27
Configuring ASP.NET Applications

Session 28
Finding and Fixing Errors

Session 29
Some Advanced Topics

Session 30
Putting It All Together

PART

V

Sunday Morning

Session 21
Understanding Databases

Session 22
Setting Up Your Databases

Session 23
Using the Data Controls

Session 24
Understanding ADO.NET

Session 25
Working with Data

Session 26
Building a Data Aware ASP.NET Page

Understanding Databases

Session Checklist

✔ Understanding the concept of relational databases

✔ Learning how to create databases

✔ Inserting, updating, retrieving, and deleting data

**30 Min.
To Go**

Most business problems that need to be solved by using software involve some type of permanent data storage. Accounting, employee management, e-commerce, and contact management are common business problems that are perfectly solved by database-aware applications. In this chapter, you will learn about databases and how to create one using SQL Server 2000.

Relational Databases

No matter what data you intend to store, you need some sort of logical way to store it. The solution arrives in the form of a database. A *database* is a collection of tables and other information that defines and stores your data. A *relational database* is a database that contains two or more tables that have defined relationships to help eliminate duplicate data and provide an easy way to change one part of a large database.

Back in the old days, databases consisted of flat text files that stored data in some kind of sequential format, usually delimited with tabs, commas, spaces, or some other character. These text files were loaded by an application and parsed, then manipulated to generate a result. For a long time, flat files were the most common (and preferred) method for storing and dealing with data.

As computing became more ubiquitous, a need arose for a more cohesive approach to data storage. Developers noticed relationships in the different text files. For instance, an automobile service center has customers, with each customer having one or more cars. Because each customer may have more than one car that is serviced, a single text file containing a list of customers would have duplicate data. Each customer who had a second car would have a second entry in the database. When you factor in the service performed on each car over multiple occasions, the file gets very large.

With relational databases, this problem is solved. Customers are stored in one table, while automobiles are stored in another table with a relationship defined between it and the customer table. A third table holds the services rendered for each automobile, with a relationship defined between the services table and the automobile table.

Applications that handle these relationships and the data are called Relational Database Management Systems (RDBMS). Microsoft SQL Server and Oracle are both examples of RDBMS. An RDBMS stores multiple tables within a single database. Old database systems like dBASE stored one table in one file.

Tables

With all this talk about tables, you may be a little confused as to what a table really is. Simply put, a *table* is a collection of data organized in columns. These columns define the data stored in the table.

For example, think of the automobile service table previously mentioned. It would contain data like:

- Date of Service
- Service Performed
- Cost of Service
- Scheduled Maintenance (yes or no)
- Warranty Service (yes or no)

By looking at that data, you can get an idea for the columns that would make up that table. Date of Service is self-explanatory. Service Performed could be a text entry or a relationship to a separate table containing information about services, depending on your needs. Cost of Service could be a numerical entry or a relationship to a table containing predefined costs, or a it could be a computed field that takes a shop rate multiplied by the hours of labor defined in the services table. Scheduled Maintenance is a Yes/No field (also called a *Boolean field*), and Warranty Service is a Yes/No field. Warranty Service could instead be a relationship to a warranty table containing individual records of warranties assigned to each customer.

As you can see, the possibilities are endless. You don't have to make your data as granular as possible if you don't want to; in the very least, however, you should move oft-duplicated data to its own table.

Tables are structured as columns, and they store data in rows.

Fields

A field is part of the structure of the table. The definition of the fields is the biggest part of creating a table. The fields are what define your data structure. Each field has a name, a type, and a maximum length. Sometimes, a field has a minimum length.

Data is stored in fields as records. Each record adheres to the list of fields defined. In the service table example, data stored in each record in the row will match the definition of the field.

Think of it all this way: A table is a large grid. The fields are columns, and the rows contain data. Anywhere the field and the row intersect is a record.

Every field has a data type. The data type particulars depend on what database system you are using. Check your database documentation to determine what your data type options are.

Try not to create fields with a space in the name. These fields can quickly become difficult to maintain and a bear to deal with if you ever decide to move your data to another RDBMS, such as Oracle or DB/2.

Keys

A key is required in order to define the uniqueness of a record. A field defined as the primary key is the field that defines the uniqueness of entries in a table. In our service example, a field would be created, probably called ID or Service_ID. Keys are often system-generated. In SQL Server, this is called an *identity*. In Access, it's called an *autonumber*. When the value of the key is system-generated, the system creates a sequential number for each record stored.

A key can also be indexed. When an index is defined on a key, the database system knows how to quickly search a table. This is important for performance considerations. A slow database can provide a miserable user experience.

You should never create a relational table without a unique index, such as a primary key, in mind. Adding an identity or autonumber as an afterthought to your table design will prove frustrating.

Relationships

A *relationship* is defined as a link between fields in two tables. The point of a relationship is to preserve data integrity. A relationship enforces rules in your database; for example, each state in an employee table must be one of the 50 states defined in the States table. In this case, a relationship would be defined between the States table and the Employees table. Relationships are defined at the field level.

Consider two tables, TableA and TableB. TableA contains a field called ID. TableB contains a field called TableA_ID. A relationship is defined between TableA.ID and TableB.TableA_ID. TableA.ID is the primary key, and TableB.TableA_ID is called the *foreign key*. With this relationship in place, each time TableB.TableA_ID is queried, it will be checked against TableA.ID to make sure it gets a legal value.

Relationships also simplify retrieval of different data from different tables.

Queries

With your data in tables and relationships defined between them, you need some way to access and manipulate that data. This is accomplished with queries.

A *query* is an instruction for the database written in some kind of query language. Microsoft SQL Server supports SQL, which stands for Structured Query Language. SQL (pronounced *sequel*) is a standard language that uses English-like syntax to simplify querying databases. Microsoft's implementation of SQL is called Transact-SQL, or T-SQL for short.

SQL can perform four different queries: SELECT, INSERT, UPDATE, and DELETE. Each one of these has a specific function.

- SELECT retrieves records based on specified criteria.
- INSERT inserts rows into a table.
- UPDATE allows you to update a specific record or set of records based on criteria.
- DELETE removes records from a table according to specified criteria.

Each of these query types will be further explained later in this chapter. Before you can do any kind of queries, you must first create your database. Fire up your database application and get ready.

The SELECT **query is the only query that returns data stored in your tables from the database. When you learn about** DataSets, **you'll understand this better. For now, just remember that the other statements *tell* the database something, while the** SELECT **statement *asks* for something.**

Create Your Database

**20 Min.
To Go**

Queries are exciting, but with no database and no data, a query is useless. Creating databases is very easy. In fact, most of the work is in the planning. You have several choices when it comes to creating a database. You can

- Use the RDBMS software to point-and-click your database.
- Use SQL scripts to build your database.
- Export from Access to a major RDBMS.
- Use a tool such as ERWin to export a database from a data model.

All of these are reasonable ways to create your database, but I'm partial to tools like ERWin. In this case, however, creating the database using SQL is the best choice because it is generally database-independent (it may not work in Access).

First, identify your table. I'll call mine Sample, and it will contain a first name, a last name, and a social security number. It will also have an identity column for the primary key.

Because I'm using SQL Server, I have to create a database before I can create a table within it. This is generally done by a DBA. If you are using SQL Server, refer to Chapter 5 to create a database yourself.

You can choose your own naming convention. The table will have these field names:

- ID
- FNAME
- LNAME
- SSN

ID is the identity, FNAME is the first name, LNAME is the last name, and SSN is the social security number. These field names are self-documenting.

Now we need to define the data types and maximum lengths of the fields. ID is an identity column in SQL Server, so it defaults to numeric. FNAME, LNAME, and SSN are all character strings, which means they store text such as letters and numbers. SSN could be numeric, but I want to include the - between sets of numbers for readability.

With that in mind, I'm ready to create my table. This is the SQL script to do just that.

```
CREATE TABLE Sample
{
    ID      numeric     IDENTITY,
    FNAME   char(10)    NOT NULL,
    LNAME   char(40)    NOT NULL,
    SSN     char(11)    NOT NULL,
    CONSTRAINT PK_SAMPLE_1 PRIMARY KEY (ID)
}
```

This SQL statement does several things.

- It defines the table name and tells SQL Server to create it.
- It specifies each field name and its data type, followed by its precision (maximum length) in parentheses.
- It specifies identity for the first column, and not null for the other columns. Not null means a value is required.
- It tells SQL Server to create a constraint called PK_SAMPLE_1 on ID. This is the primary key.

This is all you need to know to get up and running with your own database. If you're curious about how relational databases are defined, then have a look at this code:

```
CREATE TABLE Sample
{
    ID      numeric     IDENTITY,
    FNAME   char(10)    NOT NULL,
    LNAME   char(40)    NOT NULL,
    SSN     char(11)    NOT NULL,
    Constraint PK_SAMPLE_1 PRIMARY KEY (ID)
}
go
CREATE TABLE SampleIQ
{
    ID        numeric     IDENTITY,
    SAMPLE_ID numeric     NOT NULL,
    IQ        numeric     NOT NULL,
    CONSTRAINT PK_SAMPLEIQ PRIMARY KEY (ID)
}
go

alter table SampleIQ
    ADD CONSTRAINT FK_SAMPLEIQ_REF_K_SAMPLE FOREIGN KEY
      (SAMPLE_ID) REFERENCES SAMPLE (ID)
go
```

The alter table statement adds the foreign key, which defines the relationship between the two tables.

Inserting and Updating Data

If you remember, inserting and updating data in a database is performed using SQL. ASP.NET supports querying databases directly using the SQL language.

When your tables are created, you most likely want to populate them with data. With SQL Server or Access installed, this is simple: Just open the application and populate the fields directly. However, ASP.NET can't populate records this way. ASP.NET relies on SQL statements, so you need to know how to properly construct an INSERT statement and an UPDATE statement so you can populate and edit your tables.

INSERT

INSERT statements insert new values into a table. An INSERT statement does not return anything from the database; it just gives the database an instruction and a set of values as parameters.

An INSERT statement is structured as:

```
INSERT INTO table(field1, field2, field3, ...) VALUES(value1, value2, value3, ...)
```

In this statement, table represents the name of the table you want to insert data into. Field1, field2, and field3 are the names of the fields you want to populate. Value1, value2, and value3 are the values for those fields.

Let's consider a more real-world example. Assume you have a table with the following structure:

```
CREATE TABLE Sample
{
    ID       numeric      IDENTITY,
    FNAME    char(10)     NOT NULL,
    LNAME    char(40)     NOT NULL,
    SSN      char(11)     NOT NULL,
    CONSTRAINT PK_SAMPLE_1 PRIMARY KEY (ID)
}
```

To insert data into this table, an INSERT statement would be structured as:

```
INSERT INTO Sample(FNAME, LNAME, SSN) VALUES('Robert', 'Standefer', '000-00-0000')
```

Because ID is an identity column, specifying a value for it is not required. The INSERT statement requires the table name first, with its columns listed in sequential order. The VALUES keyword tells SQL that you are now specifying the values for the columns.

You can also get away with structuring a SQL statement like so:

```
INSERT INTO Sample('Robert', 'Standefer', '000-00-0000')
```

This INSERT statement will always make the assumption that each piece of data immediately following the table name will correspond to the same order of column names in the table's schema.

UPDATE

An UPDATE statement is designed to provide editing capability. In other words, it lets you edit, or update, an existing record. Like INSERT, UPDATE does not return anything from the database. It just tells the database, "Here, take this value and stuff it in to this field, and forget about what was already in that field."

An UPDATE statement is structured as:

```
UPDATE table SET field1 = value1 [WHERE field1=criteria]
```

UPDATE requires the table name, the SET keyword, the field you want to update, and the new value. The WHERE clause in the UPDATE statement is optional. The UPDATE statement will accept more than one `field = value` directive:

```
UPDATE table SET field1 = value1, field2 = value2 [WHERE field1=criteria]
```

When you want to update more than one record, the WHERE clause still matters for both of them. This means that the UPDATE will only run if the WHERE clause evaluates. Considering our Sample table from earlier, let's look at some queries. The table:

```
CREATE TABLE Sample
{
    ID      numeric     IDENTITY,
    FNAME   char(10)    NOT NULL,
    LNAME   char(40)    NOT NULL,
    SSN     char(11)    NOT NULL,
    CONSTRAINT PK_SAMPLE_1 PRIMARY KEY (ID)
}
```

Let's first update an SSN value. We'll assume that the ID corresponding to the entry is 5.

```
UPDATE Sample SET SSN = '111-11-1111' WHERE ID=5
```

This statement will update SSN to 111-11-1111 for the record with an ID of 5. Now, what would happen if we executed this statement?

```
UPDATE Sample SET SSN = '111-11-1111'
```

This statement would set SSN to 111-11-1111 for every record in the database. This is most likely not the desired result.

Always test your SQL statements before you execute them in production. It will save you headaches and protect you from the wrath of your database administrator.

Now, assume a need to update both the first name (FNAME) and social security number in the sample table. The ID of 5 is still valid. To do this, the UPDATE would be:

```
UPDATE Sample SET FNAME = 'Rob', SSN='111-11-1111' WHERE ID = 5
```

This will only update FNAME and SSN for the specified record. If the WHERE clause were omitted, all of the FNAME and SSN entries would be updated.

Retrieving Data

Getting data out of the database can prove to be much more complicated than putting it in. SELECT queries can vary from the sublimely simple to the nerve-wrackingly complex. In fact, for the novice, a SQL building tool such as Seagate Analysis, Microsoft Query, or the query builder in Visual Interdev 6.0 is advisable. Microsoft Access also has a good query builder, but the queries often don't translate very well to SQL Server.

At its most basic, a SELECT query requires two things: the fields you want returned and the table you want them returned from.

```
SELECT [*][field] FROM table
```

This query shows that you can tell SELECT you want one of two things. The asterisk (*) represents all fields:

```
SELECT * FROM table
```

The field is the specific fieldname you want data from:

```
SELECT fieldname FROM table
```

Considering our Sample database once again:

```
CREATE TABLE Sample
{
    ID      numeric     IDENTITY,
    FNAME   char(10)    NOT NULL,
    LNAME   char(40)    NOT NULL,
    SSN     char(11)    NOT NULL,
    CONSTRAINT PK_SAMPLE_1 PRIMARY KEY (ID)
}
```

We can construct a simple SELECT query:

```
SELECT * FROM Sample
```

This query will return all fields in all rows. If you want something more specific, just tell SELECT:

```
SELECT FNAME FROM Sample
```

You can also specify more than one field at a time:

```
SELECT FNAME, LNAME FROM Sample
```

This is fine, but it's not too often that you need all rows returned. The power of the SELECT statement lies in its WHERE clause. As it is with UPDATE, the WHERE clause takes a fieldname and some kind of criteria:

```
SELECT FNAME FROM Sample WHERE ID = 5
```

This will return 'Robert.' As you can see, SELECT queries can be very simple. It's not until you consider relationships that SELECT queries become complex.

 A discussion of JOIN queries is really out of the scope of this book. I recommend you try a tool such as one mentioned in this chapter, or read one of the fine SQL books from HungryMinds, such as *SQL For Dummies*.

Deleting Data

Deleting records is the simplest of all, and that simplicity is what does a lot of people in. Consider this statement:

```
DELETE FROM Sample
```

What do you think this statement does? If you guessed that it deletes every single row from Sample, you are correct. This is a very dangerous statement, especially when you aren't using transactions.

The DELETE statement takes a WHERE clause, just like SELECT and UPDATE. The WHERE clause tells DELETE what records to destroy.

```
DELETE FROM Sample WHERE ID = 5
```

In some programming circles, the use of the DELETE statement is heavily frowned upon. I find it much more practical to add a field to my table that marks the data as active or inactive. I then simply add the active field to my SELECT clause depending on my needs. Consider:

```
CREATE TABLE Sample
{
   ID      numeric      IDENTITY,
   FNAME   char(10)     NOT NULL,
   LNAME   char(40)     NOT NULL,
   SSN     char(11)     NOT NULL,
   ACTIVE  char(1)      NOT NULL,
   CONSTRAINT PK_SAMPLE_1 PRIMARY KEY (ID)
}
```

It's a good idea to set the ACTIVE field to have a default value of 'Y.' Then when you "delete" a record, you could execute this script:

```
UPDATE Sample SET ACTIVE = 'N' WHERE ID = 5
```

This will set the value of ACTIVE to 'N.' Anytime I want to query values in my database that I know aren't deleted, I execute this statement:

```
SELECT * FROM Sample WHERE ACTIVE = 'Y'
```

Use DELETE at your discretion.

Most database administrators disable DELETE capability to protect you from yourself. Check with your DBA.

Done!

REVIEW

In this chapter, you learned about relational databases and how to work with them. We talked about the importance of relational databases and what kinds of problems they solve. We discussed the parts of a database, including tables, keys, fields, relationships, and queries. You created a sample database in SQL Server 2000 (or Access if necessary). We discussed the four types of queries and looked at examples of each. Finally, we looked at how to retrieve data, as well as how to delete data.

QUIZ YOURSELF

1. What is a relational database? (See "Relational Databases.")
2. What are some current RDBMS products? (See "Relational Databases.")
3. What does SQL stand for? (See "Queries" under "Relational Databases.")
4. How do you add data to a table? (See "Inserting and Updating Data.")
5. How do you get data from a table? (See "Retrieving Data.")

Setting Up Your Database

Session Checklist

✔ Installing SQL Server 2000

**30 Min.
To Go**

ASP.NET is perfect for building database applications. Using ASP.NET and the ADO.NET classes, it's possible to build powerful, robust applications that work with real-time data transactions. This chapter shows you how to install SQL Server 2000 and set up an environment for your ASP.NET database applications.

Preparing for SQL Server 2000

Microsoft SQL Server 2000 is a powerful relational database management system. Although SQL Server 2000 is definitely not the only database server you can use for your ASP.NET applications, it is an excellent choice. It's reliable, powerful, and fully integrated into the Microsoft .NET Enterprise Servers suite, which is Microsoft's next generation platform for hosting, servicing, and delivering .NET applications.

Acquiring SQL Server 2000

SQL Server 2000 is available from the Microsoft SQL Server Web site at www.microsoft.com/ sql/default.asp. It comes in several flavors: Evaluation Edition for a free 120-day trial, Developer Edition, Standard Edition, and Enterprise Edition. These different editions vary in cost and capability. If you don't already have SQL Server 2000, get the Evaluation Edition. This will let you run SQL Server 2000 for 120 days, which is plenty of time to decide if you want to lay down the cash for a "full" version.

SQL Server 2000 also comes in two smaller versions: Personal Edition and Desktop Engine. Personal Edition is for users who want to use SQL Server 2000 for very small database applications; it lacks many of the features of its bigger brothers. Desktop Engine is designed for applications that need SQL Server 2000 built in; it allows applications to be deployed in environments absent of SQL Server 2000.

The Developer Edition includes several tools for database developers. The Standard and Enterprise Editions are for production databases, like e-commerce sites and workgroup applications. The Evaluation Edition is a 120-day evaluation version of SQL Server 2000 Enterprise Edition.

System requirements

SQL Server 2000 Evaluation Edition requires an Intel Pentium 166 or higher processor, 250 megabytes of hard disk space (as much as 380 if you install all the optional add-ons), and at least 64 megabytes of RAM. It runs on Windows NT Server 4.0 SP5 or later, Windows 2000 Server, Advanced Server, and Datacenter Server.

 The Personal and Developer editions of SQL Server 2000 will run on Windows NT Workstation and Windows 2000 Professional; if you have either of these versions, your operating system requirements are relaxed.

SQL Server 2000also requires Internet Explorer 5.0 or greater, VGA or higher-resolution display, and a CD-ROM or DVD-ROM drive.

Installing SQL Server 2000

**20 Min.
To Go**

Installing SQL Server 2000 is a simple process. You need to know a few things about your machine and the network it sits on, and you need to know to what username and password you want to give administrator privileges.

If you have the SQL Server 2000 installation CD, insert it into your CD-ROM drive. It will automatically start. If you have downloaded SQL Server 2000, run its setup program. After the CD is inserted or the setup program is started, you seethe screen shown in Figure 22-1.

Figure 22-1 *SQL Server 2000 Startup splash screen*

This screen provides five choices that let you install SQL Server 2000, read its prerequisites, and a few other things. On this screen, click SQL Server 2000 Components. The screen in Figure 22-2 appears.

Figure 22-2 SQL Server 2000 Installation choices

Now we want to install the database server, so click Install Database Server. For our purposes, we don't need Analysis Services, although you can install it later if you want. After clicking Install Database Server, you see the screen in Figure 22-3.

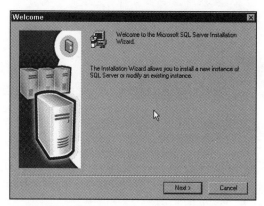

Figure 22-3 SQL Server 2000 Welcome screen

Click Next to continue the installation. The screen in Figure 22-4 appears.

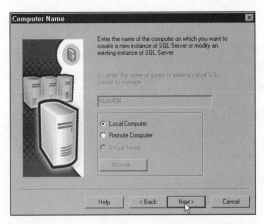

Figure 22-4 *SQL Server 2000 Computer Name*

This part of the installation wants to know where you want to install SQL Server 2000, on a remote machine or locally. In this screen, KLAVEN is the name of my server, and that's where I chose to install SQL Server 2000. Select Local Computer and click Next. The screen in Figure 22-5 appears.

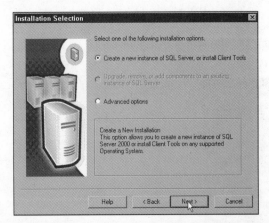

Figure 22-5 *SQL Server 2000 Installation Selection*

When this window appears, choose "Create a new instance of SQL Server, or install Client Tools" and click Next. The screen in Figure 22-6 appears.

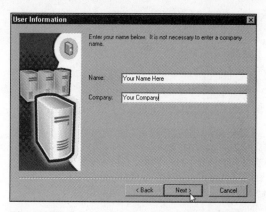

Figure 22-6   *SQL Server 2000 User Information*

Type your name and organization name into the text boxes and click Next. The screen in Figure 22-7 appears.

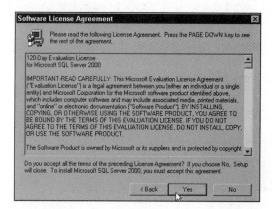

Figure 22-7   *SQL Server 2000 License agreement*

This is the SQL Server 2000 License Agreement. Read it and if you decide to continue the installation, click Yes. The screen in Figure 22-8 appears.

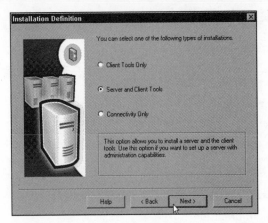

Figure 22-8 SQL Server 2000 Installation Definition

This part of the installation asks you what you want to install. Picking "Client Tools" just installs the client-based tools like SQL Query Analyzer. Picking "Server and Client Tools" installs the database server and the client-based tools. "Connectivity Only" just installs the files necessary to connect to a remote SQL Server. Choose "Server and Client Tools" and click Next. The screen in Figure 22-9 appears.

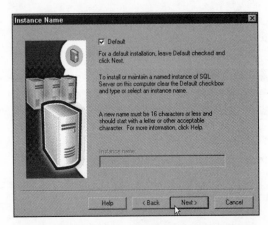

Figure 22-9 SQL Server 2000 Instance Name

This screen allows you to name your SQL Server 2000 instance. SQL Server 2000 (except the Windows CE version) supports named instances so you can run more than one instance of SQL Server. You can name your instance, or pick "Default" on this window and click Next. The screen in Figure 22-10 appears.

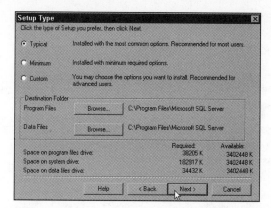

Figure 22-10 *SQL Server 2000 Setup Type*

This screen allows you to customize your installation. It allows you to pick which components are installed, where the SQL Server program files go, and where the SQL Server data will reside. Make your customizations as you see fit; I recommend choosing Typical to ensure everything you need is installed. Make your selection and click Next. The screen in Figure 22-11 appears.

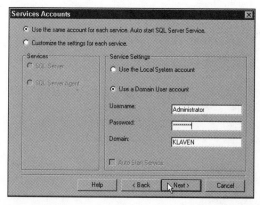

Figure 22-11 *SQL Server 2000 Services Accounts*

This screen gives you the opportunity to set security on the SQL Server 2000 service, which is the program that runs in Windows NT or Windows 2000 to provide SQL Server services. You can make your own decisions here, but be very sure you know what you are doing. If your machine is on a network, you can elect to use a Domain User account. Otherwise, you can use the locally logged in account. Make your selection and click Next. The screen in Figure 22-12 appears.

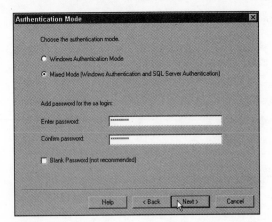

Figure 22-12   *SQL Server 2000 Authentication Mode*

This screen allows you to decide on an authentication scheme for your SQL Server. This governs connectivity to the server. Choosing Windows Authentication Mode forces SQL Server to rely on Windows to authenticate users. Choosing Mixed Mode increases diversity by allowing both Windows authentication and SQL Server authentication (for the sa username). Make your selection and click Next. The screen in Figure 22-13 appears.

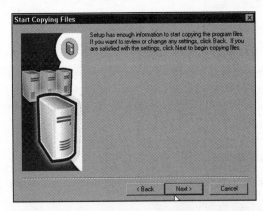

Figure 22-13   *SQL Server 2000 Start Copying Files*

We're almost done. Clicking Next on this screen will start the file copy selection. When it has completed, you will see the screen in Figure 22-14.

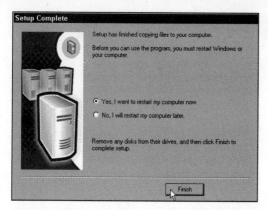

Figure 22-14   *SQL Server 2000 Setup Complete*

SQL Server 2000 setup has completed and all you have to do is restart your system.

If you don't want to download SQL Server 2000 or install it for any reason, you can use the scaled-down version that's included with the .NET Framework. You'll have to create your databases using SQL scripts rather than the visual tools.

Creating Your Database

10 Min. To Go

Now that SQL Server 2000 is installed, you're ready to create your database. In SQL Server 2000, a database consists of one or more tables. When you create a database, you'll create a table and define its properties.

The first thing to do is start Enterprise Manager. Choose Start ⇨ Programs ⇨ Microsoft SQL Server ⇨ Enterprise Manager. Enterprise Manager will start and in the left pane, you'll see some text with little plus signs next to them. Click the plus sign next to "Microsoft SQL Servers," and then click the plus sign next to "SQL Server Group." You should see the SQL Server you set up with either its instance name or the computer name, depending on what you selected in the installation. Click the plus sign next to your server name and you should see something very similar to the screen shown in Figure 22-15.

The first thing to do is create a database. Click the plus sign next to "Databases." You'll see a list of built-in databases. We want to create our own, so right-click Databases with your mouse and select New Database. The window in Figure 22-16 appears.

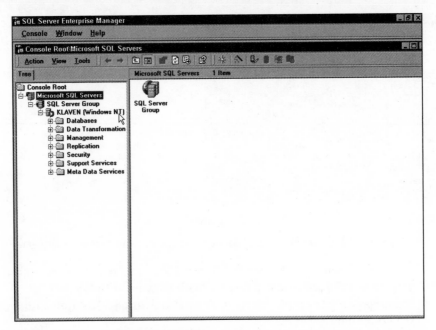

Figure 22-15   *A SQL Server machine*

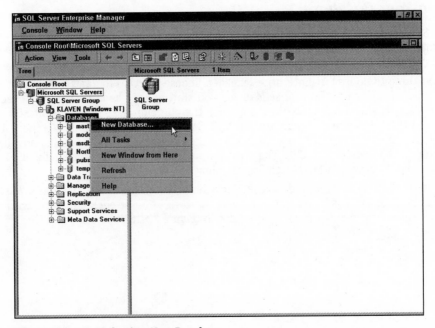

Figure 22-16   *Selecting New Database*

In this window, you can set the properties for your database. Accept the default properties and type ASPNET WCC into the Name field (see Figure 22-17).

Figure 22-17   *Naming the database*

Click OK. The ASPNET WCC database will now be listed under Databases for your server.

Now, click the plus sign next to ASPNET WCC. You'll see a listing that says Tables. This is a list of all the tables in your database, ASPNET WCC. Right-click Tables with your mouse and select New Table... (see Figure 22-18).

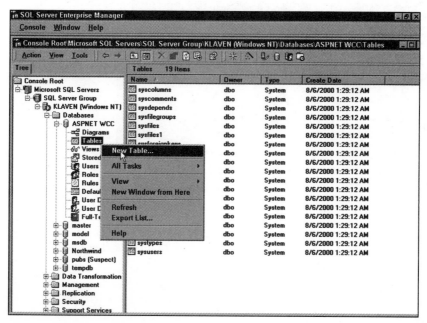

Figure 22-18   *Selecting New Table...*

A window appears that allows you to define your new table in ASPNET WCC on your SQL Server (mine is named KLAVEN). This window is shown in Figure 22-19.

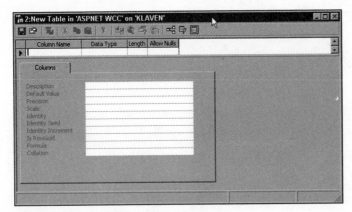

Figure 22-19   *The New Table window*

Because we're going to use this table in a later example, we'll need three columns. First select the solid gray bar beneath the first entry and drag it down. This will give you some more room. Now, type the column names and data types to match what is shown in Figure 22-20.

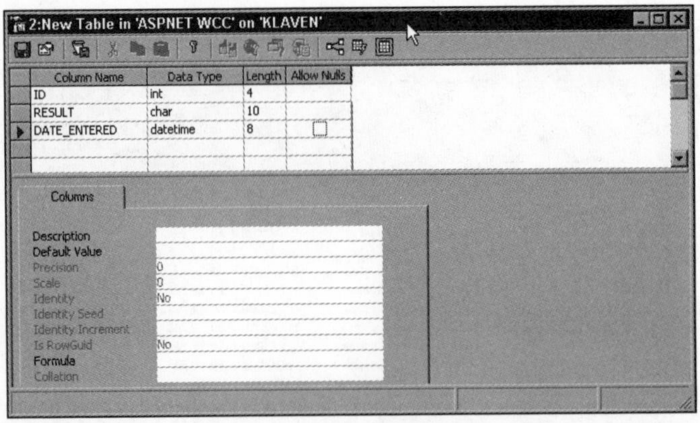

Figure 22-20   *Our New Table properties*

Make sure that Nulls is not checked for any of the columns. All of our fields will be required. After you have entered the text and made sure Nulls isn't checked for each column, click Save. You'll see the window shown in Figure 22-21.

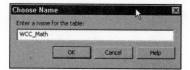

Figure 22-21 *Name the table*

This window lets you name the new table. Name it WCC_Math and click OK. The table will appear in the list of tables for the ASPNET WCC table and you are done!

Done!

REVIEW

In this chapter, we covered installing SQL Server 2000, creating a database, and creating a table. Specifically we covered:

- How to acquire SQL Server 2000
- The different versions of SQL Server 2000
- SQL Server 2000 system requirements
- Installing SQL Server 2000 step by step
- Creating a database
- Creating a table in the database

Chapter 23 covers using the data controls to work with data.

QUIZ YOURSELF

1. What is Microsoft's next generation platform for hosting, servicing, and delivering .NET applications? (See "Preparing for SQL Server 2000.")
2. Name the different versions of SQL Server 2000. (See "Preparing for SQL Server 2000.")
3. What does the Evaluation Edition require that the Developer Edition does not? (See "Preparing for SQL Server 2000.")
4. How do you create a database in Enterprise Manager? (See "Creating Your Database.")
5. How do you create a table in Enterprise Manager? (See "Creating Your Database.")

Using the Data Controls

Session Checklist

✔ Understanding data binding

✔ Learning about the data controls

✔ Applying the DataGrid and DataList controls

✔ Understanding how the data controls work with data

**30 Min.
To Go**

The .NET Framework exposes a set of controls for providing interface elements and working with forms. These are the Web controls discussed in Chapter 18. In this chapter, we'll take a look at binding the Web controls to databases, as well as a set of Web controls specifically designed to simplify working with data.

Data Binding

Data binding, in the context of Web controls, is the idea of attaching a control to a piece of data. This data can come from a result from a method call, a simple property, a collection, or an expression. The data binding is performed using a simple syntax:

```
<%# [value] [expression] [property] [method call] [collection] %>
```

The data binding does not occur when the page is processed. It only occurs when the DataBind() method is called. To invoke data binding when the page is loaded, you simply place the DataBind() method in the page's Page_Load event:

```
Sub Page_Load(Src As Source, e As EventArgs)
    Page.DataBind()
End Sub
```

DataBind() is a method of the Page class and all Web controls. DataBind() is a cascading method, which means that when you call it on a parent class it is cascaded down to all of the child classes. For example, if you call Page.DataBind(), or call DataBind() in the Page_Load event, then all the data binding expressions on the page are evaluated.

Data binding can be used almost anywhere within an ASP.NET page. The only requirement is that it evaluates to the expected data type at runtime. Let's say you have a data binding expression that uses a method call, and the method call returns text. In this case, the expected data type of the data binding expression is String. If the expression returns an integer, it must evaluate to a value of the type Integer. All you have to do to ensure this is use the appropriate type converter in your expression. For example, if you want to return an integer and display it as text:

```
<%# nValue.ToString() %>
```

This will write out your integer value as a string.

Binding to data from a database

Most developers will find they use Web control data binding with databases as the data sources. Data binding with the Web controls is a simple process that requires only three high-level steps: connecting to the database, selecting the data, and binding the control to the data.

In this section, I don't use the `<%# %>` syntax for data binding, instead choosing to control the data binding in the code. It's all a matter of personal preference; if you want to use `<%# %>`, you have that option and your results should be the same as mine.

The best way to explore data binding with Web controls is by looking at an example. Let's build a simple page that queries a SQL Server database and populates a list box with the result data. First, we build the shell of our page:

```
<%@ Import namespace="System.Data" %>
<%@ Import namespace="System.Data.OleDb" %>
<html>
<head>
<script language="VB" runat="server">
Sub Page_Load(Src As Source, e As EventArgs)
'Our code will go here
End Sub
</script>
</head>
<body>
<form>
</form>
</body>
</html>
```

The first thing we did was import the two namespaces we need for working with data, System.Data and System.Data.OleDb. These two namespaces expose the core objects we need to perform data access with ASP.NET. The rest of the page is your standard ASP.NET fare, with an empty Page_Load event that we will add code to in a moment.

The next step is to define the database connection. For this example, I'm using the Northwind database included in SQL Server 2000, because it is already populated with data.

When I installed SQL Server 2000, it automatically set up a DSN called NWIND on my machine pointing to the Northwind database, so I will use that DSN as well. This is the code:

```
<script language="VB" runat="server">
Dim strConn As String
Dim strSQL As String
Dim objConn As OleDbConnection
Dim objAdp As New OleDbDataAdapter()
Dim dsNW As DataSet

strConn = "DSN=Northwind"
strSQL = "SELECT * From Products"

objConn = New OleDbConnection(strConn)
```

This code also includes the text for our SQL statement, which we will issue to the server to retrieve the data:

```
Dim objCmd As New OleDbCommand(strSQL, objConn)
Dim objAdp As New OleDbDataAdapter()
objCmd.CommandType = CommandType.Text
objAdp.SelectCommand = objCmd
dsNW = New DataSet("Products")
objAdp.Fill(dsNW)
</script>
```

The DataSet now has data in it and all we have to do is define our control and bind it to the data. The first step is actually creating the control:

```
<form method="post" runat="server">
<asp:ListBox id="lbDataBindSample" runat="server">
<DataTextField="ProductName" DataValueField="ProductID" />
<asp:ListBox>
</form>
```

Now bind it after the DataSet is filled:

```
lbDataBindSample.DataSource = dsNW.Tables("Products").DefaultView
lbDataBindSample.DataBind()
```

That's all there is to it!

The data binding code

```
<%@ Import namespace="System.Data" %>
<%@ Import namespace="System.Data.OleDb" %>
<html>
<head>
<script language="VB" runat="server">
Sub Page_Load(Src As Source, e As EventArgs)
```

```
<script language="VB" runat="server">
Dim strConn As String
Dim strSQL As String
Dim objConn As OleDbConnection
Dim objAdp As New OleDbDataAdapter()
Dim dsNW As DataSet

strConn = "DSN=Northwind"
strSQL = "SELECT * From Products"

objConn = New OleDbConnection(strConn)

Dim objCmd As New OleDbCommand(strSQL, objConn)
Dim objAdp As New OleDbDataAdapter()
objCmd.CommandType = CommandType.Text
objAdp.SelectCommand = objCmd
dsNW = New DataSet("Products")
objAdp.Fill(dsNW)


lbDataBindSample.DataSource = dsNW.Tables("Products").DefaultView
lbDataBindSample.DataBind()

End Sub
</script>
</head>
<body>
<form method="post" runat="server">
<asp:ListBox id="lbDataBindSample" runat="server">
<DataTextField="ProductName" DataValueField="ProductID" />
</asp:ListBox>
</form>
</body>
</html>
```

**20 Min.
To Go**

Data Controls and Classes

Although data binding with Web controls provides a great way to work with data from a user interface perspective, there are controls built into the .NET Framework that are specifically designed for working with data.

System.Web.UI.WebControls exposes a set of classes and two controls designed for working with data. The classes expose objects that provide further programmatic control over the data controls.

BoundColumn

When a DataGrid (discussed below) is bound to a data source, its columns are bound to data fields. BoundColumn represents each column in the DataGrid.

ButtonColumn

ButtonColum represents each column in the bound `DataGrid` with a set of push button controls.

DataGridColumn

Column represents a column in a `DataGrid`. It is the base class for all `DataGrid` column types.

DataGridColumnCollection

This is a collection containing all of the columns to be displayed in a `DataGrid` control.

DataGrid

`DataGrid` is a control that displays data via ADO.NET in a scrollable grid.

DataGridItem

The `DataGridItem` represents an individual item in a `DataGrid` control.

DataGridItemCollection

This is a collection of `DataGridItem` objects.

DataGridPagerStyle

This specifies the pager style for the `DataGrid` control.

DataKeyCollection

The `DataKeyCollection` object represents a collection of primary key field names.

DataList

`DataList` is a control that displays a data-bound list.

DataListItem

DataListItem represents an individual item in a `DataList` control.

DataListItemCollection

This class represents a collection of `DataListItem` objects.

EditCommandColumn

EditCommandColumn creates a special column with buttons to edit items within the selected row. The buttons provide functionality for and are labeled as Edit, Update, and Cancel.

HyperLinkColumn

HyperLinkColumn creates a column in the DataGrid containing hyperlinks.

TemplateColumn

This class defines the template for a control's layout within a DataGrid column.

Using the Controls

There are two base controls in the System.Web.UI.WebControls namespace that are designed for displaying data on a form. These controls use what I call auxiliary controls and classes, such as the ButtonColumn. The two base controls are DataGrid and DataList. DataGrid displays data in a grid fashion, with configurable columns. DataList displays data in a list with configurable rows (like alternating colors).

DataGrid

A DataGrid is placed on a form using the <asp:DataGrid> syntax. It accepts several properties, including Width, BackColor, CellPadding, and CellSpacing. The DataGrid renders as a table on the client, so whatever properties can be set for the <table>, <td>, and <tr> tags can be set for the DataGrid. DataGrid also has some properties of its own:

```
<asp:DataGrid id="DataGridID" runat="server"
BorderColor="black"
BorderWidth="2"
GridLines="Both"
CellPadding="2"
CellSpacing="1"
Font-Name="Arial"
Font-Size="12pt"
HeaderStyle-BackColor="#C0C0C0"
AutoGenerateColumns="false">
</asp:DataGrid>
```

The DataGrid control is very flexible. It's possible to write code to provide custom sorting, item selection, and events, and the control supports data binding.

**10 Min.
To Go**

Data binding with DataGrid

Data binding with the DataGrid is as easy as using any other control. System.Data.OleDb exposes the DataView class, which simplifies data binding. Using the DataView class in conjunction with the DataGrid provides a rich environment for displaying records in a table. Consider this code:

```
<script runat="server">
Dim strConn As String
Dim strSQL As String
Dim objConn As OleDbConnection
Dim objCmd As OleDbDataSetCommand
Dim dvNW As DataView
Dim dsNW As DataSet

strConn = "DSN=Northwind"
strSQL = "SELECT * From Products"

objConn = New OleDbConnection(strConn)
objCmd = New OleDbCommand(strConn, objConn)
dsNW = New DataSet()
objCmd.FillDataSet(dsNW, "Products");

dvNW = New DataView(dsNW.Tables[0])
dgSample.DataSource = dvNW
dgSample.DataBind()

End Sub
</script>
<form runat="server">
<asp:DataGrid id="dgSample" runat="server"></asp:DataGrid>
</form>
```

This code takes our existing connection code and adds a DataView object to the mix. The DataView object provides some extra functionality that you can use in your application, such as sorting. This functionality essentially provides instant capabilities for your DataGrid, created with the <asp:DataGrid> code.

Manipulating Columns

The Columns templates allow you to add formatting to a DataGrid. It is simple to add a column to the DataGrid in the above code:

```
<asp:DataGrid id="dgSample" runat="server">
<property name="Columns">
<asp:HyperLinkColumn
DataNavigateUrlField="productid"
DataNavigateUrlFormatString="http://localhost/show.aspx?id={0}"
Text="Details"
/>
</property>
</asp:DataGrid>
```

This code will specify that one column of the DataGrid shall contain links to a page named show.aspx, and pass the value of the productid field. The {0} at the end of the link indicates to ASP.NET that it should plug in the value of the field specified in DataNavigateUrlField.

Editing, deleting, and sorting data

The `DataGrid` control exposes a set of events that a developer can use to spawn actions such as editing, deleting, or sorting data. The events are `EditCommand`, `DeleteCommand`, and `SortCommand`.

 `DataGrid` **has other events, such as** `ItemCommand`, **but they're not discussed here.**

To use the events, you simply specify a `ButtonColumn` for the `DataGrid` and set the value of the `CommandName` to a specified value, depending on what you want to do. In the `DataGrid` itself, you specify a function to run when the event occurs. Here's a code sample:

```
<asp:DataGrid id="dgSample" runat="server"
AutoGenerateColumns="false"
OnEditCommand="EditData">
<property name="Columns">
<asp:ButtonColumn HeaderText="Edit" Text="Edit"
      CommandName="edit" />
</property>
</asp:DataGrid>
```

In this code, I've specified the `OnEditCommand` attribute with the value `EditData`, which could be a method that carried out the data edit. A `ButtonColumn` was created with the value `edit` specified for the `CommandName` attribute. The valid `CommandName` values for our purposes are `edit`, `delete`, and `sort`.

It's possible to specify all three event attributes in a single `DataGrid` control. Just be sure you have written the methods that correspond to the events. Here's the code:

```
<script runat="server">
Sub Page_Load(src As Object, e As EventArgs)
'Page_Load code here
End Sub

Sub EditData(Sender As Object, e As DataGridCommandEventArgs)
'Data edit code here
End Sub

Sub SortData(Sender As Object, e As DataGridSortCommandEventArgs)
'Data sort code here
End Sub

Sub DeleteData(Sender As Object, e As DataGridCommandEventArgs)
'Data delete code here
End Sub
</script>
<form runat="server">
<asp:DataGrid id="dgSample" runat="server"
AutoGenerateColumns="false"
```

```
OnEditCommand="EditData"
OnSortCommand="SortData"
OnDeleteCommand="DeleteData">
<property name="Columns">
<asp:ButtonColumn HeaderText="Edit" Text="Edit"
    CommandName="edit"/>
<asp:ButtonColumn HeaderText="Delete" Text="Delete"
    CommandName="delete" />
<asp:ButtonColumn HeaderText="Sort" Text="Sort"
    CommandName="sort" />
</property>
</asp:DataGrid>
</form>
```

You may have noticed in the functions above the code e As DataGridCommandEventArgs. The DataGridCommandEventArgs class provides data for the CancelCommand, EditCommand, DeleteCommand, UpdateCommand, and ItemCommand events of a DataGrid. DataGridSortCommandEventArgs provides data for the SortCommand event.

DataList

The DataList control facilitates easy displaying of data as lists. It's good for generating lists of data that are in alternating colored rows, such as in a check register. This is code for creating a DataList with some commonly used attributes:

```
<asp:DataList id="DataList1" runat="server"
BorderColor="black"
CellPadding="3"
Font-Name="Arial"
Font-Size="10pt"
HeaderStyle-BackColor="White"
AlternatingItemStyle-BackColor="Green">
</asp:DataList>
```

The DataList also accepts templates for defining styles for parts of a list such as the header and footer:

```
<template name="HeaderTemplate">
Entries
</template>
```

The accepted templates are ItemTemplate, AlternatingItemTemplate, SeparatorTemplate, SelectedItemTemplate, EditItemTemplate, HeaderTemplate, and FooterTemplate. If you don't specify a template, the default template is used. In other words, if you don't specify an AlternatingItemTemplate, then ASP.NET uses a default style.

In the case of HeaderTemplate and FooterTemplate, **if you don't specify a style for these templates, then no header or footer is displayed.**

Done!

REVIEW

In this chapter, we looked at how specific Web controls are used to access data. These controls, which include `DataGrid` and `DataList`, are commonly called data controls. We covered these items in detail:

- Data binding
- The data controls and classes exposed by `System.Web.UI.WebControls`
- Using the `DataGrid` control
- Using the `DataList` control

QUIZ YOURSELF

1. What is the syntax for data binding a control? (See "Data Binding.")
2. What method do you call to perform data binding? (See "Data Binding.")
3. What is a `BoundColumn`? (See "Data Controls and Classes.")
4. What event represents an update in a `DataGrid`? (See "Using the Controls.")
5. What happens if you don't specify a style for the header template? (See "Using the Controls.")

Understanding ADO.NET

Session Checklist

✔ Understanding the concept of modifying data

✔ Reviewing ADO and how it uses Recordsets

✔ Examining the ADO.NET namespaces

✔ Exploring the ADO.NET classes

**30 Min.
To Go**

When you write an ASP.NET application, you have at your fingertips some of the most innovative ways of handling data, but eventually, the n-tier of business logic and workflow objects must end with something new for your data tier. This chapter discusses the internals of inserts, updates and deletes as a general aspect of an ADO.NET connection. When you have an understanding of the basics, I will introduce the data modification enhancements available in ADO.NET.

What Happens When I Modify Data?

We have been using a math-based application throughout this book. Suppose we wanted to log the problems people have tried. In a test environment, having one person modify a table is easy to manage; just give them exclusive access and a change is possible. However, this scenario does not translate well to a multi-user environment, where hundreds (if not thousands) of connections are managed simultaneously to one database, and often one table! Your database server's resources can quickly become very scarce, so it is worth some time to discuss conceptually all stages of a database modification.

Four transactional properties

You may hear people discuss transactions when discussing changes to a table. The most common example is an ATM withdrawal. You have several expectations about the data in our account when you withdraw money. We will discuss these expectations under the umbrella concept of ACID, which stands for Atomicity, Consistency, Isolation, and Durability.

Atomicity

This aspect is a fancy way of saying that a transaction is all or nothing. If you request $20 from a bank machine, you would not stay a customer if you received $0 and had $20 deducted from your account because of an error somewhere down the chain of computers. A transaction for $20 is said to *commit* when all criteria are met, or *roll back* to the initial state if there was some reason to abort.

Consistency

Being consistent means that the only change made is the change requested. If you request $20 from a bank machine, you have a reasonable expectation that $20 and not $12 will be deducted from your account and logged against your particular time at the ATM.

Isolation

This aspect is the most difficult part of a transaction from a resource management perspective because it means that every connection can only see what transactions have been committed instead of incomplete transactions or transactions in the middle of execution. In our ATM scenario, you expect that any check that was presented to your account before the ATM request has been withdrawn and shows a true available balance. You also expect that any checks posted afterward will be posted against a balance that reflects your ATM withdrawal. This is where a database will use a lock to preserve a specific state for records involved in a transaction until it is committed.

Durability

Finally, this property of a transaction suggests that the committed transaction will be permanent and available. You have confidence that if your ATM is struck by lightning or a truck hits your home branch, somebody somewhere will be able to see that you did withdraw the $20. From a database management perspective, this is where disaster recovery, network connectivity, and distributed transactions play into the success of a transaction.

Updating a Recordset using ADO

Now that you understand the architectural issues in data modification, let's see this process in action using ADO in an ASP page. The following code builds an automatic insertion of rows for every page browse:

```
<!-- #include file="adovbs.inc" ‡
<html>
<body>
<script LANGUAGE ="VB" runat="server">
Dim oConn
Dim cmdSQL
Dim rsPubs
Dim strConn
```

```
Set oConn = Server.CreateObject("ADODB.Connection")
cmdSQLSet cmdSQL = Server.CreateObject("ADODB.Command")
Set rsPubs = Server.CreateObject("ADODB.Recordset")

'Connection shows data source and execution context
strConn = "Provider=SQLOLEDB;Server=.;username=sa;password=;database=pubs"
oConn.Open strConn

'Recordset object manages insertion
rsPubs.CursorType = adOpenKeyset
rsPubs.LockType = adLockOptimistic
rsPubs.Open "authors", oConn, , , adCmdTable
rsPubs.AddNew
rsPubs("au_fname") = "Duplicate"
rsPubs("au_lname") ="Author"
rsPubs.Update

'Command shows the execution content
cmdSQL.CommandText = "SELECT * FROM authors WHERE au_id > 10"
cmdSQL.ActiveConnection = oConn
rsPubs = cmdSQL.Execute
rsPubs.CursorLocation = adUseClient
rsPubs.Open cmdSQL, , adOpenStatic, adLockBatchOptimistic
rsPubs("au_lname").Properties("Optimize") = True
rsPubs.Sort = "au_lname"
rsPubs.MoveFirst
Response.Write "<p>ADO Inserts in ASP.NET</p>"
if rsPubs.BOF and rsPubs.EOF then ' Query didn't return any records.
Response.Write "<p>No Records</p>"
else
Do While Not rsPubs.EOF
Response.Write "<br>" & rsPubs("au_fname").Value & _
" " & rsPubs("au_lname").Value & "</br>"
rsPubs.MoveNext
Loop
end if
rsPubs.Close
Set rsPubs = nothing
oConn.Close
Set oConn = Nothing
Set cmdSQL = Nothing
</script>
</body>
</html>
```

This code is classic ADO code. It uses several different objects to get data, it uses EOF and BOF to check for the presence of data, and it uses a Do...Loop to output data. These are the issues that have made many ASP developers throw in the towel.

The code uses the Open method of the Connection object to establish a connection to a database. It then creates a Recordset object that explicitly opens the Authors table through the Connection object.

After the recordset is created and populated via its Open method, a new record is created in the table via the recordset's AddNew method. The code then populates each field, and calls the Update method of the recordset after the fields are all populated.

Alternately, a cmdSQL.CommandText statement like the example below could be built:

```
"BEGIN TRANSACTION
 INSERT INTO authors (au_fname, au_lname) VALUES ('Duplicate', 'Author')
IF @@ERROR=0 COMMIT TRANSACTION
ELSE ROLLBACK TRANSACTION"
```

The results are the same. It depends on how the data that you need to communicate comes in to the data access component. If you are modifying data based on the contents of a recordset already returned, then it will be easier to make changes within this subset to update later than to extract information into a query and execute separately.

20 Min. To Go

Using ADO.NET to Access Data

ADO.NET is different from ADO in many ways. Most importantly, ADO.NET deals with disconnected data, while ADO focuses on active connections. ADO can be summarized in a series of steps:

1. Open a connection to the database.
2. Retrieve data.
3. Loop through the information.
4. Close the connection.

ADO.NET takes these steps and goes farther via the DataSet. The DataSet could be viewed as a disconnected recordset. It's filled with data, and it doesn't rely on an open connection to work with that data. ADO.NET's first step is to open a connection to a database. Then, it retrieves data. Third, it populates a DataSet. After the DataSet is populated, it can request more data, or move on. The next step closes the database connection. You now have a DataSet that you can work with however you please, and you don't have to have an open connection to a database.

ADO.NET namespaces

ADO.NET exposes a host of objects that let you work with data in different ways. The .NET Framework exposes three key namespaces for accessing data: System.Data, System.Data.OleDb, and System.Data.SqlClient. System.Data is the root ADO.NET class. It contains the core classes that the other two namespaces derive (actually, overload) new classes from. System.Data.OleDb is intended for accessing OLE DB databases (that is, a database with an OLE DB provider). System.Data.SqlClient is intended for accessing SQL Server databases.

ADO.NET utilizes four primary types of classes (note that these aren't actually classes exposed by the ADO.NET namespaces; rather, they are concepts):

- Connection
- Command

- DataReader
- DataAdapter

These classes are derived for each data provider from the System.Data namespace. These are called the Data Provider Classes. For example, System.Data.OleDb represents the OLE DB Data Provider, while System.Data.SqlClient represents the SQL Server Data Provider. Each of the primary classes is derived from these interfaces, which are exposed by System.Data:

- IDbConnection (Connection)
- IDbCommand (Command)
- IDataReader (DataReader)
- IDbDataAdapter (DataAdapter)

Because System.Data.OleDb and System.Data.SqlClient represent specific data providers, the namespaces each implement the primary class interfaces in their own way. System.Data.OleDb exposes:

- OleDbConnection (from IDbConnection)
- OleDbCommand (from IDbCommand)
- OleDbDataReader (from IDbDataReader)
- OleDbDataAdapter (from IDbDataAdapter)

Likewise, System.Data.SqlClient exposes the primary class interfaces:

- SqlConnection (from IDbConnection)
- SqlCommand (from IDbCommand)
- SqlDataReader (from IDbDataReader)
- SqlDataAdapter (from IDbDataAdapter)

These classes provide the core database functionality you will need in your data-aware applications.

**10 Min.
To Go**

Using the ADO.NET classes

Each class exposed by ADO.NET has its own specific functionality. The core interfaces (IDbConnection, IDbCommand, and so on) provide the root functionality, and the classes exposed by System.Data.OleDb and System.Data.SqlClient override the methods exposed by the primary interfaces. For example, IDbConnection exposes a method called Open(). Thus, SqlCommand and OleDbCommand both have methods called Open(), which is the Open() method exposed by IDbConnection.

This can all get pretty complicated, so let's focus on using the ADO.NET classes. Because System.Data.OleDb and System.Data.SqlClient both instantiate the classes exposed by System.Data, this discussion will focus only on System.Data.OleDb. System.Data.OleDb is more versatile than System.Data.SqlClient, and for all intents and purposes, the key differences between the two namespaces (from a coding syntax standpoint) are in the names of the objects.

This discussion will focus on the most commonly used ADO.NET classes: `DataSet`, `DataTable`, `OleDbConnection`, and `OleDbDataAdapter`.

DataSet

It's easy to think of DataSet as the most important ADO.NET class; it's certainly the basis for accessing data in an ASP.NET page. The `DataSet`, exposed by `System.Data`, is a cache of data retrieved from a database. It follows the "disconnected recordset" paradigm previously mentioned.

But in all actuality, the `DataSet` is much more than a disconnected recordset, especially considering that a recordset can only store one set of data. A `DataSet` consists of a collection of `DataTable` objects. The `DataTable` objects can relate to each other. The `DataSet` represents a complete set of data without regard to the type of data it contains (for example, text, XML, binary files, and so on.).

A `DataSet` can be created three different ways: programmatically creating `DataTables`, `DataRelations`, and `Constraints` within the `DataSet`; loading and persisting the `DataSet` using XML; and populating the `DataSet` with tables of data from an existing database through a `DataAdapter` (`OleDbDataAdapter` or `SqlDataAdapter`).

The `DataSet` is stateless; it can be passed between calling applications without tying up resources like database connections. The `DataSet` is also formatted as an XML document and not a binary stream of data.

DataTable

A `DataTable` represents one table of relational data. `DataTables` are typically created within a `DataSet`, either through a `DataAdapter` or from an XML schema using a method such as `ReadXML`.

OleDbConnection

`OleDbConnection` simply represents an open connection to a data source, a unique connection to a database. A connection is opened through an `OleDbConnection` by using its `Open()` method and passing a connection string. An `OleDbConnection` does not close itself when it goes out of scope; thus, it must be closed using the `Close()` or `Dispose()` method.

OleDbDataAdapter

`OleDbDataAdapter` could be regarded as the workhorse of ADO.NET. It serves as the bridge between a `DataSet` object and a data source. The `OleDbAdapter` class exposes the `Fill` method for retrieving data into a `DataSet` and the `Update` method for sending changes in the `DataSet` back to the data source.

Creating and Filling DataSets

The process of creating a `DataSet` in code is actually quite simple. Let's examine each step:

1. Use a DataAdapter (such as OleDbDataAdapter) to build and fill each DataTable in a DataSet with data from a data source such as a database or XML document using the Fill method.
2. Use DataRow objects to change the data in individual DataTable objects.
3. Create a second DataSet that contains only the changed data using the GetChanges method.
4. Check the DataSet HasErrors property to determine if any errors occurred. If errors are present, check each DataTable HasErrors property.
5. Merge the first and second DataSets using the Merge method.
6. Call the DataAdapter Update method and pass the second DataSet as an argument.
7. Invoke the Merge method to merge the changes from the second DataSet into the first.
8. Commit the changes using AcceptChanges or roll them back using RejectChanges.

That's all there is to it. The next chapter examines this process in more detail and covers how to write the code to create DataSets.

Done!

REVIEW

This chapter introduced you to ADO.NET, its key concepts, and its core objects. Specifically, we covered:

- Core data-access concepts
- Some of the limitations of ADO
- Using ADO.NET to access data
- The ADO.NET namespaces
- Using the ADO.NET classes
- Creating and populating a DataSet

The next chapter puts into practice what you have learned in this chapter. Part of this practice involves converting the ADO-based ASP page at the beginning of this chapter to ADO.NET-based ASP.NET

QUIZ YOURSELF

1. In terms of database activity, what does ACID mean? (See "Four transactional properties.")
2. What are some of the issues of ADO that frustrated ASP developers? (See "Updating a Recordset using ADO.")
3. What are the steps that summarize ADO.NET? (See "Using ADO.NET to Access Data.")
4. Which namespace exposes the ADO.NET interfaces? (See "ADO.NET namespaces.")
5. Which class is the "workhorse" of ADO.NET? (See "Using the ADO.NET classes.")

Working with Data

Session Checklist

✔ Learning more about ADO.NET

✔ Converting the ADO application to ADO.NET

I n the previous chapter, you learned about ADO.NET and the namespaces and classes that expose ADO.NET to developers. In this chapter, you will learn how to apply ADO.NET to creating database applications. You'll start by revisiting the ADO application from the previous chapter and exploring how to convert it to ADO.NET.

ADO Revisited

The discussion of ADO in the previous chapter resulted in a sample ASP page that used ADO to retrieve values from a table in a database. This is the ASP page:

```
<!-- #include file="adovbs.inc" -->
<html>
<body>
<script LANGUAGE ="VB" runat="server">
Dim oConn
Dim cmdSQL
Dim rsPubs
Dim strConn

Set oConn = Server.CreateObject("ADODB.Connection")
cmdSQLSet cmdSQL = Server.CreateObject("ADODB.Command")
Set rsPubs = Server.CreateObject("ADODB.Recordset")

'Connection shows data source and execution context
strConn = "Provider=SQLOLEDB;Server=.;username=sa;password=;database=pubs"
oConn.Open strConn

'Recordset object manages insertion
```

```
rsPubs.CursorType = adOpenKeyset
rsPubs.LockType = adLockOptimistic
rsPubs.Open "authors", oConn, , , adCmdTable
rsPubs.AddNew
rsPubs("au_fname") = "Duplicate"
rsPubs("au_lname") ="Author"
rsPubs.Update

'Command shows the execution content
cmdSQL.CommandText = "SELECT * FROM authors WHERE au_id > 10"
cmdSQL.ActiveConnection = oConn
rsPubs = cmdSQL.Execute
rsPubs.CursorLocation = adUseClient
rsPubs.Open cmdSQL, , adOpenStatic, adLockBatchOptimistic
rsPubs("au_lname").Properties("Optimize") = True
rsPubs.Sort = "au_lname"
rsPubs.MoveFirst
Response.Write "<p>ADO Inserts in ASP.NET</p>"
if rsPubs.BOF and rsPubs.EOF then ' Query didn't return any records.
Response.Write "<p>No Records</p>"
else
Do While Not rsPubs.EOF
Response.Write "<br>" & rsPubs("au_fname").Value & _
" " & rsPubs("au_lname").Value & "</br>"
rsPubs.MoveNext
Loop
end if
rsPubs.Close
Set rsPubs = nothing
oConn.Close
Set oConn = Nothing
Set cmdSQL = Nothing
</script>
</body>
</html>
```

This code uses the Connection, Recordset, and Command objects exposed by ADO and familiar to practically every ASP developer. It opens a connection to a database server via the Connection object, adds a new record to the database using a Recordset, and then gets data from the server using a Command.

If you look at the end of the code, you'll see a Do...Loop block with a MoveNext statement inside it. This little piece of code has maddened plenty of ASP developers. After the Loop statement, notice the several lines of code that close the objects and then destroy them.

ADO Code Rewritten

**20 Min.
To Go**

You know there's plenty to not like about the ADO code, but don't disparage it; for a long time, it was the best method for accessing data from an ASP page and it's still a viable, widespread solution. This chapter, however, is about using ADO.NET to work with data, so let's jump into it.

Following the ADO.NET paradigm, you can identify the classes you will need to use in the converted code. They are OleDbConnection, OleDbDataAdapter, OleDbCommand, OleDbCommandBuilder, DataSet, and DataRow. OleDbConnection, OleDbCommand, OleDbCommandBuilder, and OleDbDataAdapter are exposed by System.Data.OleDb, and DataSet and DataRow are exposed by System.Data.

```
<html>
<head>
<title>ADO.NET Conversion</title>
<script language="vb" runat="server">
Dim oConn As OleDbConnection
oConn = New
OleDbConnection("Provider=SQLOLEDB;Server=.;username=sa;password=;database
=pubs")
oConn.Open()

Dim adpPubs As New OleDbDataAdapter()
Dim dsPubs As New DataSet()
Dim strSQL As String = "SELECT * FROM Authors"
Dim odbPubs As OleDbCommandBuilder = New OleDbCommandBuilder(adpPubs)

adpPubs.SelectCommand = New OleDbCommand(strSQL, oConn)
adpPubs.Fill(dsPubs)

Dim rowPubs As New DataRow = dsPubs.Tables("Authors").NewRow
rowPubs("au_fname") = "Duplicate"
rowPubs("au_lname") = "Author"
dsPubs.Tables("Authors").Rows.Add(rowPubs)
adpPubs.Update(dsPubs, "Authors")

oConn.Close
oConn = Nothing

DataSampleGrid.DataSource = dsPubs
DataSampleGrid.DataBind()
</script>
</head>
<body>
<asp:DataGrid ID="DataSampleGrid" Runat="server"></asp:DataGrid>
</body>
</html>
```

**10 Min.
To Go**

As you can see, this code is quite different from the ADO code. It uses several different objects, as well as a DataGrid and data binding.

Let's explore the code in more detail:

```
<html>
<head>
<title>ADO.NET Conversion</title>
<script language="vb" runat="server">
```

These lines simply define the HTML structure and open the <script> block.

```
Dim oConn As OleDbConnection
oConn = New OleDbConnection("Provider=SQLOLEDB;Server=.;" & _
"username=sa;"password=;database=pubs")
oConn.Open()
```

These lines define and open the connection to the database using an OleDbConnection object.

```
Dim adpPubs As New OleDbDataAdapter()
Dim dsPubs As New DataSet()
Dim strSQL As String = "SELECT * FROM Authors"
Dim odbPubs As OleDbCommandBuilder = New OleDbCommandBuilder(adpPubs)
```

This code defines the various ADO.NET objects we need for our page. strSQL is populated with a basic SELECT query.

```
adpPubs.SelectCommand = New OleDbCommand(strSQL, oConn)
adpPubs.Fill(dsPubs)
```

This code executes a command, passing the SQL query and the connection objects as parameters. It then fills the DataSet with the results.

```
Dim rowPubs As New DataRow = dsPubs.Tables("Authors").NewRow
rowPubs("au_fname") = "Duplicate"
rowPubs("au_lname") = "Author"
dsPubs.Tables("Authors").Rows.Add(rowPubs)
adpPubs.Update(dsPubs, "Authors")
```

This code handles updating the DataSet with new data. The rows are populated, the Add method of the Rows object is called, and the Update method of the OleDbDataAdapter is called, accepting the DataSet and the table name as parameters.

```
oConn.Close
oConn = Nothing
```

This code simply closes the Connection object and then destroys it.

```
DataSampleGrid.DataSource = dsPubs
DataSampleGrid.DataBind()
</script>
```

This code fills the DataGrid control on the Web form by pointing it to a datasource (in this case, dsPubs, a DataSet) and then calling the DataBind() method.

```
</head>
<body>
<asp:DataGrid ID="DataSampleGrid" Runat="server"></asp:DataGrid>
</body>
</html>
```

The DataGrid now contains data that was added to the database at the beginning of the page. This completes the conversion of the ADO page to ADO.NET!

Done!

REVIEW

This chapter was short and to the point. It was intended to help you get a good, quick understanding of how ADO.NET works in comparison to ADO. Specifically, we covered

- A few problems with the ADO implementation
- The objects need for the rewrite
- The actual code for the rewrite
- Using DataGrid and DataBind()

The next chapter puts everything together and lets you apply your newfound ADO.NET knowledge.

QUIZ YOURSELF

1. What are some sources of chagrin for ASP developers caused by ADO? (See "ADO Code Revisited.")
2. What are some of the objects used in the ADO.NET conversion? (See "ADO Code Rewritten.")
3. How is the OleDbDataAdapter populated with data? (See "ADO Code Rewritten.")
4. Which ADO.NET object is used to add new rows? (See "ADO Code Rewritten.")
5. Which namespace exposes the DataSet and DataRow classes? (See "ADO Code Rewritten.")

Building a Data Aware ASP.NET Page

Session Checklist

✔ Revisiting the existing ASP.NET application

✔ Applying database support to the application

**30 Min.
To Go**

By now you should have a solid understanding of ASP.NET concepts, such as creating pages, building Web forms, and working with databases. This chapter combines what you have learned with the page that you've already constructed, math.aspx.

A Quick Recap

The original plan for this application, called ASP.NET Math Program, was to satisfy some basic requirements using a form and an ASP.NET page. We built that application as two files, and then we decided later to alter the requirements and reconstruct the application using ASP.NET Web forms. To that end, we did away with the HTML page entirely and put several `<asp:ControlName>` tags in our ASP.NET page. We also retained the existing functions for performing the math calculations. This is how our application currently looks:

```vb
<%@Import Namespace="System" %><html>
<head>
<title>ASP.NET Math Program</title>
<script language="vb" runat="server">
Sub Page_Load(Source as Object, e As EventArgs)

End Sub
Sub btnGetResult_OnClick(Source As Object, e As EventArgs)
decValue1 = txtValue1.Text
decValue2 = txtValue2.Text
strOperator = MathOperator.SelectedItem.Text
Dim decResult As Decimal

Try
Select Case strOperator
```

```
Case "multiply"
decResult = MultiplyValues(decValue1, decValue2)
Case "divide"
decResult = DivideValues(decValue1, decValue2)
Case "add"
decResult = AddValues(decValue1, decValue2)
Case "subtract"
decResult = SubtractValues(decValue1, decValue2)
End Select
Catch myEx As OverflowException
Response.Write("The result was too large to represent" & _
"as a decimal.")
Catch myEx As DivideByZeroException
Response.Write("You cannot divide by zero.")
Finally
Response.Write("The result of your calculation is: " & _
decResult)
End Try
End Sub
Function MultiplyValues(decValue1 As Decimal, decValue2 As _
Decimal)
Dim decResult As Decimal
decResult = Multiply(decValue1, decValue2)
Return decResult
End Function

Function DivideValues(decValue1 As Decimal, decValue2 As _
Decimal)
Dim decResult As Decimal
decResult = Divide(decValue1, decValue2)
Return decResult
End Function

Function AddValues(decValue1 As Decimal, decValue2 As _
Decimal)
Dim decResult As Decimal
decResult = Add(decValue1, decValue2)
Return decResult
End Function

Function SubtractValues(decValue1 As Decimal, decValue2 As _
Decimal)
Dim decResult As Decimal
decResult = Subtract(decValue1, decValue2)
Return decResult
End Function

Sub CheckValue(objValue As Object, args As EventArgs) As Boolean
If IsNumeric(objValue) Then
Return True
Else
Return False
```

```
End If
End Sub
</script>
</head>
<body>
<form runat="server">
Please enter your values and click Get Results.
<br/>
<asp:TextBox id="txtValue1" runat="server"></asp:TextBox>
<asp:DropDownList id="MathOperator" runat="server">
<asp:ListItem>x</asp:ListItem>
<asp:ListItem>/</asp:ListItem>
<asp:ListItem>+</asp:ListItem>
<asp:ListItem>-</asp:ListItem>
</asp:DropDownList>
<asp:TextBox id="txtValue2" runat="server" ></asp:TextBox>
<asp:Button id=btnGetResult runat="server" Text="Get Result"
OnClick="btnGetResult_OnClick"></asp:Button>

<asp:RequiredFieldValidator id="Value1HasValue" runat="server"
ControlToValidate="txtValue1"
ErrorMessage="You must enter value in the first box."
Display="none">
</asp:RequiredFieldValidator>

<asp:CustomValidator id="Value1IsNumber" runat="server"
ControlToValidate="txtValue1"
OnServerValidate="CheckValue(" & txtValue1.Text & ")"
ErrorMessage="The first value does not contain a number."
Display="None">
</asp:CustomValidator>

<asp:RequiredFieldValidator id="Value2HasValue" runat="server"
ControlToValidate="txtValue2"
ErrorMessage="You must enter value in the second box."
Display="none">
</asp:RequiredFieldValidator>

<asp:CustomValidator id="Value1IsNumber" runat="server"
ControlToValidate="txtValue1"
OnServerValidate="CheckValue(" & txtValue2.Text & ")"
ErrorMessage="The second value does not contain a number."
Display="None">
</asp:CustomValidator>

<asp:RequiredFieldValidator id="MathOperatorHasValue"
runat="server"
ControlToValidate="MathOperator"
ErrorMessage="You must choose an operator."
Display="none">
</asp:RequiredFieldValidator>
```

```
<asp:ValidationSummary id="MathSummary" runat="server"
HeaderText="The following errors were encountered:"
ShowSummary="True"
DisplayMode="BulletList">
</asp:ValidationSummary>
</form>
</body>
</html>
```

Our mission in this chapter is to add database functionality to the ASP.NET application. The idea is to store our mathematical results in a table. We'll use ADO.NET to accomplish this. In Chapter 30, we'll wrap everything up and build another page to act as a client.

Redefining the Requirements, Again

**20 Min.
To Go**

We started this development process with a set of requirements, which we redefined to include Web forms and form validation. We removed some of the original requirements, such as the one requiring that data be transmitted on the query string. To make our application database-aware, we don't need to remove anything. We just have to add some requirements that pertain to the new database functionality.

The updated requirements from Chapter 20 read as:

- The page must be able to perform four different mathematical operations: multiplication, division, addition, and subtraction.
- The page must be complete; only one page shall be used for the application.
- The page must use server-side controls.
- The instruction must indicate to the page what mathematical operation to perform.
- The form must allow for entry of two values.
- The form must allow for the selection of an operator.
- The form must offer validation.
- The page must perform the mathematical operation on the two values.
- The page must output the result of the mathematical operation.

The new requirements state that the application must store the mathematical result in a table in SQL Server 2000. We're going to use the ASPNET WCC database you created in Chapter 22, as well as the WCC_Math table you created in that same chapter. WCC_Math has three fields: ID, RESULT, and DATE_ENTERED.

We'll add these requirements:

- The page must store the result of a calculation in a table.
- The table must be called WCC_Math.
- The table must be stored in a database called ASPNET WCC.
- The page should update the fields RESULT with the calculation's result, and DATE_ENTERED with the date the calculation was performed. ID is an identity column and automatically updates itself.

These requirements are simple in scope. Note that SQL Server 2000 is not a requirement; I realize that not everyone uses SQL Server 2000 (or wants to) so the code won't be using the SQL Managed Provider. With the requirements specified we're ready to get started.

Building the Connection Code

Because we want the code to be database-independent, we'll focus on using the ADO.NET Managed Provider. This provider allows for connecting to any ODBC or OLE DB data store. If you're running DB/2, Informix, or any other ODBC-compliant database (or a database with an OLE DB provider, such as Microsoft Access, SQL Server, or Oracle), you'll be able to use this code.

The code in this chapter will use SQL Server 2000. If you use something different, all you'll need to do is change the connection string to your database's settings.

 Using an OLE DB provider instead of ODBC can increase performance almost 90 percent. Using the SQL Server Managed Provider instead can increase performance over OLE DB by 300 percent.

Using the ADO.NET managed provider

The plan is to use ADO.NET to connect to our database. ADO.NET exposes OleDbConnection, which could be considered a replacement of the old ADO Connection object. We can use the ConnectionString property, then use the Open() and Close() methods of the OleDbConnection object to control the life of the connection to our database.

All we have to do is set the ConnectionString property and then call the Open() method, right? Well, not exactly. To use ADO.NET, we have to import the System.Data and System.Data.OleDb namespaces:

```
<%@ Import namespace="System.Data" %>
<%@ Import namespace="System.Data.OleDb" %>
```

Importing these two namespaces gives us everything we need to access the database and manipulate its tables.

Defining the connection

At its simplest, you have two choices for defining your connection. You can use a Data Source Name (DSN), which is a file that stores database information, such as location (IP address, for example), username, and password. You can define a DSN using the ODBC Administrator in Windows. The alternative is to use a DSN-less connection.

DSNs have the advantage of simplifying connecting to ODBC-compliant databases. If you are using ODBC, use a DSN. If we used a DSN named "WCC" in our application, the code would look like this:

```
<script language="vb" runat="server">
Sub Page_Load(ByVal Sender As Object, e As EventArgs)
Dim oConn As OleDbConnection
```

```
oConn = New OleDbConnection("DSN=WCC")
oConn.Open()
End Sub
</script>
```

The advantage to using a DSN-less connection is that it makes your code more portable. If you use a DSN, deploying the ASP.NET application to another server will require you to set up the DSN on that server. If you use a DSN-less connection, the connection is defined in your code and you don't have to set up a DSN.

Because our example uses SQL Server as its database, we can use a DSN-less connection. To do this, we simply build a connection string that uses the SQL Server OLE DB provider:

```
<script language="vb" runat="server">
Sub Page_Load(ByVal Sender As Object, e As EventArgs)
Dim oConn As OleDbConnection
oConn = New OleDbConnection("provider=SQLOLEDB.1;Data
Source=Default;Initial Catalog=ASPNET WCC;uid=sa;pwd=testbox")
oConn.Open()
End Sub
</script>
```

This code will establish our connection so we can begin to update data. It's possible to store the connection string in the Web.config and then reference it from here; it's also possible to store the connection string in the global.asax file. For these examples, we'll keep the connection string in our code so you won't have any difficulty figuring out what's going on. In Chapter 30, we'll look at how to streamline our application, and moving the connection string to another location may be one part of that.

 If you are using SQL Server 2000, you must have it set up to use SQL Server authentication instead of Windows authentication in order for these examples to run. This was covered in setup; if you have your own SQL Server already set up, then open SQL Server Enterprise Manager, right-click your server name, and click Properties. Under the Security tab, change the Authentication to "SQL Server and Windows."

Building the Update Code

To update the database from this application, we'll use classes provided by System.Data.OleDb, specifically the OleDbAdapter, DataSet, and DataRow.

The code we'll use to update our table works like this:

```
Dim objAdp As New OleDbDataAdapter()
Dim dsWCC As New DataSet()
Dim strSQL As String = "SELECT * FROM Math_WCC"
Dim odbWCC As OleDbCommandBuilder = New OleDbCommandBuilder(objAdp)

objAdp.SelectCommand = New OleDbCommand(strSQL, oConn)
objAdp.Fill(dsWCC)
```

```
Dim rowWCC As New DataRow = dsWCC.Tables("Math_WCC").NewRow
rowWCC("RESULT") = decResults 'Our results will go here
rowWCC("DATE_ENTERED")= System.DateTime.Now.ToShortDateString
dsWCC.Tables("Math_WCC").Rows.Add(rowWCC)
objAdp.Update(dsWCC, "Math_WCC")
End Sub
```

When we plug this code into our Math.aspx page, we'll add in the variables that contain the result of the calculation and the date the calculation was performed.

The data update should go into its own subroutine:

```
Sub UpdateTableWithResult(decResults As Decimal)
Dim objAdp As New OleDbDataAdapter()
Dim dsWCC As New DataSet()
Dim strSQL As String = "SELECT * FROM Math_WCC"
Dim odbWCC As OleDbCommandBuilder = New OleDbCommandBuilder(objAdp)

objAdp.SelectCommand = New OleDbCommand(strSQL, oConn)
objAdp.Fill(dsWCC)

Dim rowWCC As New DataRow = dsWCC.Tables("Math_WCC").NewRow
rowWCC("RESULT") = decResults 'Our results will go here
rowWCC("DATE_ENTERED")= System.DateTime.Now.ToShortDateString
dsWCC.Tables("Math_WCC").Rows.Add(rowWCC)
objAdp.Update(dsWCC, "Math_WCC")
End Sub
```

The routine will be called in the `Click` event of `btnGetResult`:

```
Sub btnGetResult_OnClick(Source As Object, e As EventArgs)
decValue1 = txtValue1.Text
decValue2 = txtValue2.Text
strOperator = MathOperator.SelectedItem.Text
Dim decResult As Decimal

Try
Select Case strOperator
Case "multiply"
decResult = MultiplyValues(decValue1, decValue2)
Case "divide"
decResult = DivideValues(decValue1, decValue2)
Case "add"
decResult = AddValues(decValue1, decValue2)
Case "subtract"
decResult = SubtractValues(decValue1, decValue2)
End Select
Catch myEx As OverflowException
Response.Write("The result was too large to represent" & __
"as a decimal.")
Catch myEx As DivideByZeroException
Response.Write("You cannot divide by zero.")
```

```
Finally
   UpdateTableWithResult(decResult)
End Try
End Sub
```

Now that we know where the code will go and how it's supposed to work, we can integrate it into our page.

Tying It All Together

We didn't write a lot of code, but we did change the way things work in our page. The first thing we need to do is import the namespaces:

```
<%@ Import namespace="System" %>
<%@ Import namespace="System.Data" %>
<%@ Import namespace="System.Data.OleDb" %>
```

The next thing to do is put the connection code in Page_Load. The connection code should only execute when the page is POSTed. Otherwise, it's a waste of resources:

```
Sub Page_Load(ByVal Sender As Object, e As EventArgs)
If Page.IsPostBack Then 'We only want to connect on post back
Dim oConn As OleDbConnection
oConn = New OleDbConnection("provider=SQLOLEDB.1;Data" & _
"Source=Default;Initial Catalog=ASPNET WCC;" & _
"uid=sa;pwd=testbox")
oConn.Open()
End If
End Sub
```

The complete page is:

```
<%@ Import namespace="System" %>
<%@ Import namespace="System.Data" %>
<%@ Import namespace="System.Data.OleDb" %>

<HTML>
<HEAD>
<title>ASP.NET Math Program</title>
<script language="vb" runat="server">
Sub Page_Load(ByVal Sender As Object, e As EventArgs)
If Page.IsPostBack Then 'We only want to connect on post back
Dim oConn As OleDbConnection
oConn = New OleDbConnection("provider=SQLOLEDB.1;Data" & _
"Source=Default;Initial Catalog=ASPNET WCC;" & _
"uid=sa;pwd=testbox")
oConn.Open()
End If
End Sub

Sub UpdateTableWithResult(decResults As Decimal)
Dim objAdp As New OleDbDataAdapter()
```

```
Dim dsWCC As New DataSet()
Dim strSQL As String = "SELECT * FROM Math_WCC"
Dim odbWCC As OleDbCommandBuilder = New OleDbCommandBuilder(objAdp)

objAdp.SelectCommand = New OleDbCommand(strSQL, oConn)
objAdp.Fill(dsWCC)

Dim rowWCC As New DataRow = dsWCC.Tables("Math_WCC").NewRow
rowWCC("RESULT") = decResults 'Our results will go here
rowWCC("DATE_ENTERED")= System.DateTime.Now.ToShortDateString
dsWCC.Tables("Math_WCC").Rows.Add(rowWCC)
objAdp.Update(dsWCC, "Math_WCC")
End Sub

Sub btnGetResult_OnClick(Source As Object, e As EventArgs)
decValue1 = txtValue1.Text
decValue2 = txtValue2.Text
strOperator = MathOperator.SelectedItem.Text
Dim decResult As Decimal

Try
Select Case strOperator
Case "multiply"
decResult = MultiplyValues(decValue1, decValue2)
Case "divide"
decResult = DivideValues(decValue1, decValue2)
Case "add"
decResult = AddValues(decValue1, decValue2)
Case "subtract"
decResult = SubtractValues(decValue1, decValue2)
End Select

Catch myEx As OverflowException
Response.Write "The result was too large to represent" & _
as a decimal."
Catch myEx As DivideByZeroException
Response.Write "You cannot divide by zero."

Finally
UpdateTableWithResult(decResult)
End Try
End Sub

Function MultiplyValues(decValue1 As Decimal, decValue2 As _
Decimal)
Dim decResult As Decimal
decResult = Multiply(decValue1, decValue2)
Return decResult

End Function
Function DivideValues(decValue1 As Decimal, decValue2 As _
Decimal)
```

```
Dim decResult As Decimal
decResult = Divide(decValue1, decValue2)
Return decResult

End Function
Function AddValues(decValue1 As Decimal, decValue2 As _
Decimal)
Dim decResult As Decimal
decResult = Add(decValue1, decValue2)
Return decResult

End Function
Function SubtractValues(decValue1 As Decimal, decValue2 As _
Decimal)
Dim decResult As Decimal
decResult = Subtract(decValue1, decValue2)
Return decResult

End Function
Function CheckValue(objValue As Object, args As EventArgs) As Boolean
If IsNumeric(objValue) Then
Return True
Else
Return False
End If
End Function
</script>
</HEAD>
<body>
<form runat="Server">
<P>Please enter your values and click Get Results. </P>
<P>
<asp:TextBox id="txtValue1" runat="server"></asp:TextBox>
<asp:DropDownList id="MathOperator" runat="server">
<asp:ListItem>x</asp:ListItem>
<asp:ListItem>/</asp:ListItem>
<asp:ListItem>+</asp:ListItem>
<asp:ListItem>-</asp:ListItem>
</asp:DropDownList>
<asp:TextBox id="txtValue2" runat="server" ></asp:TextBox>
<asp:Button id=btnGetResult runat="server" Text="Get Result"
OnClick="btnGetResult_OnClick"></asp:Button>

<asp:RequiredFieldValidator id="Value1HasValue" runat="server"
ControlToValidate="txtValue1"
ErrorMessage="You must enter value in the first box."
Display="none">
</asp:RequiredFieldValidator>

<asp:CustomValidator id="Value1IsNumber" runat="server"
ControlToValidate="txtValue1"
```

```
OnServerValidate="CheckValue(" & txtValue1.Text & ")"
ErrorMessage="The first value does not contain a number."
Display="None">
</asp:CustomValidator>

<asp:RequiredFieldValidator id="Value2HasValue" runat="server"
ControlToValidate="txtValue2"
ErrorMessage="You must enter value in the second box."
Display="none">
</asp:RequiredFieldValidator>

<asp:CustomValidator id="Value1IsNumber" runat="server"
ControlToValidate="txtValue1"
OnServerValidate="CheckValue(" & txtValue2.Text & ")"
ErrorMessage="The second value does not contain a number."
Display="None">
</asp:CustomValidator>

<asp:RequiredFieldValidator id="MathOperatorHasValue"
runat="server"
ControlToValidate="MathOperator"
ErrorMessage="You must choose an operator."
Display="none">
</asp:RequiredFieldValidator>

<asp:ValidationSummary id="MathSummary" runat="server"
HeaderText="The following errors were encountered:"
ShowSummary="True"
DisplayMode="BulletList">
</asp:ValidationSummary>
</form>
</body>
</html>
```

That's it! The page is complete. We'll revisit this application in Chapter 30 and add performance enhancements, as well as rewrite certain parts that are bloated and unnecessary. There is some code in math.aspx that may cause problems when using SQL Server and decimals. We'll address that and a lot more in Chapter 30.

Done!

REVIEW

In this chapter, we revisited the math.aspx application and made some changes to make it work with a database. Specifically, we

- Reviewed the existing math.aspx application
- Analyzed our new requirements
- Wrote the new requirements
- Defined our database connection

- Defined the database update code
- Integrated the database code with the existing math.aspx application

Chapter 27 covers using Web.config. You're almost finished!

Quiz Yourself

1. How much faster can OLE DB be than ODBC? (See "Building the Connection Code.")

2. What object exposed by System.Data.ADO do we use to define a connection? (See "Building the Connection Code.")

3. What namespaces are needed to work with data, specifically using ADO? (See "Building the Connection Code.")

4. Why should the data connection code go in Page.IsPostBack? (See "Tying It All Together.")

5. How do you set the authentication in SQL Server 2000 to "SQL Server and Windows"? (See "Building the Connection Code.")

PART

V

Sunday Morning Part Review

1. What was the most common format for data before relational databases?
2. How are tables structured?
3. What is a key?
4. What type of query retrieves data from a database?
5. What is the difference between INSERT and UPDATE?
6. What is data binding?
7. What is the syntax for data binding?
8. What is the DataBind() method?
9. Where can data binding be used within a Web page?
10. What is the difference between DataGrid and DataList?
11. What happens if you don't specify HeaderTemplate and FooterTemplate styles for a DataGrid control?
12. What namespaces expose ADO.NET and data access objects?
13. Where does a DataSet object get source data?
14. What namespace exposes classes designed for working with SQL Server 2000?
15. What does the OleDbDataAdapter object act as?
16. Name the four transactional properties and the acronym to help you remember them.

PART

VI

Sunday Afternoon

Session 27
Configuring ASP.NET Applications

Session 28
Finding and Fixing Errors

Session 29
Some Advanced Topics

Session 30
Putting It All Together

Configuring ASP.NET Applications

Session Checklist

✔ Configuring ASP.NET applications

✔ Understanding the purpose and structure of Web.config

**30 Min.
To Go**

B y now you are well prepared to tackle creating an ASP.NET application on your own. Throughout this book, reference has been made to Web.config, a file storing configuration information for an ASP.NET application. This chapter explores the Web.config and explains how it is structured.

What Is Web.config?

Web.config is a file ASP.NET refers to for configuration information. In other words, it's an XML document used to configure ASP.NET applications. All configuration information for your application exists in Web.config.

Each time an ASP.NET application is launched, the ASP.NET runtime refers to the application's Web.config file. Based on the information in that file, ASP.NET starts certain services, puts data in memory, and does all kinds of other things.

The Web.config file has two major advantages: First, it provides a centralized location for application configuration. Second, it's written in XML, which makes the actual file very easy to read and understand.

Because the Web.config file is globally available to your application, whatever you specify in the Web.config will be applied to your application. For example, you can specify the languages accessible by your application in the Web.config file. By putting the tags for the languages in the Web.config file, all the ASP.NET pages in your application will be able to use the languages you specify.

The Web.config file essentially provides one-stop shopping for your application configuration. Security, supported browsers, tracing, and everything else you may need to configure for your application will be in Web.config.

The Web.config Structure

The Web.config file is simply a text file and you open or create it in any plain old text editor, like Notepad. The first thing you'll notice about Web.config is that it's written in XML. Each section of the Web.config file exists as a set of tags.

Let's examine a Web.config file piece by piece. This Web.config file is not necessarily ready to be dropped into your application; it has had extra (as in duplicate) tags removed so we can focus on the meat and potatoes. The first tag in Web.config is

```
<configuration>
```

This is the root tag for the Web.config file. Without this tag, your ASP.NET application will return an error.

```
    <configsections>

<add name="browserCaps"
type="System.Web.HttpBrowserCapabilities$SectionHandler"/>
    </configsections>
```

`<configsections>` contains a list of configuration section handlers, specified in the `<add>` tags. Each configuration section of Web.config has a handler in the `<configsections>` tag.

```
    <trace
        enabled="false"
        requestlimit="10"
        pageoutput="false"
        traceMode="SortByTime"
    />
```

The `<trace>` tag determines whether tracing is turned on for an application. Tracing is covered in the next session.

```
    <globalization
        requestEncoding="iso-8859-1"
        responseEncoding="iso-8859-1"
    />
```

The `<globalization>` tag sets the globalization for your application. "Globalizing" your application means enabling it to be accessible by users who read and write other languages. The `<globalization>` tag sets the encoding for the information coming into your application and the information going out. The encoding attributes accept an ISO character set, which ultimately lets ASP.NET work with something like the Greek alphabet or the Cyrillic character set.

The `requestEncoding` attribute specifies the default encoding for all requests; `responseEncoding` specifies the default encoding for all responses. The `<globalization>`

tag also supports three other attributes, which set globalization attributes for files and culture.

```
<httpRuntime executiontimeout value="90" />        <!-- 90 seconds -->
```

This tag simply sets the timeout value for execution of an ASP.NET page. In this example, the timeout is set to 90 seconds; if nothing happens with the page for 90 seconds, the page times out.

```
<compilation debug="false">
```

The `<compilation>` tag supports one attribute. It is a top-level element for two subelements. The debug attribute tells the compiler to compile in debug mode, which produces slower code. The debug mode allows you to view more information about your code as it is executed. Debug should only be used in development.

```
<compilers defaultLanguage="vb">
```

The `<compilers>` element supports three subelements, `<compiler>`, `<assemblies>`, and `<namespaces>`. Specifying a defaultlanguage attribute for `<compilers>` tells your ASP.NET application to use a default language at compilation.

```
<compilers>
<compiler
language="vb"
extension=".vb"
type=
  "Microsoft.VB.VBCodeProvider.System">
</compiler>
</compilers>
```

The `<compiler>` subelement allows you to define compilers supported by your application. These can point to any of the 30 languages supported by .NET. You specify how the compiler is referred to in your ASP.NET pages by setting the values of the attributes of the `<compiler>` tag. The `<compilers>` tag can take as many `<compiler>` subelements as you need.

```
<compilation>
        <assemblies>
        <add assembly="System.Data"/>
    </assemblies>
  </compilation>
```

The `<assemblies>` subelement allows you add and remove assembly references. An assembly is used during dynamic class compilation.

```
<customErrors mode="RemoteOnly" defaultRedirect="error.aspx">
   <error statusCode="404" redirect="error.aspx?code=404"/>
</customerrors>
```

If you desire page redirects when an error is encountered, the `<customErrors>` element is for you. A good use for `<customErrors>` is to redirect a user to a custom page for 404 File

Not Found, as the above entry shows. <customErrors> has one subelement, <error>, which allows you to specify what page to redirect to on a specific error (like 404 or 400). <customErrors> takes two attributes: mode and defaultRedirect. Mode tells ASP.NET whether to turn custom error pages On (all users are redirected), Off (no users are redirected), or RemoteOnly (only non-local, or remote, users are redirected). Defaultredirect points to the default page for redirection when an error is encountered; using this redirects users to the default page whenever an error is encountered and that error is defined in the <error> subelement.

```
<security>

    <authentication mode="Windows"/>

    <authorization>
        <allow users="*" /> <!-- Allow all users -->
    </authorization>

    <identity>
        <impersonation enable="false" />
    </identity>

</security>
```

The <security> block enables security for your ASP.NET application. It lets you specify the authentication and authorization levels for your application. One of the greatest things about Web.config is its simplification of site security.

The <security> element has three subelements: <authentication>, <authorization>, and <identity>. <authentication> has one attribute, mode, which can be Windows, Passport, or cookie. Specifying Windows will make your ASP.NET application require Windows authentication (a login). Specifying Passport makes use of Microsoft's Passport authentication system. If you've used Hotmail, you've used Passport. Specifying cookie will make your ASP.NET application look in a cookie for authentication information.

<authorization> is different from <authentication>. Whereas <authentication> ensures the validity of a user, <authorization> controls access to the site (or parts of the site). For example, a user named John Doe may have an account on your server (he's authenticated), but he is not authorized to use your application (he's not authorized).

```
Author:          <authentication mode="Windows"/>

        <authorization>
            <allow users="*" /> <!-- Allow all users -->
        </authorization>

        <identity>
            <impersonation enable="false" />
        </identity>
```

Security is enabled through three elements in your ASP.NET application. You can specify the authentication and authorization levels for your application. One of the greatest things about Web.config is its simplification of site security.

Web.config three elements: `<authentication>` , `<authorization>`, and `<identity>`. `<authentication>` has one attribute, mode, which can be Windows, Passport, or cookie. Specifying Windows will make your ASP.NET application require Windows authentication (a login). Specifying Passport makes use of Microsoft's Passport authentication system. If you've used Hotmail, you've used Passport. Specifying cookie will make your ASP.NET application look in a cookie for authentication information.

`<authorization>` is different from `<authentication>`. While `<authentication>` ensures the validity of a user, `<authorization>` controls access to the site (or parts of the site). For example, a user named John Doe may have an account on your server (he's authenticated), but he is not authorized to use your application (he's not authorized).

```
<sessionState
    mode="inproc"
    cookieless="false"
    timeout="20"
    sqlConnectionString="data source=127.0.0.1;
        userid=sa;password="
    server="127.0.0.1"
/>
```

The `<sessionState>` element controls the session-level options for your application. `<sessionState>` is discussed in Chapter 14.

```
<httpHandlers>
    <add verb="*" path="trace.axd"
        type="System.Web.IHttpHandler.GetHandler" />
</httpHandlers>
```

**10 Min.
To Go**

`<httpHandlers>` lets you map incoming requests to httpHandlers. Trace.axd, discussed in Chapter 28, is an httphandler. Httphandlers are basically like custom filters for your application. The Trace.axd handler, for example, intercepts http requests (GET, POST, and PUT) and passes control to the handler, which is either a built-in class or one you define.

The `<httphandler>` element has three subelements: `<add>`, `<remove>`, and `<clear>`. The `<add>` subelement allows you to add httpHandlers, like Trace.axd, to your application. This is called a handler definition.

The `<add>` subelement has three attributes: verb, path, and type. Verb tells the runtime when to process the request, on GET, POST, or PUT. Using an asterisk specifies all three methods. The path attribute points to a file that contains whatever you want processed. The third attribute, type, points to the assembly and class that will handle the request.

```
<httpModules>
    <add
     type=
        "System.Web.SessionState.CookielessSessionModule" />
</httpModules>
```

`<httpModules>` lets you `<add>`, `<remove>`, and `<clear>` modules. In this example, the `CookielessSessionModule` class is added in the `<httpModules>` section. Many of the classes are included by default.

```
<processmodel
    enable="true"
    timeout="1000000"
    idleTimeout="1000000"
    shutdownTimeout="5"
    requestLimit="10000000"
    requestQueueLimit="1000"
    memoryLimit="40"
    webGarden="false"
    cpuMask="0xffffffff"
/>
```

`<processmodel>` provides features to customize the process model of your applications. It lets you set things like `timeout` (the number of minutes until a new IIS worker process is spawned to replace the current one), `shutdowntimeout` (the number of minutes to wait until a process shuts down before killing it), and `memoryLimit` (the percentage of memory that can be used before a process is shut down and restarted).

These attributes allow you to exert more control over how your application works within IIS. For example, there have been many reports of significant performance increases by configuring the `memoryLimit` attribute.

```
<browserCaps>
    <result type="System.Web.HttpBrowserCapabilities" />
    <use var="HTTP_USER_AGENT" />

    browser=Unknown
    version=0.0
    majorversion=0
    minorversion=0
    frames=false
    tables=false
    cookies=false
    backgroundsounds=false
    vbscript=false
    javascript=false
    javaapplets=false
    activexcontrols=false
    win16=false
    win32=false
    beta=false
    ak=false
    sk=false
    aol=false
    crawler=false
    cdf=false
    gold=false
    authenticodeupdate=false
    platform=Unknown
```

```
<filter>
    <case match="Windows 95|Win95">
        platform=Win95
    </case>
</filter>
</browserCaps>
```

The `<browserCaps>` section can easily grow to the biggest section of the Web.config file. This is where you put all of your browser capabilities settings. The `<browserCaps>` section exposes the settings in the `HttpBrowserCapabilities` class. The example above specifies the `HTTP_USER_AGENT` server variable be referenced for browser type, and a filter is applied using `<filter>` to check for `Windows 95|Win95`.

Going over every detail of the Web.config file, and specifically the `<browserCaps>` section, would easily swallow up several chapters. Feel free to refer to the .NET Framework SDK for more in-depth coverage of each element and subelement within Web.config. This chapter should help you get a solid understanding of how its structured and what it's good for.

Now we reach the final tag of Web.config:

```
</configuration>
```

This tag closes the `<configuration>` top-level element and finalizes the file. Without this closing tag, you'll encounter an exception, so be sure it's there!

At the time of this writing, Microsoft was promising a graphical tool for manipulating Web.config. That should make your configuration management go much smoother, but if you do have to open the Web.config in Notepad and make changes, you're armed with the knowledge you need to get stuff done. Just be careful, and make sure you back up your Web.config before you make changes.

Done!

REVIEW

In this chapter, you learned about the Web.config file and how it works. Although we didn't cover every single minute configuration possibility, we did cover the parts you need to get your own applications up and running. Specifically, we looked at

- What the Web.config is
- What the Web.config file is for
- The Web.config structure, including most of the elements

You're almost ready to configure and deploy an entire application. The next chapter covers error handling, which we have touched on a few times.

QUIZ YOURSELF

1. In what format is Web.config? (See "What Is Web.config?")
2. What program can you use to view Web.config? (See "What Is Web.config?")
3. How do you add an httpHandler? (See "Web.config Structure.")
4. What does `<httpRuntime executiontimeout>` do? (See "Web.config Structure.")
5. What is the advantage of `<processModel>`? (See "Web.config Structure.")

Finding and Fixing Errors

Session Checklist

✔ Examining the origin of errors

✔ Identifying common types of errors

✔ Exploring ASP.NET error handling

✔ Learning how to use tracing

**30 Min.
To Go**

Programming can be very fun and rewarding. The feeling of accomplishment when a project is delivered on time and with full functionality is exhilarating. Unfortunately, even the best programmers are not perfect and that brings us to the topic of errors and how to fix them.

Where Do Errors Come From?

The origin of the word *bug* to describe an error in a program dates back to the ENIAC/ UNIVAC days. The story goes like this: Computer operators were expecting the computer to perform a certain calculation, but every time the calculation was run the results were incorrect. They input the program several times and each time it didn't work. Deciding that it wasn't a code issue, they opened up the panel and discovered a dead moth amongst the tubes. The rest is history.

While that story may or not be true, it demonstrates two frustrating aspects of programming: encountering errors and trying to fix them. For as long as computers have been around, all kinds of problems have plagued their use. The ancient Chinese probably ran into similar problems with the abacus — perhaps a stuck bead or an abacus that was being held incorrectly.

Examples of problems can vary from the trite to the dangerous. The important thing to understand about bugs is that while the bug's affect may yield different outcomes, the approach to debugging a program stays consistent. There are even whole methodologies that define debugging.

Some of the common errors in programs are

- Typos
- Incorrect syntax
- Endless loops

Typographical errors are the most common of all errors in programming. In today's complex and powerful IDEs, typos are relatively easy to find. The compiler usually issues a warning when it encounters a typo. Back in the days of edlin and line-by-line programming (such as in BASIC), typos could cripple the development process and force programmers to use the "pencil method," which involved reading the entire program line by line using a pencil as a guide.

This is a basic typographical error in ASP:

```
<%

Option Explicit
Dim strName
strName = "This car is fast."
strName = Repalce(strName, "this", "that")

%>
```

In this code, the function name `Replace` is spelled as `Repalce`. Making that mistake is easy, and it's easy to fix as well. A typographical error is commonly referred to as a *coding error*.

Incorrect syntax is also common, and, like a typo, it's usually caught by the compiler. In some IDEs, such as Visual Basic, syntax mistakes are caught as they are typed. This comes in very handy. Incorrect syntax can be very easy to catch, and sometimes it can be a real pain.

This code has a syntax error that is legal, but it yields the wrong result.

```
<%

Option Explicit
Dim strName
strName = "This car is fast."
strName = Replace("this", "that", strName)

%>
```

The intention is to replace instances of the word *this* with the word *that* in the variable `strName`. However, the programmer has made a syntax error and the code is attempting to replace instances of the word *that* with the string contained in `strName`. The compiler won't return an error because, technically, the syntax is correct. This type of error is caused by the programmer and is thus a coding error.

Endless loops are common and easily the most frustrating. They can be easy to find and fix, but when they occur, they typically crash the whole program. Endless loops are typically not caught by the compiler. Endless loop errors are of a special type of coding error known as a *runtime error*.

In the grand scheme of things, all errors caused by code are programmer errors. There are some errors, however, that are caused by the operating environment. These fall under the execution error moniker. When it comes right down to it, they all have to be fixed, regardless of the cognomen.

An endless loop can be tricky to spot. Try to find it in this ASP code:

```
<%

'Connection code here...
objRS.Open "database", oConn 'objRS is our recordset object

Do Until objRS.EOF
Response.Write "This is the data:" & objRS("data")
Loop

objRS.Close

%>
```

The Do...Loop is an endless loop because objRS.EOF will never be true. A very important line of code, objRS.MoveNext, is absent from this code block. This code tells ASP that it should move to the next record in the recordset. As it moves through the records, it will eventually reach the end of the data, or EOF. Without this code, EOF will never happen.

ASP.NET Error Handling

**20 Min.
To Go**

ASP.NET offers a wide range of tools and functionality for finding and reporting errors. The error handling in ASP.NET allows a developer to define custom messages for errors and deal with errors gracefully as they occur, known as *custom error pages*.

Custom error pages aren't a new concept. ASP offered support for custom error pages. The idea behind custom error pages is better error reporting on the client. Each error has its own page. In ASP, setting up custom error pages consists of defining them in Internet Service Manager, with one page for each error.

In ASP.NET, custom error pages are defined in the Web.config file for the application. This makes the custom error pages available application-wide.

```
<configuration>
<customErrors defaultRedirect="http://sitename/errorpage.aspx"
mode="on" />
</configuration>
```

Setting the mode attribute to "on" activates custom error pages. The "on" value specifies that custom error pages should be delivered whenever an error occurs. The "off" value specifies that a custom error will never be displayed; it is default. Setting the mode attribute to RemoteOnly tells ASP.NET to deliver custom error pages only to clients who come to the site using a URL other than localhost or 127.0.0.1; in other words, from other machines.

The defaultredirect attribute specifies the error page that will be loaded for every error that does not have its own specified error page. Expanding on the Web.config entry to include custom error pages, we have this XML:

```
<configuration>
<customErrors
 defaultredirect="http://sitename/defaulterror.aspx"
mode="on" />
<error statusCode="403" redirect="/customerrors/denied.aspx" />
<error statusCode="404" redirect="/customerrors/fnf.aspx" />
<error statusCode="500" redirect="/customerrors/busy.aspx" />
</customErrors>
</configuration>
```

Notice there are three entries for specified errors: one each for 403, 404, and 500. When the ASP.NET application encounters one of these three errors, it will load the custom error page specified in the redirect attribute for that error. When the ASP.NET application encounters an error that isn't specified in an <error> tag, it will load the page specified in the defaultredirect attribute of the <customErrors> tag.

Occasionally, it's necessary to override the custom error page settings in the Web.config file. For example, you may have pages that are password protected, but you want to allow users to e-mail the administrator for access. You can specify a special error page to handle the 403 error for this page, and set up a custom error page in the Web.config for all other 403 errors.

This is done in the @Page directive by adding the ErrorPage attribute:

```
<%@Page ErrorPage="accessdeniedandrequested.aspx" %>
```

The accessdeniedandrequested.aspx page could contain a message saying that access was denied, and provide an e-mail link or telephone number for users to request access to that resource.

Using custom error pages in ASP.NET is a great way to improve the user experience. Because custom error pages can be written in HTML and ASP.NET, developers can code special error handling within the custom error page.

Custom error pages generally meet two different needs. The first need is improving the user experience. Delivering a custom error page with support information is a lot more user-friendly than the plain white page with code in the upper left corner. The second need is gathering and accessing information about the errors encountered.

ASP.NET provides information about errors via the Form collection. Using specific items within the collection, a developer can get information about the error, including its code and its source.

 An error code in ASP.NET exists as "ASPxxxx," where "xxxx" represents the number of the error. Using this number, you can cross-reference it against the complete list of ASP.NET error codes and instantly know what went wrong.

This ASP.NET code snippet retrieves the error code and error source (the page experiencing the error) from the Form collection and displays a special message:

```
<%

Dim strErrorCode As String
Dim strErrorSrc As String

strErrCode = Request.Form.Item("ErrorCode")
strErrSrc = Request.Form.Item("ErrorPage")

%>
<FONT COLOR="Red">
An error occurred while processing <%= strErrorSrc %>
</FONT>
<P/>
<I>Error code: <%=strErrorCode%></I>
```

You can get more creative and add whatever HTML code you want in your error message, and you can add more information about the error such as its description.

Solid error handling is vital to a successful software application deployment. Nothing is more frustrating than using an application and encountering errors that are handled gracefully. It can be downright embarrassing for a customer to call Technical Support about a blank white page.

One thing I do in my ASP.NET applications is build a custom error page that e-mails me whenever a 404 is encountered. The e-mail contains the name of the missing page, and I'm able to immediately fix it.

Tracing

10 Min.
To Go

ASP.NET offers an excellent trace utility that provides a "debug-as-you-go" facility for developers. This trace utility allows developers to insert debugging statements directly into the code. The debugging statements can output variables and structures, determine if a condition is met, or simply step through the execution of an application.

This type of functionality was somewhat available in ASP by using response.write statements. This method of debugging yielded mixed results, and when the application was deployed with the response.write statements mistakenly left in (as they often were), the users received debugging messages that were nothing short of confusing.

The ASP.NET trace utility is much simpler to use and can be turned on and off in one line of code at the top of the page. By contrast, the response.write statements in ASP were embedded throughout the code. To remove them, the developer had to search for each entry, one by one.

The ASP.NET trace facility supports tracing at two levels: application and page. Tracing functionality differs greatly between the two levels. Simply put, application-level tracing provides statistics about a page's execution, as well as its inputs and outputs, while page-level tracing outputs custom debugging statements on a page.

Let's look at the two methods specifically.

Application-level tracing

Application-level tracing is designed to allow developers to monitor page usage. It is activated in the Web.config file with the <trace> tag:

```
<configuration>
<trace enabled="true" pageOutput="true" requestLimit="15"
traceMode="SortByCategory" />
</configuration>
```

The enabled attribute sets the on/off status for application-level tracing. True turns on tracing, False turns it off. The default value of enabled is False.

Setting the second attribute, pageOutput, to True tells ASP.NET to display the table of trace values on each page. Setting it to False tells ASP.NET to write the trace information to the trace log. The trace log is a file stored on the server containing trace information for your application. It's accessed using a special utility called trace.axd, which we'll get to in a moment.

Enabling application-level tracing turns on tracing for every page in your application. However, all trace information is sent to the trace log rather than the page. If you don't want this to happen, set the pageoutput attribute to True in the <trace> **tag in Web.config.**

The third attribute, requestLimit, sets the number of trace requests that should be stored. The default is 10.

The fourth attribute, traceMode, tells ASP.NET how to sort the trace results. The default for this attribute is SortByTime.

The trace.axd utility provides access to the trace log for your application. Trace.axd is generated any time application-level tracing is activated. It's accessible in the root directory of your ASP.NET application. If your URL is http://localhost/wccapp/, then trace.axd is accessible at http://localhost/wccapp/trace.axd. Figure 28-1 shows what you see when you visit trace.axd after you load a few pages.

Each request made to the application is logged and accessible via trace.axd, up to the limit specified in the <trace> tag in Web.config. Trace.axd will list the requests in the order they were made, with a View Details link next to each request.

After you click a View Details link, trace.axd will display detailed information about that request. The information about the request is comprised of seven sections, in the order listed here: Request Detail, Trace Information, Control Hierarchy, Session State, Application State, Cookies Collection, Headers Collection, Forms Collection, QueryString Collection, and Server Variables. Figure 28-2 illustrates the output of View Details.

View Details shows you the same kind of information that is available at the page level (discussed in the following section), but with the added benefit of allowing you to compare trace results of different pages and track the results of a single page over several requests.

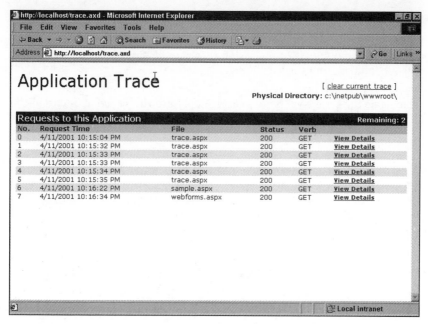

Figure 28-1   Trace.axd output

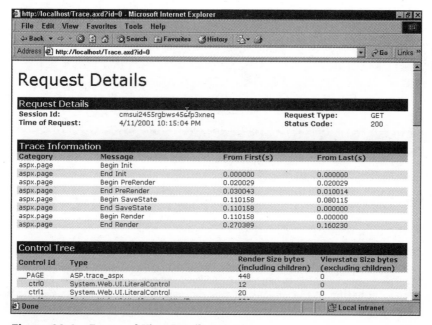

Figure 28-2   Trace.axd View Details output

Page-level tracing

Page-level tracing allows developers to write custom debugging statements that appear at the bottom of the rendered ASP.NET page. Using these statements, developers can view information about the page and track down bugs.

Because tracing is disabled by default, you must turn it on for your page to use it. Turning on tracing at the page level is very easy. Simply use the `Trace` attribute of the `@Page` directive.

```
<%@Page Language="VB" Trace="True" %>
```

With this statement present in your code, ASP.NET will output a table at the bottom of the page. This table provides information about your page, such as the session ID, the time of request, and the request type. It also contains a section broken into categories. This section is where your custom trace information would reside.

Figure 28-3 shows the output of a trace on an ASP.NET page.

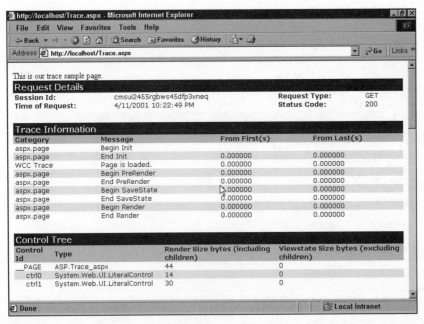

Figure 28-3   *ASP.NET Trace=On output*

Look at the table with the heading "Trace Information." You should see a category called WCC Trace. This category contains the text "Page is loaded." This trace information was created using the Trace object, which is exposed to ASP.NET pages and your code. The code to create the trace information in the screenshot was defined in the `Page_Load` event of the `tracedemo.aspx` page:

```
Sub Page_Load(Sender As Object, e As EventArgs)
Trace.Write("WCC Trace", "Page is loaded.")
End Sub
```

This code shows the `Trace` object and its `Write` method. The `Write` method of the `Trace` object takes two parameters. The first parameter is the name of the category. The second parameter is the output for that category, its message.

The second parameter does not have to be text. You can stuff a variable name in there and it will print out next to the category name, but you must convert it to a string first. Here's a sample code snippet:

```
<script language="VB" runat="server">
'Write the value of a long variable
Dim lngValue As Long
lngValue = 2038420
Trace.Write("Long Variable", CStr(lngValue))
</script>
```

The `Trace` object includes several other methods and properties to assist you in debugging. There are four properties and eight primary methods. These four properties and eight primary methods provide the core functionality of the `Trace` object within an **ASP.NET** page.

The four properties are `AutoFlush`, `Indent`, `IndentSize`, and `Listeners`:

- `AutoFlush` determines whether the `Flush` method should be called on the `Listeners` after every write.
- `Indent` gets or sets the indent level for the trace information.
- `IndentSize` specifies the number of spaces in an indent
- `Listeners` gets the collection of listeners that is monitoring the trace output.

The eight primary methods are `Assert`, `Close`, `Fail`, `Flush`, `Write`, `WriteIf`, `WriteLine`, and `WriteLineIf`:

- `Assert` checks for a condition and displays a message if the condition is false.
- `Close` flushes the output buffer and closes the Listeners so they no longer receive debug output.
- `Fail` issues an error message.
- `Flush` empties the output buffer and causes the buffered data to be written to the Listeners.
- `Write` is the most commonly used method, because it writes information about the trace to the trace listeners in the Listeners collection.
- `WriteIf` writes information about the trace if a condition is true.
- `WriteLine` writes information about the trace followed by a line terminator.
- `WriteLineIf` writes information about the trace followed by a line terminator if the condition is true.

Done!

REVIEW

This chapter covered error handling and debugging in ASP.NET. Specifically, we covered

- Where errors come from
- Some basic types of errors
- ASP.NET custom error pages
- The ASP.NET debugger
- Application-level tracing and how to use it
- Using the trace.axd utility
- Page-level tracing and how to use it, including the Trace object

This chapter provided an introduction and discussion of how to handle bugs in ASP.NET. From this point, you should be able to use the Trace functionality in your own ASP.NET applications.

QUIZ YOURSELF

1. What are three common sources of program errors? (See "Where Do Errors Come From.")
2. What is the basic idea behind custom error pages? (See "ASP.NET Error Handling.")
3. How do you turn on the ASP.NET debugger? (See "Tracing.")
4. What are the two types of tracing in ASP.NET? (See "Tracing.")
5. How do you view the trace log? (See "Application-level tracing.")

SESSION

29

Some Advanced Topics

Session Checklist

✔ Going over Web services and how they work

✔ Learning about SOAP and how it works with Web services

✔ Exploring ASP.NET caching

**30 Min.
To Go**

You have seen that ASP.NET is a powerful and useful tool for creating Web applications. You have learned many things in these lessons so far, and there is still a lot out there. This chapter covers some of the more advanced ASP.NET topics for you to explore.

Web Services

The idea behind software as a service is built on the availability of the technology for sharing application functionality across the Internet. The concept of a company such as eBay sharing its auction software is becoming a reality as Web services take hold.

A Web service is application logic that is programmatically available and exposed to the Internet. Web services further separate application from presentation, enabling developers to create new software without being tied to a browser.

Web services could be compared to DCOM, which was essentially COM over a network. The Web service is the equivalent of the COM object in the DCOM model, with SOAP (explained in the next section) acting as the protocol for retrieving information from the Web service. The Web service sends data back and forth as XML. This promotes platform independence.

How do Web services work?

A Web service relies on the presence of a provider and a consumer. The consumer contains code that makes use of the provider's service. In order for the consumer code to make use of the provider's service, it must first discover the service, and a contract, or service description, between the service and consumer must be present. The contract outlines what the provider exposes, such as its methods, and how the consumer uses them.

When the consumer has discovered the service and a contract has been issued, it can make a request of the service. This is where the contract is important, because without it, the consumer doesn't know how to request data.

The client sends the request encoded as XML through http. The provider receives the request, decodes the XML, and assembles the http packets in the correct order. It then does whatever extra work is needed in order to invoke the logic that actually makes up the service.

When the provider has processed the request, it encodes and transports the response back to the consumer. The consumer then decodes and assembles the message, which contains the results of its request. For example, let's say you have a Web service called `Trimmer` that trims the first letter off of a string. `Trimmer` receives a request to execute the method `TrimFirstLetter()` with the argument "software." `Trimmer` decodes the request, executes the method, and returns an encoded message to the consumer. The consumer then decodes and assembles the message, which evaluates to "software."

Supported protocols

ASP.NET supports three protocols for accessing Web services: HTTP-POST, HTTP-GET, and SOAP. All three protocols return XML in the body of an http message.

HTTP-POST

ASP.NET supports using the POST verb for encoding and passing parameters. POST sends the encoded request in the http headers.

HTTP-GET

ASP.NET supports using the GET verb for encoding and passing parameters in the querystring.

SOAP

SOAP (Simple Object Access Protocol) describes a platform-neutral contract for transporting data as XML through http.

What's next?

Creating a Web service is not a simple process, but with some practice and studying it's not something out of your reach. You'll have to create a class, and save your Web service as a file with the .asmx extension. You'll also have to do some configuring in the Web.config. Creating Web services is out of the scope of this book, but I hope this section has whetted your appetite. The next section discusses some more of the technical aspects of Web services, specifically SOAP and the Web Services Description Language.

**20 Min.
To Go**

SOAP

Three technologies combine to complete the interoperability puzzle: SOAP (Simple Object Access Protocol), WSDL (Web Services Description Language), and WSML (Web Services Meta Language). Figure 29-1 shows the relationship between the technologies:

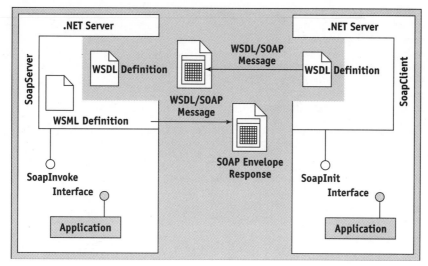

Figure 29-1   *SOAP architecture*

As you can see, SOAP is used for the exchange between applications. WSDL is the public definition of the interaction between server and client. WSML is the private implementation of what actual work occurs on the server's programs.

The documentation on WSDL and WSML is based on the Beta Release of SOAP Toolkit 2.0. This is anticipation of the WSDL specification superceding SOAP encoding and the SDL definitions. Check your final ASP.NET documentation for the most accurate results.

SOAP operations

The Simple Object Access Protocol (www.w3.org/TR/soap) is an XML-based proposal for standardizing communication between two applications. Although there are ways to bind a SOAP message to a network connection, the SOAP protocol is fundamentally designed around two one-way document creations: a request and a response. Each direction of communication involves several steps. The application must read the SOAP message and determine the components of the message. Then it must respond to all mandatory and optional parts as designed or discard the message and finally remove all parts and forward the message if it is not the ultimate destination. This chain of events is possible because of the components of a SOAP-based message

Document-oriented operations

SOAP has three components: a SOAP envelope, SOAP encoding, and a SOAP transport mechanism. The encoding, or content of the document, closely mirrors and may someday completely be included in the XSD Schema specification, but currently it offers element definitions for `array` and `struct`. We will concentrate on the uniquely SOAP components of the envelope.

The following sample SOAP message shows the three aspects of the header:

```
<? xml version="1.0" ?>
<!-- SOAP wrapper -->
<soap:Envelope xmlns:soap="urn:schemas-xmlsoap-org:soap.v1"
xmlns="http://www.w3.org/1999/XMLSchema"
xmlns:app="http://localhost/ " >
  <soap:Header app:name="BookApp" >
     <soap:Body app:data="BookSummary">
         <!-- SOAP payload -->
         <Book Author="Rob Standefer">
            <Title="ASP.NET Weekend Crash Course"/>
            <Chapter="Introducing.NET"/>
            <Chapter="The Evolution of Server-Side Scripting"/>
            <Chapter="Programming Basics"/>
            <Chapter="Setting Up ASP.NET"/>
            <Chapter="Working with the .NET Platform"/>
            <Chapter="Choosing a .NET Language"/>
            <Chapter="Understanding XML and SOAP"/>
            <Chapter="Programming with VB.NET"/>
         </Book>
     </soap:Body>
  </soap:Header>
</soap:Envelope>
```

Although the schema book.xsd are not defined in the example above, the burden of validation is on the server receiving the message. The Envelope element is a designation for routing, as the SOAP listening application, sometimes called a listener, will use to determine the destination. The Header element is the first child element that can be used to include any non-application destination information requirements, such as authentication and transactional identification. The Body element wraps around the document payload, as seen in the hypothetical BookApp expecting a book description.

RPC-Oriented Operations

Messages are said to be delivered in two generic categories: *synchronous,* in which the program delivering the message expects a response before it will continue with another activity, and *asynchronous,* in which another activity will execute on the sender before a message is received. Logging in to a network is an example of synchronous calls, whereas any e-mail activity is an example of asynchronous delivery. SOAP transport can occur via two synchronous methods: HTTP and Remote Procedure Call. RPC is a protocol based on a client/server model where a stub acts as the representative of the remote procedure code.

While the structure of SOAP does not change depending on the method of transport, it is important to understand the different delivery methods.

Web Services Description Language (WSDL) and Web Services Meta Language (WSML)

Figure 29-1 shows the translation of a SOAP message to an application execution. Because the two document specifications are not at recommendation phase, you should be familiar with the general elements of both schemas.

- `<types>`: User-definable data type definitions for the messages in a document.
- `<message>`: An abstract (external XSD referencing) definition of the message containing a `<part>` for each piece of the message described.
- `<porttype>`: An abstract definition that will contain an `<operation>` with at least one pair of `<input>` and `<output>` elements for each `<message>`.
- `<binding>`: A concrete (internal XSD referenced) protocol and data format specifications for the `<operation>` and `<message>` defined by a particular `<porttype>`.
- `<port>`: A connection of a `<binding>` to a URI.
- `<service>`: A collection of all of the `<port>` elements.

This stuff is somewhat high-level, but it should help you gain an understanding of a technology that applies not just to the .NET Framework but to the whole concept of software as a service.

ASP.NET Caching

10 Min. To Go

The idea behind caching is to speed up page access and delivery by caching its contents in memory for a specified duration. ASP has no caching abilities built in; developers had to write custom caching algorithms. ASP.NET, however, supports caching intrinsically via two methods of caching: page output caching and page data caching.

Why cache?

The answer is simple: It speeds things up. For example, say you set caching duration on your page for five minutes. This means that for five minutes after the page is first requested, ASP.NET will serve a cached version of that page regardless of the client. A user visits the page for the first time and the cache countdown begins. The page can receive millions of hits in those five minutes and each time, it's serving the cached page.

There are caching policies to help ease your worries about caching a page for five minutes and the data changing in the first four. These policies can be set to watch your page for changes, causing a "dirty cache." Pages can also be cached in sections so your static content can be cached for hours, while your dynamically generated navigation menu can be cached for seconds, or not at all.

Page output caching

Output caching is the caching of content generated by dynamic pages. Output caching on the response is activated using this syntax:

```
<%@ OutputCache Duration="360" %>
```

Duration is in seconds, so 360 seconds is six minutes. Requests received while the page is still cached will receive the cached page. After 360 seconds, the page will be removed from the cache and the next request will be handled explicitly. The page is then cached again.

Page data caching

Page data caching is different from page output caching in that it allows the developer to explicitly cache objects. This allows developers to store and retrieve objects across http requests. Don't confuse this with Session variables; the page data cache is a special section of memory maintained by ASP.NET for the sole purpose of caching objects. The lifetime of the cache is tied to the lifetime of the application; when the application is restarted, the cache is recreated.

Using page data caching is very similar to using a collection. You simply use Cache():

```
Cache("DataKey") = DataValue
```

Retrieving the data is simple: Simply switch the two sides of the = sign:

```
DataValue = Cache("DataKey")
Response.Write DataValue
```

The page data cache supports other methods for things such as scavenging and expiration. Scavenging lets the cache remove data that is old, or not used very often. Expiration allows you to add a lifetime to the page data cache, so it empties itself after a duration (like page output caching).

 The Cache class supports some other methods for working with caching, such as Insert(). Consult the .NET Framework documentation for more information on these methods.

Done!

REVIEW

In this chapter, we briefly covered some advanced ASP.NET topics. These topics are ready for your further study. Specifically, we covered:

- What a Web service is
- How Web services work
- Protocols supported by Web services
- The Simple Object Access Protocol

- Web Services Description Language
- Web Services Meta Language
- ASP.NET caching

The next chapter is the final session.

QUIZ YOURSELF

1. What is a Web service? (See "Web Services.")
2. What happens when a Web service provider receives a request? (See "How do Web services work?")
3. What three protocols does ASP.NET support for accessing Web services? (See "Supported protocols.")
4. What does SOAP stand for? (See "SOAP.")
5. What are the two types of ASP.NET caching? (See "ASP.NET Caching.")

Putting It All Together

Session Checklist

✔ Analyzing the Math ASP.NET application

✔ Improving the code

✔ Increasing performance

This chapter analyzes our math.aspx application and applies some more of what you have learned in this book to increasing performance and maintainability.

30 Min.
To Go

The Application

This is the application in its entirety. We're going to make several changes to how this program works:

```
<%@ Import namespace="System" %>
<%@ Import namespace="System.Data" %>
<%@ Import namespace="System.Data.OleDb" %>

<HTML>
<HEAD>
<title>ASP.NET Math Program</title>
<script language="vb" runat="server">
Sub Page_Load(ByVal Sender As Object, e As EventArgs)
If Page.IsPostBack Then 'We only want to connect on post back
Dim oConn As OleDbConnection
oConn = New OleDbConnection("provider=SQLOLEDB.1;Data" & _
"Source=Default;Initial Catalog=ASPNET WCC;" & _
"uid=sa;pwd=testbox")
oConn.Open()
End If
End Sub
```

```
Sub UpdateTableWithResult(decResults As Decimal)
Dim objAdp As New OleDbDataAdapter()
Dim dsWCC As New DataSet()
Dim strSQL As String = "SELECT * FROM Math_WCC"
Dim odbWCC As OleDbCommandBuilder = New OleDbCommandBuilder(objAdp)

objAdp.SelectCommand = New OleDbCommand(strSQL, oConn)
objAdp.Fill(dsWCC)

Dim rowWCC As New DataRow = dsWCC.Tables("Math_WCC").NewRow
rowWCC("RESULT") = decResults 'Our results will go here
rowWCC("DATE_ENTERED")= System.DateTime.Now.ToShortDateString
dsWCC.Tables("Math_WCC").Rows.Add(rowWCC)
objAdp.Update(dsWCC, "Math_WCC")
End Sub

Sub btnGetResult_OnClick(Source As Object, e As EventArgs)
decValue1 = txtValue1.Text
decValue2 = txtValue2.Text
strOperator = MathOperator.SelectedItem.Text
Dim decResult As Decimal

Try
Select Case strOperator
Case "multiply"
decResult = MultiplyValues(decValue1, decValue2)
Case "divide"
decResult = DivideValues(decValue1, decValue2)
Case "add"
decResult = AddValues(decValue1, decValue2)
Case "subtract"
decResult = SubtractValues(decValue1, decValue2)
End Select

Catch myEx As OverflowException
Response.Write "The result was too large to represent" & _
as a decimal."
Catch myEx As DivideByZeroException
Response.Write "You cannot divide by zero."

Finally
UpdateTableWithResult(decResult)
End Try
End Sub

Function MultiplyValues(decValue1 As Decimal, decValue2 As _
Decimal)
Dim decResult As Decimal
decResult = Multiply(decValue1, decValue2)
Return decResult
```

```
End Function
Function DivideValues(decValue1 As Decimal, decValue2 As _
Decimal)
Dim decResult As Decimal
decResult = Divide(decValue1, decValue2)
Return decResult

End Function
Function AddValues(decValue1 As Decimal, decValue2 As _
Decimal)
Dim decResult As Decimal
decResult = Add(decValue1, decValue2)
Return decResult

End Function
Function SubtractValues(decValue1 As Decimal, decValue2 As _
Decimal)
Dim decResult As Decimal
decResult = Subtract(decValue1, decValue2)
Return decResult

End Function
Function CheckValue(objValue As Object, args As EventArgs) As Boolean
If IsNumeric(objValue) Then
Return True
Else
Return False
End If
End Function
</script>
</HEAD>
<body>
<form runat="Server">
<P>Please enter your values and click Get Results. </P>
<P>
<asp:TextBox id="txtValue1" runat="server"></asp:TextBox>
<asp:DropDownList id="MathOperator" runat="server">
<asp:ListItem>x</asp:ListItem>
<asp:ListItem>/</asp:ListItem>
<asp:ListItem>+</asp:ListItem>
<asp:ListItem>-</asp:ListItem>
</asp:DropDownList>
<asp:TextBox id="txtValue2" runat="server" ></asp:TextBox>
<asp:Button id=btnGetResult runat="server" Text="Get Result"
OnClick="btnGetResult_OnClick"></asp:Button>

<asp:RequiredFieldValidator id="Value1HasValue" runat="server"
ControlToValidate="txtValue1"
ErrorMessage="You must enter value in the first box."
Display="none">
</asp:RequiredFieldValidator>
```

```
<asp:CustomValidator id="Value1IsNumber" runat="server"
ControlToValidate="txtValue1"
OnServerValidate="CheckValue(" & txtValue1.Text & ")"
ErrorMessage="The first value does not contain a number."
Display="None">
</asp:CustomValidator>

<asp:RequiredFieldValidator id="Value2HasValue" runat="server"
ControlToValidate="txtValue2"
ErrorMessage="You must enter value in the second box."
Display="none">
</asp:RequiredFieldValidator>

<asp:CustomValidator id="Value1IsNumber" runat="server"
ControlToValidate="txtValue1"
OnServerValidate="CheckValue(" & txtValue2.Text & ")"
ErrorMessage="The second value does not contain a number."
Display="None">
</asp:CustomValidator>

<asp:RequiredFieldValidator id="MathOperatorHasValue"
runat="server"
ControlToValidate="MathOperator"
ErrorMessage="You must choose an operator."
Display="none">
</asp:RequiredFieldValidator>

<asp:ValidationSummary id="MathSummary" runat="server"
HeaderText="The following errors were encountered:"
ShowSummary="True"
DisplayMode="BulletList">
</asp:ValidationSummary>
</form>
</body>
</html>
```

Have you noticed anything about the application that should be done differently? The glaring issue is the use of System.Decimal to perform mathematical calculations.

The Changes

**20 Min.
To Go**

Several changes can be made to this application to make it look and perform better. Removing extraneous code, rewriting functions, and changing the naming convention are some of the things we can do to make our code more manageable.

Too much code

There is simply too much code in this one page. That's not to say that there are too many lines; rather, there is a lot of extraneous code that could be pared down to simpler code.

One example is the use of the System.Decimal methods to perform basic mathematical operations. It's perfectly reasonable to use the basic operators /, *, -, and + to perform these operations on the decimal data type.

There are four functions that perform our mathematical operations. Here's the code:

```
Function MultiplyValues(decValue1 As Decimal, decValue2 As _
Decimal)

Dim decResult As Decimal
decResult = Multiply(decValue1, decValue2)
Return decResult

End Function

Function DivideValues(decValue1 As Decimal, decValue2 As _
Decimal)

Dim decResult As Decimal
decResult = Divide(decValue1, decValue2)
Return decResult

End Function

Function AddValues(decValue1 As Decimal, decValue2 As _
Decimal)

Dim decResult As Decimal
decResult = Add(decValue1, decValue2)
Return decResult

End Function

Function SubtractValues(decValue1 As Decimal, decValue2 As _
Decimal)

Dim decResult As Decimal
decResult = Subtract(decValue1, decValue2)
Return decResult

End Function
```

We have two choices with this code. We can eliminate the functions entirely and put the operations in the Select...Case construct, or we can rewrite the functions to accept the two values and perform the basic arithmetic function.

I think the best idea is to remove the functions entirely, because they offer no advantage other than modularity. Because the arithmetic functions are single-line operations, the modularity of the separate functions simply extends the size of our page.

Rewriting the Select...Case construct to reflect the change, we get

```
Dim decResult As Decimal
Try
```

```
Select Case strOperator
Case "multiply"
decResult = decValue1 * decValue2
Case "divide"
decResult = decValue1 / decValue2
Case "add"
decResult = decValue1 + decValue2
Case "subtract"
decResult = decValue1 - decValue2
End Select

Catch e As OverflowException
Response.Write("The result was too large to represent" & _
          "as a decimal.")

Catch e As DivideByZeroException
Response.Write("You cannot divide by zero.")

Finally
    UpdateTableWithResult(decResult)

End Try
```

Now the arithmetic functions are performed inline, greatly simplifying our code. Because we're not using the methods in System.Decimal to perform our operations, why bother declaring the variables as Decimals? Using the Single data type offers a few advantages, such as the simplicity in converting it to a string, and it's 32 bits in length as opposed to the 96-bit length of a Decimal. The Single data type supports single-precision floating point numbers; its C# equivalent is float.

To reflect the change to Single, we'll replace the As Decimal declaration with As Single, and change the variable prefix dec to sng:

```
Dim sngResult As Single
Try

Select Case strOperator
Case "multiply"
sngResult = sngValue1 * sngValue2
Case "divide"
sngResult = sngValue1 / sngValue2
Case "add"
sngResult = sngValue1 + sngValue2
Case "subtract"
sngResult = sngValue1 - sngValue2
End Select

Catch e As OverflowException
Response.Write("The result was too large to represent " & _
          "as a single.")

Catch e As DivideByZeroException
Response.Write("You cannot divide by zero.")
```

```
Finally
     UpdateTableWithResult(sngResult)
End Try
```

Also be sure to convert the rest of the code from Decimal to Single.

Performance enhancement

**10 Min.
To Go**

Because the page is initially always the same, meaning there is no result the first time
the page is visited, it makes sense to turn on output caching. This can be done using the
@ OutputCache directive:

```
<%@ OutputCache Duration="600" %>
```

Setting the duration to 600 makes ASP.NET store the page in cache for ten minutes. That
way, each time a user visits the page in that ten-minute span, the user is seeing the cached
version of the page. When the user clicks Get Result, a new version of the page will be sent
and the cache is restarted.

What's the advantage of this if the point is for the user to click the button? Well, sometimes users visit pages and don't do anything. It makes sense to not deliver the page fresh
on every visit, even if the idea is to let them use the page as an application.

As an exercise on your own, figure out how to cache pieces of the page.

Another good performance enhancement is to convert the application from System.Data.
OleDb toSystem.Data.SqlClient, if you're using SQL Server. System.Data.SqlClient can
offer 300 percent more performance than System.Data.OleDb. To use System.Data.
SqlClient, you use the SqlConnection instead of OleDbConnection:

```
<%@ Import System.Data.SqlClient %>
<script language="VB" runat="server">
Sub Page_Load(ByVal Sender As Object, e As EventArgs)
If Page.IsPostBack Then 'We only want to connect on post back
   Dim oConn As SQLConnection
   oConn = New SqlConnection("Data Source=KLAVEN;" & _
        "Initial Catalog=ASPNET WCC;" & _
        "uid=sa;pwd=testbox")
     oConn.Open()
End If
End Sub
</script>
```

Whether you use System.Data.OleDb or System.Data.SqlClient, another way to
increase performance is to use INSERT statements directly, or use a stored procedure. These
can be performed via the OleDbCommand and SQLCommand objects. If you decide to use
System.Data.SqlClient, you will have to convert the rest of the ADO.NET objects from
OleDb to their SqlClient counterparts.

**To gain a better understanding of database programming with ASP.NET, take
a look at *ASP.NET Database Programming Weekend Crash Course*.**

The End Result

Considering all of our changes, how does the code look?

```
<%@ Import namespace="System.Data" %>
<%@ Import namespace="System.Data.OleDb" %>
<%@ OutputCache Duration="600" %>
<html>
<head>
<title>ASP.NET Math Program</title>
<script language="VB" runat="server">
Sub Page_Load(ByVal Sender As Object, e As EventArgs)
If Page.IsPostBack Then 'We only want to connect on post back
    Dim oConn As OleDbConnection
    oConn = New OleDbConnection("provider=SQLOLEDB.1;Data " & _
        "Source=KLAVEN;Initial Catalog=ASPNET WCC;" & _
          "uid=sa;pwd=testbox")
        oConn.Open()
End If
End Sub


Sub UpdateTableWithResult(sngResults As Single)

Dim objAdp As New OleDbDataAdapter()
Dim dsWCC As New DataSet()
Dim strSQL As String = "SELECT * FROM Math_WCC"
Dim odbWCC As OleDbCommandBuilder = New OleDbCommandBuilder(objAdp)

objAdp.SelectCommand = New OleDbCommand(strSQL, oConn)
objAdp.Fill(dsWCC)


Dim rowWCC As New DataRow = dsWCC.Tables("Math_WCC").NewRow
rowWCC("RESULT") = sngResults 'Our results will go here
rowWCC("DATE_ENTERED")= System.DateTime.Now.ToShortDateString
dsWCC.Tables("Math_WCC").Rows.Add(rowWCC)
objAdp.Update(dsWCC, "Math_WCC")
End Sub


Sub btnGetResult_OnClickClick(Source As Object, e As EventArgs)
Dim sngFirstValue As Single = txtValue1.Text
Dim sngSecondValue As Single =As Single = txtValue2.Text
Dim strOperator As String = MathOperator.SelectedItem.Text

Dim sngResult As Single
Try

Select Case strOperator
Case "multiply"
sngResult = sngValue1 * sngValue2
```

```
Case "divide"
sngResult = sngValue1 / sngValue2
Case "add"
sngResult = sngValue1 + sngValue2
Case "subtract"
sngResult = sngValue1 - sngValue2
End Select

Catch e As OverflowException
Response.Write("The result was too large to represent" & _
            as a single.")

Catch e As DivideByZeroException
Response.Write("You cannot divide by zero.")

Finally
     UpdateTableWithResult(sngResult)
End Try


Function CheckValue(objValue As Object, args As EventArgs)
If IsNumeric(objValue) Then
Return True
Else
Return False
End If
End Function
</script>
</head>
<body>
<form runat="server">
Please enter your values and click Get Results.
 <br/>
<asp:TextBox id="txtValue1" runat="server"></asp:TextBox>
<asp:DropDownList id="MathOperator" runat="server">
<asp:ListItem>x</asp:ListItem>
<asp:ListItem>/</asp:ListItem>
<asp:ListItem>+</asp:ListItem>
<asp:ListItem>-</asp:ListItem>
</asp:DropDownList>
<asp:TextBox id="txtValue2" runat="server" ></asp:TextBox>
<asp:Button id=btnGetResult runat="server" Text="Get Result"
OnClick="btnGetResult_OnClick"></asp:Button>

  <asp:RequiredFieldValidator id="FirstValueHasValue"
      runat="server"
      ControlToValidate="txtValue1"
      ErrorMessage="You must enter value in the first box."
      Display="none">
  </asp:RequiredFieldValidator>
```

```
<asp:CustomValidator id="FirstValueIsNumber" runat="server"
    ControlToValidate="txtValue1"
    OnServerValidate="CheckValue(" & txtValue1.Text &_
    ")"
    ErrorMessage="The first value does not contain a " & _
        number."
    Display="None">
</asp:CustomValidator>

<asp:RequiredFieldValidator id="SecondValueHasValue"
    runat="server"
    ControlToValidate="txtValue2"
    ErrorMessage="You must enter value in the second box."
    Display="none">
</asp:RequiredFieldValidator>

<asp:CustomValidator id="FirstValueIsNumber" runat="server"
    ControlToValidate="txtValue2"
    OnServerValidate="CheckValue("&_
        txttxtValue2.Text & _ ")"
    ErrorMessage="The second value does not contain " & _
        number."
    Display="None">
</asp:CustomValidator>

<asp:RequiredFieldValidator id="MathOperatorHasValue"
    runat="server"
    ControlToValidate="MathOperator"
    ErrorMessage="You must choose an operator."
    Display="none">
</asp:RequiredFieldValidator>

<asp:ValidationSummary id="MathSummary" runat="server"
    HeaderText="The following errors were encountered:"
    ShowSummary="True"
    DisplayMode="BulletList">
</asp:ValidationSummary>
</form>
</body>
</html>
```

That's it! You're finished!

Done!

REVIEW

In this chapter, we revisited math.aspx one last time and made several changes to it. Specifically, we:

- Simplified the code
- Changed data types for compatibility and performance

- Changed the naming convention
- Turned on output caching
- Discussed the performance improvement of using `System.Data.SqlClient`

This is the last chapter. I hope you gained a solid understanding of ASP.NET and an unquenchable thirst to learn all there is to learn!

QUIZ YOURSELF

1. What are the advantages of using a `Single` data type over a `Decimal` data type? (See "The Changes.")

2. How does using the `Decimal` data type affect working with SQL Server 2000? (See "The Changes.")

3. What is the SQL Server 2000-specific data namespace? (See "Performance enhancement.")

4. What will output caching do? (See "Performance enhancement.")

5. What are the three things we did to make this application's code more manageable? (See "The Changes.")

PART

VI

Sunday Afternoon
Part Review

1. What kind of information does Web.config contain, and in what format is it stored?
2. What are the two major advantages of Web.config?
3. What is the root tag of Web.config?
4. How would you define compilers for your ASP.NET application?
5. What section of Web.config allows you to define browser capabilities?
6. What is a runtime error?
7. What section of Web.config allows you to define custom error pages?
8. The trace facility supports tracing at two levels. What are they?
9. With application-level tracing turned on, where is the trace information sent?
10. How do you write trace statements to a page?
11. What does a Web service need to work?
12. What happens after a client sends a request to a Web service?
13. What does SOAP do?
14. What is the difference between output caching and data caching?
15. How do you enable output caching in an ASP.NET page?

Answers to the Part Reviews

Friday Evening Review Answers

1. The .NET Framework is an environment for building, deploying, and running applications, and specifically, Web Services.

2. The .NET Framework provides an environment that could be seen as combining the mainframe and client/server computing paradigms.

3. .NET is Microsoft's strategy for delivering software as a service. The .NET Framework is the environment for creating software that adheres to the .NET model.

4. Answers will vary.

5. No, ASP.NET does not replace ASP. Instead, ASP.NET is an evolution of ASP.

6. It must be an application that is delivered via a Web browser.

7. Perl offers excellent support for string processing and regular expressions.

8. NSAPI is Netscape's implementation of a Web server programming interface. ISAPI is Microsoft's implementation for their Internet Information Server product.

9. An ASP file is a text file that contains one or more of the following: script code, HTML formatting tags, and content.

10. The Request object exposes user data to the server. The Response object exposes server data to the client.

11. A computer program is a set of instructions for a computer to carry out.

12. Answers will vary.

13. When a program is compiled, the text file containing the source code is compiled and linked, and a machine-code executable is produced. When a program is interpreted, the compiler processes the program line by line, and a machine-code executable is not produced.

14. There are eight steps in the Software Development Lifecycle: Requirements analysis, design, specification, development, testing, production, maintenance, and enhancement.

15. Select...Case can accept multiple conditions, while If...Then can only handle one at a time.

16. No, ASP.NET pages are processed on the server, and HTML is sent to the client browser.

17. Currently, the .NET Framework is supported on Windows 98, Windows ME, Windows NT 4.0, Windows 2000, and Windows XP. There are plans for a version that supports Linux.

18. Absolutely nothing. ASP.NET is configured automatically.

Saturday Morning Review Answers

1. The .NET Framework acts as an interface between applications and the Windows operating system. It could be regarded as a middleware layer.

2. ASP.NET pages are typically named with the extension .aspx. However, you can use whatever extension you want, as long as you specify it in IIS. Web services have an extension of .asmx and user controls have the extension .ascx.

3. The CLR takes input source code and compiles it to intermediate language (IL), which is then compiled to a library or executable.

4. Garbage collection is intended to clean up after your application. It eliminates memory leaks by managing object lifetimes.

5. The Standard JIT and EconoJIT are the two JIT compilers included in .NET.

6. The three built-in .NET languages are Visual Basic.NET, C#, and JScript.NET.

7. The .NET implementation of Eiffel is called Eiffel#.

8. Simply set the @Page language to COBOL, or specify the language as COBOL in a script block:

```
<%@Page Language="COBOL" %>
```

or

```
<script language="COBOL" runat="server">
</script>
```

9. C# natively supports .NET features such as built-in garbage collection and scalability support.

10. Free threading, operator overloading, and object-orientation.

11. Extensible Markup Language

12. ASP.NET uses the MSXML parser.

13. An XML document requires a DTD or schema to be considered valid.

14. The XML DOM is a document object model that exposes pieces of an XML document to programming languages.

15. The <xsl> tag indicates to the parser that the enclosed content (that is, between <xsl> and </xsl>) is XSL code.

16. `Dim VariableName As DataType = Value`
17. Constant declarations require a name, a data type, and a value.
18. Use the `Return` statement and make sure the return value is the same type as the function.
19. The code in the `Finally` block always executes.
20. Microsoft.VisualBasic.Compatibility.VB6 provides compatibility between VB6 and VB.NET.
21. You use the `System.IO` namespace to work with the server's file system.
22. `<input type="file" id="some_id">`
23. The `SmtpMail` class performs the action of sending a mail message.
24. `StreamWriter` exposes the File class.
25. The SMTP service must be installed on the server for an ASP.NET page to send e-mail.
26. The class is the foundation of object-oriented programming.
27. A method is a function performed by an object.
28. A property is a definable variable stored by an object.
29. The four tenets are abstraction, inheritance, encapsulation, and polymorphism.
30. Answers will vary. Some examples are C++, Java, VB.NET, and C#.

Saturday Afternoon Review Answers

1. ASP.NET can be extended through httpHandlers, which are high-level programs that can be written in Visual Basic.
2. ASP.NET supports multiple interfaces and multiple inheritance.
3. ASP.NET simplifies configuration by encapsulating all of it into one or more XML-based text files.
4. All you have to do is copy the component's files to your Web server. ASP.NET handles the rest.
5. A Web garden is a Web server with more than one processor.
6. `<script runat="server"></script>`
7. Code render blocks are delimited using `<% %>`.
8. The Language attribute of the `@Page` directive tells ASP.NET what language is used on the page so it knows how to compile it.
9. `<object id="object_id" runat="server" class="System.Data.SqlClient" />`
10. `<!-- #include file="filename.inc"-->`
11. Namespaces are grouped by functionality.
12. Namespaces are stored in portable executable (PE) files.
13. There are over 80 namespaces included in the .NET Framework.

14. `HttpApplicationState` enables developers to share information across sessions and multiple requests within an ASP.NET application.

15. The `Directory` class exposes methods for creating directories and moving through them.

16. An application domain guarantees against version conflicts, and tightens security by providing application autonomy.

17. All a text file needs to be considered an ASP.NET page is the .aspx filename extension.

18. You deploy an ASP.NET application with an XCOPY command.

19. Application events fire the first time an ASP.NET application is accessed, and the last time an application is accessed (that is, an application restart).

20. Session events fire per user; `Session_OnStart` is fired each time a user session is instantiated, and `Session_OnEnd` fires when the user session ends.

21. The three main problems in ASP session management are process dependence, cookie dependence, and lack of scalability.

22. Use the `<sessionstate>` tag in Web.config to configure session state management in ASP.NET.

23. The Mode attribute accepts three values: `inproc`, `stateserver`, and `sqlserver`.

24. The `sqlserver` mode is good for reducing overhead and providing reliability and stability in session state management.

25. Session variables are referenced by using the syntax Session("`session_variable`"). If you are using C#, the syntax is Session["`session_variable`"].

Saturday Evening Review Answers

1. Web forms provide an event-based model, similar to Visual Basic, for ASP.NET applications.

2. The `Page_Load` event fires when the ASP.NET page is accessed. It provides an entry point to the page.

3. Unmapped tags, such as `<div>` and `<span>`, can be derived from `HtmlGenericControl`.

4. Code-behind simplifies maintenance and improves security.

5. To "hide" the code-behind file, compile it into the application's DLL and leave the `Src` attribute off the @Page directive (but be sure to include the full namespace for the class in the Inherits attribute).

6. System.Web.UI.WebControls exposes the ASP.NET Web controls.

7. `<asp:TextBox id="textbox" runat="server" />`

8. The panel control is designed to group other controls.

9. The `AdRotator` control gets information about what ads to show via an XML file specified in the AdRotator tag.

10. `<asp:WebControlType id="webcontrol_id" runat="server" />`

11. The six validating controls are `CompareValidator`, `CustomValidator`, `RangeValidator`, `RegularExpressionValidator`, `RequriedFieldValidator`, and `ValidationSummary`.

12. More than one validation control can be linked to a control on a Web form.

13. Use `<%@ Page ClientTarget="DownLevel" %>`

14. The `ValidationSummary` control outputs the results of validation on the form.

15. Use `Page.IsValid` to check the validity of a form.

Sunday Morning Review Answers

1. The most common database format before relational databases was flat-files.

2. Tables are structured into rows and columns.

3. A key is a row that defines the uniqueness of an entry.

4. A `SELECT` query retrieves data from a database.

5. `INSERT` adds new data, and `UPDATE` changes existing data.

6. Data binding is the concept of binding a control to a piece of data.

7. `<%# [value] [expression] [property] [method call] [collection] %>`

8. The `DataBind()` method, when executed, initializes all data binding on the page.

9. Data binding can be used anywhere within an ASP.NET page, as long as it evaluates to the expected data type at runtime.

10. `DataGrid` displays data in a scrollable grid, and `DataList` displays a data-bound list.

11. If you don't specify `HeaderTemplate` and `FooterTemplate`, no header or footer is displayed.

12. `System.Data`, `System.Data.OleDb`, and `System.Data.SqlClient` expose ADO.NET and data access methods.

13. The `DataSet` can get data from a data source using `SqlDataAdapter`, `OleDbDataAdapter`, `OleDbCommand`, or `SqlCommand`.

14. `System.Data.SqlClient` exposes classes designed for working with SQL Server 2000.

15. `OleDbDataAdapter` acts as a broker between a `DataTable` class and the data source.

16. ACID: Atomicity, Consistency, Isolation, and Durability.

Sunday Afternoon Review Answers

1. Web.config contains configuration information for an application, and stores it as an XML-based text file.

2. The two major advantages of Web.config are centralized management and simplified maintenance.

3. The root tag of Web.config is <configuration>.

4. Each compiler would be defined with a <compiler> tag under the <compilers> tag. For example:

```
<compilers defaultlanguage="vb">
<compiler
language="cobol"
extension=".cbl"
type="Fujitsu.Cobol"
/>
</compilers>
```

5. The <browsercaps> section allows you to set the capabilities of an application on a per-browser basis.

6. A runtime error is an error that occurs when an application is executed. This error is generated by the runtime environment.

7. <customerrors> will allow you to define custom error pages.

8. Tracing is supported at the application level and at the page level.

9. With application-level tracing turned on, trace information is sent to the trace log.

10. Use Trace.Write to write trace statements to a page.

11. A Web service requires a consumer, a provider, and a contract.

12. The provider receives the request, then encodes and transports the request back to the consumer.

13. SOAP provides an XML-based, platform-neutral, standardized way for two applications to communicate.

14. Page data caching allows the developer to explicitly cache objects, while output caching caches the entire page.

15. Use <%@OutputCache Duration="time" %>, where "time" is a numeric value representing seconds.

What's on the CD

This book's CD-ROM includes all of the source code from all of the examples in this book and the ASP.NET Weekend Crash Course Assessment test. For the latest and greatest information, please refer to the ReadMe file located at the root of the CD.

System Requirements

The programs on the CD-ROM require one of these operating systems:

- Windows 95
- Windows 98
- Windows ME (Millennium Edition)
- Windows 2000
- Windows XP

You'll also need a Pentium 166 or better and at least 64 megabytes of RAM. The source code files, if you wish to copy them to your machine, will occupy around 3 megabytes of hard disk space.

Using the CD with Windows

To view the source code or use any of the existing programs, insert the CD-ROM into your CD-ROM drive. The CD will automatically run and provide a user interface that includes the following options: Install, Explore, Links, and Exit

- **Install:** Gives you the option to install the supplied software and/or the author-created code from the CD-ROM.
- **Explore:** Allows you to view the contents of the CD-ROM in its directory structure.
- **Links:** Opens a hyperlinked page of web sites.
- **Exit:** Closes the autorun window.

If you do not have autorun enabled or if the autorun window does not appear, follow the steps below to access the CD.

1. Choose Start ➪ Run.
2. In the dialog box that appears, type d:\setup.exe, where d is the letter of your CD-ROM drive. This will bring up the autorun window described above.
3. Choose the Install, Explore, Links, or Exit option from the menu. (See "Explore" in the preceding list for a description of these options.)

Source Code

The example code written for this book is included on the CD-ROM. Each session in the book has its own folder on the CD-ROM. You'll find all the code from each session in its folder. The source code examples are listed in the CD file in the same order they appear in the book.

You'll also find several SQL files on the CD-ROM. These SQL files perform the database creation from Part V. Running these SQL files in SQL Server 2000 will generate the tables for the sample application.

Applications

This CD contains Wiz.Net, a great utility for creating database applications with Visual Basic .NET.

Troubleshooting

If you have difficulty installing or using any of the materials on the companion CD, try the following solutions:

- **Turn off any anti-virus software that you may have running.** Installers sometimes mimic virus activity and can make your computer incorrectly believe that it is being infected by a virus. (Be sure to turn the anti-virus software back on later.)
- **Close all running programs.** The more programs you're running, the less memory is available to other programs. Installers also typically update files and programs; if you keep other programs running, installation may not work properly.
- **Reference the ReadMe:** Please refer to the ReadMe file located at the root of the CD-ROM for the latest product information at the time of publication.

If you still have trouble with the CD, please call the Hungry Minds Customer Care phone number: (800) 762-2974. Outside the United States, call 1 (317) 572-3994. You can also contact Hungry Minds Customer Service by e-mail at techsupdum@hungryminds.com. Hungry Minds will provide technical support only for installation and other general quality control items; for technical support on the applications themselves, consult the program's vendor or author.

If you have problems using the source code, e-mail the author directly at rob@standefer.com.

Index

Symbols & Numbers

"" (double quotes), in XML documents, 58
% (percent) character, in code syntax, 111
() (parentheses) characters, in Visual Basic
.NET procedure calls, 71
@Assembly directive, 113
@Control directive, 113
@Import directive, 113, 146–147
@OutputCache directive, 114, 295
@Page directive, 112–113
   adding ErrorPage attribute, 274
   bypassing browser checks using, 179
   with code behind files, 166
@Register directive, 113
' (apostrophe) character, in Visual Basic
.NET, 68
<% %> code block, 16
<%# %> syntax, 226
404 errors, 275

abstraction, in programming
   classes for, 87
   namespaces and, 91–92
   in object-oriented programming, 88
Access databases, autonumber key, 203
AccessKey property (WebControl), 168
action-performing Web controls, 172

Active Server Pages (ASP). See ASP (Active
Server Pages) applications
ActiveX Data Objects (ADO). See ADO
(ActiveX Data Objects)
ad rotator (Web controls), 167
Add/Remove Windows Components,
enabling, 29–30
addition function, in math.aspx, 148
addresses, assembly, 85–86
ADO (ActiveX Data Objects), 17–18
   ADO.NET comparison, 238
   ASP database access using, 99
   ASP support for, 15
   Command object, 18
   Connection object, 18
   Errors object, 18
   Parameter object, 18
   Recordset object, 18
   updating recordsets using, 236–238
ADO.NET, 99
   accessing data using, 236–237
   ADO comparison, 238
   data access interface classes, 238–239
   recoding ASP as, 244–247
   using data access classes, 239–240
adovbs.inc (sample ASP page)
   creating with ADO, 236–237
   recoding as ADO.NET application, 244–247
AdRotator control, 174
aggregate objects, 91
AlternatingItemTemplate (DataList
control), 233

apostrophe (') character, in Visual Basic .NET, 68
application development, .NET Framework, 40
application events, 128
application logic, sharing, 127
Application object (ASP), 16, 99–100, 102
Application Server Provider business model, 5
application settings, storing, 137–138
application-level tracing, 276–277
Application_OnStart/_OnEnd events, 128–129
applications, preexisting, using with .NET programs, 41
arithmetic functions, replacing with Select...Case conditional, 293–294
ArithmeticException (System namespace), 119
Array class (System namespace), 119
ASP (Active Server Pages) applications, 6–7, 15–16
  <% %> code block, 16
  ADO with, 17
  Application object, 16
  ASP.NET compared with, 8–9, 97–98
  browser support, 100
  configuring, 101
  database support, 99
  deploying, 101
  error handling tools, 104–105
  error sources, 272
  execution requirements, 97–98
  language support/interoperability, 98
  pages in, examples of, 15–16, 241
  Response object, 17
  scalability, 102
  script for, 15–16
  Server object, 16
  Session object, 17
  session state, 136
  stability of, 103
  VBScript and, 17
  versioning, 102
  Web forms, coding for, 162–163
asp.dll, 13
ASP.NET applications, 6, 8, 125
  accessing .NET Framework classes, 75–76
  browser-detection requirements, 100
  client view of, 109
  code checking procedures, 103

  code declaration blocks, 110–111
  code render blocks, 111–112
  comments, server-side, 115
  comparison with ASP, 8–9
  compilation persistence, 98
  configuring, 101, 263–269
  creating, 125
  custom server control syntax, 114
  data binding expressions, 114
  data-aware Web pages, 91–92
  database support, 99
  debugging, 104
  deploying, 101, 126–127
  directives, 112–114
  e-mail sending functionality, 76–78
  error handling tools, 104–105, 273–275
  error messages, 275
  features/advantages of, 8, 107–108
  file system access, 81–83
  file upload functionality, 79–81
  HTML control syntax, 114
  include directives, server-side, 115
  language support/interoperability, 41–42, 98
  <object> elements, server-side, 114–115
  object support, 99, 100
  scalability, 103
  security advantages/tools, 108, 129
  server process, 109–110
  session state settings, 141–142
  versioning, 102
  Web forms, 159–160
  XML document access tool, 66
ASP.NET caching, 285–286
ASP.NET, comparison with ASP
  browser-detection requirements, 100
  configuration requirements, 101
  execution requirements, 97–98
  languages, built-in, 98
  object support, 99
  programming environment, 97–98
ASP.NET Math Program example
  addition function, creating, 148
  building page skeleton, 146–147
  calling functions, 150–152
  completed code for, 249–252
  connection code, 253–254
  creating, initial code for, 163–164
  division function, creating, 148
  exception handling, 152–153
  HTML code, 146

integrating code elements, 256–259
integrating functions, 149–150
multiplication function, creating, 148
requirements for, initial outline, 145–146
requirements for, redefining, 252–253
subtraction function, creating, 148–149
updates to, coding, 254–256
ASP.NET Premium Edition, 29–34
ASP.NET session state
   mode settings, 138–140
   Web.config file for, 137–138
ASP.NET validation controls, 177–180
   using, 180–184
ASPNET WCC database, creating using
    Enterprise Manager, 219–223
ASPState service (Windows NT), 139
.aspx filename extension, 125
ASPxxxx error code, 274
assemblers, function of, 87
assemblies, 117
   <assemblies> subelement, 265
   assembly addresses, 85–86
   relationship to namespaces, 91
Assert method (Trace object), 279
asynchronous communications, using SOAP,
   284–285
atomicity, in transactions, 236
attributes
   @Page directive, 112–113
   XML documents, 58
Attributes property (WebControl base
   class), 169
<authentication> element (Web.config), 267
authentication tools, 130–131
   selecting during SQL Server installation, 218
authorization, 131–132
<authorization> element (Web.config),
   266–267
AutoFlush property (Trace object), 279

BackColor property (WebControl base
   class), 169
binary streams, ASP.NET support for, 99
binding, data, 225–226
<binding> element (WSDL/WSML), 285
Boolean type variables, 24

BorderStyle/BorderWidth properties
   (WebControl base class), 169
BoundColumn control (data controls), 228
browser support, ASP.NET vs. ASP, 100
browser-independence, Web form code, 160
<browserCaps> element (Web.config),
   268–269
bugs. See errors, sources of
built-in languages. See languages,
   programming
Business Modeling (Rational Unified
   Process), 23
business-to-business applications, 7
Button control (data controls), 172
   adding to ASP.NET applications, 82
ButtonColumn control (data controls), 229
byte type variables, 24–25

C# programming language, 8, 42, 54
C++ programming language, 52–53
   Common Language Runtime support, 42
   managed extensions, C# comparison, 54
Cache class, 286
caching
   applying to math.aspx program, 295
   ASP.NET support for, 103
   reasons for, 285–286
calendar control (Web controls), 167,
   173–174
calling sub procedures (Visual Basic .NET),
   70–71
Cascading Style Sheet (CSS) class, 169
case sensitivity, in well-formed XML, 59
CGI (Common Gateway Interface) programs
   compiled programs, 12
   scripting, using Perl, 12–13
   server-side scripting, 11–12
char type variables, 24
CheckBox control, 170
CheckBoxList control, 171
child nodes (CXML documents), 58
classes, 75–76. See also specific classes and
   namespaces
   abstraction and, 87
   ADO.NET data access, 238–239

Continued

classes (continued)
    in object-oriented programming, 88
    in System namespace, 119–120
    in System.IO namespace, 121
    in System.Web namespace, 121–122
    in System.Web.UI namespace, 122
    in Systems.Collections namespace, 120
    WebControl base class, 167–168
Client Tools installation option (SQL Server 2000), 216
client-side input validation, 177–178
client-side view of ASP.NET applications, 109
Close method
    File class, 83
    Trace object, 279
CLR (Common Language Runtime), 41
    compilation process, 42–43
    elimination of DLLs with, 43
    elimination of runtime requirements
        with, 43
    garbage collection, 44
    managed code, 42
    memory allocation/deallocation, 44
    performance advantages, 108
    platform independence, 45
CLS (Common Language Specification), 41
COBOL.NET programming language, 51–52
code
    ADO, recordset updating example, 236–237
    application logic, sharing, 127
    CLR (Common Language Runtime),
        performance advantages, 108
    intermediate language (IL) code, 42
    managed, 42, 44
    safe vs. unsafe, 44
    session state settings in, 141–142
    simplifying, 292–295
    Web forms, browser-independence, 160
    XML, well-written, 68–69
code, ASP.NET applications
    code declaration blocks, 110–111
    code render blocks, 111–112
    comments, server-side, 115
    custom server control syntax, 114
    data binding expressions, 114
    directives, 112–114
    HTML control syntax, 114
    include directives, server-side, 115
    <object> tags, server-side, 114–115

code behind
    deploying, 166
    developing, 164–166
    using, 165–166
code checking procedures, 103
code/content separation, 8
code declaration blocks, 110–111
code examples
    basic ASP.NET page, 126
    coding errors, handling, 272
    data binding with Web controls, 226–228
    e-mail functionality, 76–77
    file system access, 81–83
    file uploading, 79–81
    math.aspx, initial form page, 187–189
    math.aspx, integrated version, 289–292
    math.aspx, simplified, final code, 296–298
    mathform_prototype.aspx, 192–193
    Web page based on database records, 91–92
code profiling (ASP.NET), 104
code render blocks, 111–112
collections, 91
Collections class, replacements for VB6 keywords, 73
columns
    bound columns, 228
    managing using DataGrid control templates, 231
    in tables, 202
COM/COM+ objects/classes
    ASP/ASP.NET support for, 15, 99–100
    legacy, wrappers for, 76
Command class (ADO.NET), data access using, 238
Command object (ADO), 18
command text, defining in ADO, 18
comments. See also code
    server-side, 115
    in Visual Basic .NET, 68–69
    in XML documents, 58
Common Business Oriented Language (COBOL), 51–52
Common Language Runtime. See CLR (Common Language Runtime)
Comparer class (System.Collections namespace), 120
CompareValidator control, 179–181
<compilation> element (Web.config), 265
compilation persistence, 98

compilation process
  ASP.NET applications, 108
  ASP.NET vs. ASP, 98
  .NET Framework, 45
<compiler> element (Web.config), 265
compilers, 20
  CLR-enabled, compilation process, 42–43
  interpreter comparison, 21
  just-in-time (JITter), 45
<compilers> tag (Web.config), 265
component support, 8
computer programs
  conditionals, 27–28
  defined, 19
  executable, 19
  loops, 25–26
  source code, 19
  variables, 23
conditionals
  If...Then, 27
  Select...Case, 27–28
<configsections> tag (Web.config), 264
<configuration> tag (Web.config), 264, 269
configuring/configuration files
  ASP.NET applications, 32, 108
  ASP.NET vs. ASP applications, 101
  IDC (Internet Database Connector), 14
connecting, to databases, ADO objects for, 17
Connection class (ADO.NET), data access using, 238
connection code, 253–254
connection files, IDC .idc files, 14
Connection object (ADO), 18
  recordset updates using, 238
connectivity, adding programs, 253–254
Connectivity Only installation option (SQL Server 2000), 216
consistency, in transactions, 236
Console object (System namespace), 118, 119
constants, in Visual Basic .NET, 70
Constants class, Visual Basic .NET replacements for VB6 keywords, 73
container objects, 91
Control class (System.Web.UI namespace), 122
ControlCollection class (System.Web.UI namespace), 122
ControlName syntax, 174

controls. *See data controls; HTML control (Web forms); server-side controls; validation controls; Web controls*
Convert class (System namespace), 120
cookie authentication, 130–131
cookieless session management, 140–141
cookies, HTTP, 136
Cookies object (ASP), 17
copying, .NET application files, 126–127
CopyTo method (File class), 82
Create method (File class), 82
CreateObject method (ASP Server object), 16, 100
CreateText method (File class), 82, 83
creating ASP.NET applications, 126
CreationTime property (FileInfo class), 82
CssClass property (WebControl base class), 169
custom controls, for Web forms, 159–160
custom error pages, 273
custom server control syntax, 114
<customErrors> tag (Web.config), 265–266
customizing
  ASP.NET applications, 108
  SQL Server 2000, 217
CustomValidator control, 179
  using, 181–182
  using with math form, 193–195

data
  structuring, 86
  in tables, 202
data, in databases
  accessing, 203–204
  adding/updating, 206–208
  deleting, 209–210
  editing/managing, 232–233
  retrieving, 208–209
data, in XML documents, 58
data, managed
  ADO objects for, 17
  in the CLR environment, 44
data, persisting, 135–136
data binding, 225–226
  in ADO.NET code, 245–247
  DataGrid control for, 230–231
  expressions for, 114

data controls
  BoundColumn, 228
  ButtonColumn, 229
  DataGrid, 99, 229, 245–247
  DataGridColumn, 229
  DataGridColumnCollection, 229
  DataGridItem, 229
  DataGridItemCollection, 229
  DataGridPagerStyle, 229
  DataKeyCollection, 229
  DataList, 229
  DataListItem, 229
  DataListItemCollection, 229
  EditCommandColumn, 229
  HyperLinkColumn, 229
  TemplateColumn, 229
  using on forms, 229–233
data input, controls for, 170–172
data modifications, transactions, 235–236
Data Source Name (DSN), 253–254
data types
  for database fields, 202–203
  linking in stuctures, 86
DataAdapter class (ADO.NET)
  creating data sets using, 241
  data access using, 239
data-aware Web pages (ASP.NET Math
     Program example)
  connection code, 253–254
  defining requirements for, 252–253
  integrating code elements, 256–259
  updating, code for, 254–256
database support, ASP.NET vs. ASP, 98–99
databases, relational, 201–203
  accessing/managing data in, 203–204
  adding data/updating, 206–208
  binding data to Web controls, 226–228
  connecting to using ADO objects, 17
  creating, 204–206
  creating using Enterprise Manager, 219–223
  data controls for, 228–233
  database structures, 86
  deleting data from, 209–210
  displaying data in, 233
  fields, 202–203
  keys, 203
  modifying, 235–236
  queries, 203–204
  relationships, 203

  retrieving data from, 208–209
  tables, 202
  updating recordsets in, 236–238
DataBind() method, 225, 245–247
DataGrid control (data controls), 99, 229
  with ADO.NET, 245–247
  Columns templates (DataGrid control), 231
  data binding using, 230–231
  editing/managing data using, 232–233
DataGridColumn control (data controls), 229
DataGridColumnCollection control (data
     controls), 229
DataGridItem control (data controls), 229
DataGridItemCollection control (data
     controls), 229
DataGridPagerStyle control (data controls),
     229
DataKeyCollection control (data controls),
     229
DataList control (data controls), 229, 233
DataListItem control (data controls), 229
DataListItemCollection control (data
     controls), 229
DataReader class (ADO.NET), 239
DataRow objects (ADO.NET)
  in data-aware applications, 254
  managing tables using, 241
DataSet class (ADO.NET), 238, 240
  creating, 240–241
  in data-aware applications, 254
  merging with other datasets, 241
DataTable class (ADO.NET), 240–241
DataView class (System.Data.OleDb
     namespace), with DataGrid control,
     230–231
Date and Time class, replacements for VB6
     keywords, 73
date type variables, 25
dbWeb, 14
debugging. See error handling
decimal type variables, 25
  declaring, 147
  replacing with Single type, 294–295
declaring/declaration syntax
  functions, 71
  sub procedures, 70–71
  variables, 69–70, 140
DefType statement (VB6), elimination of,
     in Visual Basic .NET, 72–73

Delete method (File class), 82
DELETE statements (SQL), 204, 209–210
DeleteCommand event (DataGrid control),
      232–233
deploying applications, 8, 101, 126–127
   code behind files, 166
design phase (SDLC), 22
destination folder, specifying during
         setup, 32
destroying object references, importance
         of, 16
development phase (SDLC), 22
development tools, Web, 6–7
DHTML, client-side validation code, 179
Dim statement, creating variables using, 69
directives
      @Assembly, 113
      @Control, 113
      @Import, 113
      @OutputCache, 113
      @Page, 112–113
      @Register, 113
Directory class (System.IO namespace), 121
DirectoryNotFoundException (System.IO
         namespace), 120
displaying database data, 233
DivideByZeroException
      System namespace, 119
      System.Decimal.Divide namespace, 152–153
division function, creating, 148
DLLs
      elimination of with CLR, 43
      ISAPI, 13
Do Until...Loop, 26
Do While...Loop, 26
Do...Loop, 26
Do...Loop Until, 26
Do...Loop While, 26
Document Object Model (DOM), 63
Document Type Definitions (DTD), 60
document-oriented operations (SOAP),
         284–285
documents, XML, features of, 58
DOM (Document Object Model), 63
Domain User accounts, with SQL Server
         2000, 218
double quotes (""), in XML documents, 58
double type variables, 25
drag-and-drop, adding controls using, 160

DropDownList control (Web controls), 171,
      190–191
DSN (Data Source Name) connections,
      253–254
DSN-less connections, 254
dt prefix (XML documents), 62
DTDs (Document Type Definitions), 60
durability, in transactions, 236

ECMA (European Computer Manufacturers'
         Association), 42
EconoJIT, 45–46
EditCommand event (DataGrid control),
         232–233
EditCommandColumn control (data
         controls), 229
editing XML documents
      DOM (Document Object Model) for, 63
      Extensible Stylesheet Language (XSL), 64
      Simple API for XML (SAX) for, 63–64
EditSelectedItemTemplate (DataList
         control), 233
Eiffel/Eiffel# programming language, 51
      integration with Visual Studio .NET, 52–53
elements, in XML documents, 58
e-mail functionality, ASP.NET program for,
         76–77
Enabled property (WebControl base class),
         169
encapsulation, in object-oriented
         programming, 88–89
endless loops, 26, 272–273
engineering software, 23
enhancement/evolution (SDLC), 23
Enterprise Manager (SQL Server), creating
         new database using, 219–223
error code, 274
error handling
      application-level tracing, 276–277
      ASP.NET vs. ASP, 104–105
      custom error pages, 273–275
      DataSet class (ADO.NET), 241
      Errors object (ADO) for, 18
      page-level tracing, 278–279
      trace utility (ASP.NET), 275
      in Visual Basic .NET procedure calls, 71–72

error messages, 275

errors, sources of, 271–272

Errors object (ADO), 18

ERWin program, exporting databases using, 204

event handling/event-handlers, 91
  defining and sharing, 127–128
  with Web forms, 161

EventArgs class (System namespace), 120

event-driven models, limits of, 6–7

events
  application events, 128
  DataGrid control (data controls), 232–233
  for objects, 90–91
  session, 128

exception handling/exceptions
  math.aspx, (example ASP.NET page), 152–153
  System namespace, 119
  in Visual Basic .NET, 71–72

executables, 19
  creating, compilers for, 20
  creating, interpreters for, 21

Execute method (ADO Connection object), 18

execution requirements, ASP.NET vs. ASP, 97–98

Exists properties (FileInfo class), 82

Extensible Schema Description (XSD), 61

Extensible Stylesheet Language (XSL), 64

Fail method (Trace object), 279

fields, database, 202–204

file authorization, 131

File class
  Streamwriter class, 82
  System.IO namespace, 121

file system access, adding to ASP.NET applications, 81–83

File System class, replacements for VB6 keywords, 73

FileInfo class (System.IO namespace), 82

filename extensions
  ASP.NET application files, 125
  IDC (Internet Database Connector), 14

FileNotFoundException (System.IO namespace), 120

files, code behind, 164–166

files, uploading
  HTML standard method, 78
  HttpPostedFile class, 79–81

filters (ISAPI), 13

Flush method (Trace object), 279

Font property (WebControl base class), 169

FooterTemplate (DataList control), 233

For...Next loops, 25–26

ForeColor property (WebControl base class), 169

foreign keys, 203

Form object (ASP), 17

FormatException (System namespace), 119

formatting files, IDC .htx files, 14

forms, HTML, linking to validation controls, 178

forms, Web
  adding dropdown list, 190–191
  adding submit button, 191
  adding text boxes, 190
  code for, 192–193
  converting XML page to, 189–190
  data controls on, 229–233
  validation controls on, 193–195

Framework Classes, 6

function pointers, 87

functions
  calling, using Page_Load function, 150–152
  integrating into applications, 149–150
  Visual Basic .NET, 71

garbage collection (CLR), 44

global.asax, 127

<globalization> element (Web.config), 264

Gosub statement (VB6), elimination of, 72–73

graphics programming, ASP.NET support for, 100

grouping Web controls, 173

Guthrie, Scott, 8

HeaderTemplate (DataList control), 233
Height property (WebControl base class), 169
high-level programming
    structures, 85
    third-generation languages, 87–88
HTML (Hypertext Markup Language), 57
    CGI handling of, 11–12
    example ASP page code, 15–16
    file upload code, 78
HTML control (Web forms), 161–162
    adding to ASP.NET applications, 80
    syntax for, 114
HTML forms, validation controls, 178
HTML output
    CGI-generated, 11
    ISAPI-generated, 13
HtmlAnchor class (HTML controls), 162
HtmlButton class (HTML controls), 162
HtmlForm class (HTML controls), 162
HtmlGenericControl class (HTML controls), 162
HtmlInputButton class (HTML controls), 162
HtmlInputCheckBox class (HTML controls), 162
HtmlInputFile class (HTML controls), 80, 162
HtmlInputHidden class (HTML controls), 162
HtmlInputImage class (HTML controls), 162
HtmlInputRadioButton class (HTML controls), 162
HtmlInputText class (HTML controls), 162
HtmlSelect class (HTML controls), 162
HtmlTable class (HTML controls), 162
HtmlTableCell class (HTML controls), 162
HtmlTableRow class (HTML controls), 162
HtmlTextArea class (HTML controls), 162
HTTP compliant Web servers, 11
HTTP cookies, using, 136
HTTP GET method, 146, 282
http header, 179
HttpApplicationState class (System.Web namespace), 121
HttpBrowserCapabilities class (System.Web namespace), 121
HttpCookie class (System.Web namespace), 121

HttpCookieCollection class (System.Web namespace), 121
Httphandlers, 98, 109, 267
HTTPModule class, 109
<httpModules> element (Web.config), 267–268
HTTP-POST, ASP.NET support for, 282
HttpPostedFile class (System.Web namespace), 80, 121
HttpRequest class (System.Web namespace), 121
HttpResponse class (System.Web namespace), 121
HttpServerUtility class (System.Web namespace), 121
.htx files (IDC), 14
HyperLink control, 172
HyperLinkColumn control (data controls), 229
Hypertext Markup Language (HTML), 57

.idc files (IDC), 14
IDC (Internet Database Connector), 14
<identity> element (Web.config), 267
If...Then conditionals, 27
IIS (Internet Information Services), 15
    ASP dependence on, 97–98
    custom error pages, 104–105
    enabling prior to installation, 29
IL (intermediate language) code, 42
    compiling, JITter for, 45–46
    platform independence, 45
Image control, 173
image displays, Web controls for, 173
ImageButton control, 172
<img scr> tag, 173
impersonation, 132
implied programming cycle, 21
@Import directive, 113
    in math.aspx example page, 146–147
include directives, server-side, 115
Indent property (Trace object), 279
IndentSize property (Trace object), 279
indexing, database keys, 203
inheritance, in object-oriented programming, 89

initializing variables, in Visual Basic
     .NET, 69
in-process session state mode, 139, 141
input controls, 170
input parameters, storing in ADO, 18
input validation, 177–178
     controls for, 178–180
Insert() method (Cache class), 286
INSERT statements/queries (SQL), 204,
     206–207
installing, SQL Server 2000 (Microsoft),
     212–219
installing ASP.NET
     configuring, 34
     setup process, 30–34
     system requirements, 29–30
instances, naming during SQL Server
     installation, 216
integer type variables, 25
Interactive Software Engineering (ISE),
     Eiffel development environment, 51
interfaces, 87. See also user interfaces
intermediate language (IL) code, 42, 44–45
Internet Database Connector. See IDC
     (Internet Database Connector)
Internet Information Server Applications,
     13
Internet Server Application Programming
     Interface (ISAPI), 6–7, 13
interpreters
     compiler comparison, 21
     performance, 21
intrinsic objects (ASP), 16
IOException (System.IO namespace), 120
ISAPI (Internet Server Application
     Programming Interface), 6–7, 13
IsNumeric function (Visual Basic .NET),
     with math form, 194
isolation, in transactions, 236
ItemTemplate (DataList control), 233

J

JITter (just-in-time compiler), 45–46
JScript, ASP support for, 15
JScript.NET, 42, 53
just-in-time compiler (JITer), 45–46

K

keys, database, 203
keywords, deprecated (VB6), replacements
     for, 73

L

Label control, 170
     adding to applications, 82
language, intermediate (IL), 44–45
language independence, 8
     .NET Framework and, 41–42
languages, programming, 19–20
     and abstraction, 87
     ASP.NET vs. ASP, 98
     built-in, 49–50
     C#, 54
     C++, 52–53
     Eiffel, 51–52
     JScript.NET, 53
     language options, 49–50
     .NET-supported, 49–50
     Perl, 12–13
     Python, 50–51
     third-generation, 87–88
     Visual Basic .NET, 54
language-specific runtimes, eliminating, 43
LastAccessedTime property (FileInfo class),
     82
layout Web controls, 173–174
legacy COM objects, incorporating, 76
libraries, available with .NET Framework,
     40
linked lists, 86
Linux.NET, 45
ListBox control, 171
Listeners property (Trace object), 279
lists, database, generating using DataList
     control, 233
logical component (Web forms), 160
logs, trace log, accessing, 276
long type variables, 25
looping/loops
     Do...Loop, 26
     Do...Loop Until, 26
     Do...Loop While, 26

Do Until...Loop, 26
Do While...Loop, 26
endless, 26, 272–273
For...Next, 25–26
recordset looping in ASP, 99

machine language, 20
machine settings, storing in Web.config,
    137–138
MailMessage class, 77
maintenance phase (SDLC), 23
managed data, in the CLR environment, 44
managed extensions (C++), C# comparison,
    54
managed provider (ADO.NET), in data-aware
    applications, 253
managing XML documents
    DOM (Document Object Model) for, 63
    Extensible Stylesheet Language (XSL), 64
    Simple API for XML (SAX) for, 63–64
mapping Web controls, 168
Math class (System namespace), 73, 120
math form Web application (ASP.NET Math
    Program)
    adding dropdown list, 190–191
    adding submit button, 191
    adding text boxes, 190
    code for, 192–193
    connection code, 253–254
    integrating code elements, 256–259
    redefining requirements for, 252–253
    specifications for, 189–190
    update code, 254–256
    validation, 193–195
math.aspx, (example application)
    addition function, creating, 148
    building page skeleton, 146–147
    calling functions, 150–152
    code for, 187–189
    converting to Web form, 189–195
    creating, HTML code for, 146
    division function, creating, 148
    exception handling, 152–153
    integrated version, 289–292
    integrating functions into application,
        149–150

multiplication function, creating, 148
simplifying code, 292–298
subtraction function, creating, 148–149
mathform_prototype.aspx
    adding dropdown list, 190–191
    adding submit button, 191
    adding text boxes, 190
    code for, 192–193
MathOperator control, validating, 194
MDAC 2.6 (Microsoft Data Access
    Components), installing prior to
    ASP.NET installation, 30
memory allocation/de-allocation, 44
merging datasets, 241
<message> element (WSDL/WSML), 285
message queue structures, 86
messages, e-mail, sending, code for, 76–78
messages, validation, separating from
    validation controls, 179
metadata, in CLR-enabled compilers, 42–43
methodology, 21
methods, of objects, 90. See also specific
    classes and objects
Microsoft Data Access Components 2.6. See
    MDAC 2.6 (Microsoft Data Access
    Components), installing prior to
    ASP.NET installation
Microsoft Internet Explorer 5.0, installing,
    29–30
Microsoft Passport, ASP.NET support for,
    108
MissingMethodException (System
    namespace), 119
Mixed Mode authentication (SQL Server
    2000), 218
modes
    authentication, 130–131
    session state settings, 139–141
modifying databases, transactions,
    235–236
modules, in Python, 51
MoveTo method (File class), 82
MSN.NET, 5
MTS, ASP 2.0 support for, 15
multiple variables, declaring in Visual Basic
    .NET, 70
multiplication function, creating for
    math.aspx example page, 148
myInteger (sub procedure), 70–71
myString parameter (sub procedure), 70–71

namespaces
  and abstraction, 91–92
  defined, 117–118
  referencing in XML documents, 61
  relationship to assemblies, 91
  storing, 117
  System, 119–120
  System.Decimal, 147–153
  System.IO, 80, 81–83
  System.Web, 80
  System.Web.Mail, 77
  System.Web.UI.HtmlControls, 80, 162
  in XML documents, purpose of, 62
navigation controls, 172
.NET Framework
  ASPState service (Windows NT), 139
  built-in classes, 41
  built-in languages, 52–55
  classes, 75–76
  CLR (Common Language Runtime), 41
  compilation process, 45
  components, 5–6
  data controls and classes, 228–230
  language support/interoperability, 49–50
  overview, 39–40
  platform independence, 45
  programming libraries, 40
  replacements for deprecated VB6
      keywords, 73
  scalability, 41
  side-by-side program execution, 41
  simplified application development, 40
  SQL Server application with, 219
  structures in, 86–87
  Web form controls, 159–160
  XML documents in, 63
.NET infrastructure, 5
.NET platform, 5–6
NetDocs, 5
**Netscape Server Application Programming
    Interface.** *See* **NSAPI (Netscape
    Server Application Programming
    Interface)**
**New Table window (Enterprise Manager),
    viewing, 221–222**
node relationships, 61

nodes, defining in XML documents, 62
nodes (XML documents), 58
**NSAPI (Netscape Server Application
    Programming Interface), 13**

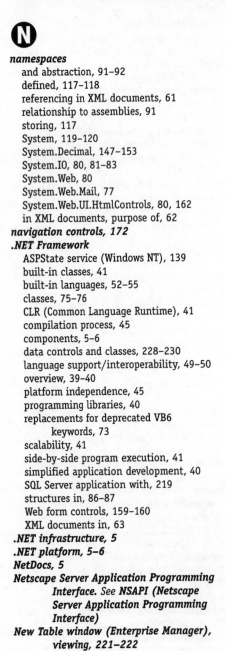

**object references, destroying, importance
    of, 16**
<object> tags, server-side, 114–115
ObjectContext object (ASP), 99–100
object-oriented programming. *See* **OOP
    (object-oriented programming)**
objects
  in ASP.NET vs. ASP, 99–100
  collections, 91
  events, 90–91
  as instances of classes, 88
  intrinsic objects (ASP), 16
  methods, 90
  namespaces for, 117–118
  properties, 89–90
  type variables, 25, 69–70
Objects class, 73
ObjectType types (Visual Basic .NET), 69
ODBC connectivity, with ADO, 99
Office.NET, 5
OLE DB connectivity, with ADO, 99
**OleDbAdapter class, using in data-aware
    applications, 254**
OleDbConnection class (ADO.NET), 240
OleDbDataAdapter class (ADO.NET), 240
OnClick event
  activating, 77, 83
  attaching to mathform_prototype.aspx
      submit button, 192
OOP (object-oriented programming)
  abstraction, 88
  C++ for, 52–53
  encapsulation, 88–89
  inheritance, 89
  polymorphism, 89
Open method
  ADO Connection object, 18, 237
  File class, 82
OpenRead method (File class), 82
OpenText method (File class), 82

OpenWrite method (File class), 82
operator, in math forms, validating,
    194–195
Oracle databases, 202
OutOfMemoryException (System
    namespace), 119
out-of-process session state mode, 139
    performance/reliability issues, 141
output parameters, storing in ADO, 18
OverflowException
    System namespace, 119
    System.Decimal namespace, 152–153

Page class (System.Web.UI namespace), 122
page data caching, 286
page output caching, 286
page-level tracing, 278–279
Page_Load event (Web forms), 161
Page_Load function, 147
    calling functions using, 150–152
pages, in ASP.NET applications
    addition function, creating, 148
    building page skeleton, 146–147
    calling functions, 150–152
    code declaration blocks, 110–111
    code render blocks, 111–112
    comments, server-side, 115
    creating, HTML code for, 146
    custom error pages, 273
    custom server control syntax, 114
    data binding expressions, 114
    division function, creating, 148
    exception handling, 152–153
    HTML control syntax, 114
    include directives, server-side, 115
    integrating functions into application,
        149–150
    multiplication function, creating, 148
    <object> tags, 114–115
    outlining goals/contents of, 145–146
    subtraction function, creating, 148–149
Page_Unload event (Web forms), 161
Panel control, 173
Parameter object (ADO), 18

parent nodes (XML documents), 58
parentheses () characters, in Visual Basic
    .NET procedure calls, 71
Passport authentication, 130
Path class (System.IO namespace), 80
PE files, storing, 117
percent (%) character, in code syntax, 111
performance
    ASP.NET application advantages, 108
    C# speed compared with C++, 54
    interpreted vs. compiled code, 21
    JIT compilers, 46
    .NET Framework scalability, 41
    and session state settings, 141
    techniques for enhancing, 295
Perl programming language, 12–13
persisting data, ASP session state for,
    135–136
platform independence, 45
polymorphism, in object-oriented
    programming, 89
<port> element (WSDL/WSML), 285
portability, of code, and DSN-less
    connections, 254
<porttype> element (WSDL/WSML), 285
post-back cycle (ASP.NET), 110
PostedFile class, 81
PostedFile property (HtmlInputFile class),
    80
primary keys, 203
processing Web forms, Page_Load/_Unload
    events, 161
<processmodel> element (Web.config), 268
processor instructions (XML documents), 58
production phase (SDLC), 22
programming, high-level, structures, 85
programming environment, ASP.NET vs.
    ASP, 97–98
programming languages. See languages,
    programming
programming libraries, .NET Framework, 40
programming process, 21
programs, computer, 19
    conditionals, 27–28
    executables, 19
    loops, 25–26
    source code, 19
    variables, 23

*properties. See also specific classes and
    objects*
  New Table window (Enterprise Manager),
      222–223
  of objects, 89–90
  WebControl base class common
      properties, 168
Python programming language, 50–51

queries, database, 203–204
Query Analyzer, running state.sql from, 140
QueryString object (ASP), 17
*Queue class (System.Collections
    namespace), 120*
QuickBasic/QBasic, 67

radio buttons (Web controls), 167
RadioButton control, 171
RadioButtonList control, 172
RangeValidator control, 179, 182–183
*Rational Unified Process (software
    engineering), 23*
*RDBMS (Relational Database Management
    Systems), 202, 204*
records, database, displaying, 230–231
recordset looping (ASP), 99
Recordset object (ADO), 18, 238
recordsets
  with ASP, 99
  updating, 236–238
Redirect method (Response object), 17
*references, to objects, destroying,
    importance of, 16*
*registry entries, ASP.NET vs. ASP
    applications, 101*
*RegularExpressionValidator control,
    179, 183*
*Relational Database Management Systems,
    202, 204*
*relational databases. See databases,
    relational*
relationships, in databases, 203

repetition. See looping/loops
Request object (ASP), 17, 99–100
*RequiredFieldValidator control, 180,
    183–184*
  with math form, 193–194
Requirements Analysis phase (SDLC), 22
Response object (ASP), 17, 99–100
Response.Redirect, 17
*Response.Write statements, for debugging
    ASP, 104*
*Return statement, in Visual Basic .NET
    functions, 71*
round trips (Web forms), 161
rows, in tables, 202
RPC-oriented operations (SOAP), 284–285
runtime errors, 272
*runtime requirements, special,
    eliminating, 43*

sample table example
  adding data/updating, 206–208
  creating, 204–206
  deleting data, 209–210
  retrieving data, 208–209
SaveAs method (PostedFile class), 81
saving, ASP.NET applications, 125
SAX (Simple API for XML), 63–64
scalability, 8, 41
  ASP.NET applications, 108
  ASP.NET vs. ASP applications, 102–103
<script> element, 111
*script files, IDC (Internet Database
    Connector), 14*
scripts
  ASP.NET for, 8
  CGI (Common Gateway Interface), 11–13
  comments in, 115
  event-handling code in, 127–128
  Perl for, 12–13
  scripting languages, 20
  SQL, creating databases using, 204–206
*SDLC (software development lifecycle),
    21–22*
  design phase, 22
  development phase, 22
  enhancement/evolution, 23

maintenance phase, 23
production phase, 22
Requirements Analysis phase, 22
specification-creation, 22
security advantages, ASP.NET
          applications, 108
<security> element (Web.config), 266
security tools
authentication, 130–131
authorization, 131–132
impersonation, 132
SQL Server 2000, 217–218
SELECT statements/queries (SQL), 204,
          208–209
Select...Case conditionals, 27–28
replacing arithmetic functions with,
          293–294
SelectedItemTemplate (DataList
          control), 233
Send Email button, activating, 77
Send method (SmtpMail class), 78
SeparatorTemplate (DataList control), 233
Server and Client Tools installation option
          (SQL Server 2000), 216
server control syntax
custom, 114
HTML for, 114
server controls, using HTML tags as, 114
Server object (ASP), 16, 99–100
Server.CreateObject statement, 16
servername variable (ASP Application
          object), 16
server-side controls, 114
ASP.NET support for, 100
HTML controls (Web forms), 161
server-side include directives, 115
server-side input validation, 177–178
automatic implementation of, 178–179
server-side <object> tags, 114–115
server-side scripting/scripts
ASP.NET for, 8
CGI (Common Gateway Interface), 11–12
comments in, 115
event-handling code in, 127–128
using Perl for, 12–13
<service> element (WSDL/WSML), 285
session events, 128
Session object (ASP), 17, 99–100, 102

session state settings
ASP, limitations, 136
ASP.NET, 137–140
coding, 141–142
cookieless, 140–141
how it works, 135–136
session variables, 129
Session_OnStart/_OnEnd events, 128–129
<sessionState> element (Web.config), 267
SGML (Standard Generalized Markup
          Language), 57
short names, in XML documents, 62
short type variables, 25
ShowMessageBox property, 184
Simple API for XML (SAX), 63–64
Simple Object Access Protocol. See SOAP
          (Simple Object Access Protocol)
Single data type, 25
replacing Decimal type with, 294–295
sizes, of variable types, 24–25
Smalltalk, 52
SmtpMail class, 77
SOAP (Simple Object Access Protocol)
architecture, 283
ASP.NET support for, 282
operations, 283–284
RPC-oriented operations, 284
SOAP encoding, 284
SOAP envelope, 284
SOAP transport mechanism, 284
translation into WSDL/WSML, 285
socket programming, ASP.NET support
          for, 100
software, delivering as a service, 5, 7–8
software development lifestyle, 21–23
software engineering, 23
software programs, features of, 19
conditionals, 27–28
loops, 25–26
variables, 23
SortCommand (DataGrid control), 232–233
SortedList class (System.Collections
          namespace), 120
source code, 19
spaces, in field names, 203
special characters, in well-formed XML, 59
specification phase (SDLC), 22
specifications
advantages of developing, 22
CLS (Common Language Specification), 41

speed. See performance
SQL (Structured Query Language)
  database support for, 203–204
  DELETE statements, 209–210
  functions of, 205–206
  INSERT statements, 206–207
  SELECT statements, 208–209
  UPDATE statements, 207–208
SQL scripts, creating databases using,
  204–206
SQL Server 2000 (Microsoft), 202
  acquiring, 211–212
  authentication, 254
  converting math.aspx to, 295
  databases in, creating, 219–223
  DSN-less connections, 254
  identity keys, 203
  installing, 212–219
  machine/application settings in, 140
  performance/reliability issues, 141
  and scalability, 103
  session state mode, 139–140
  system requirements, 212
SQL Server Desktop Engine, 211–212
SQL Server Personal Edition, 211–212
stability, ASP.NET vs. ASP applications, 103
Standard JIT, 45–46
state management
  ASP session state settings, 136–137
  ASP.NET session state settings, 137–140
  cookieless session management, 140–141
  Web forms, 161
StateBag class (System.Web.UI
  namespace), 122
state.sql, 140
stored procedures, 18
storing namespaces, 117
Stream object, 83
StreamWriter class (System.IO namespace),
  81–83
string type variables, 25
StringReader/Writer classes (System.IO
  namespace), 121
structural validation standards (XML
  documents), 59–61
structures, in .NET Framework applications,
  86. See also namespaces
Stuctured Query Language (SQL), database
  support for, 203–204
stylesheet element (XSLT), 65–66

stylesheets, XSL, 64, 65
sub procedures (Visual Basic .NET), 70–71
subelements (XML documents), 58
Submit button, adding to math form,
  190–191
subscribing to software, 7
subtraction function, creating, 148–149
synchronous communications, using SOAP,
  284–285
syntax
  @Import directive, 113
  @Page directive, 112
  code declaration blocks, 111
  code render blocks, 111–112
  data binding, 225–226
  exception handling (Visual basic .NET),
    71–72
  HTML/custom server control, 114
  INSERT statements (SQL), 206
  <object> tag, 114–115
  server-side HTML controls (Web forms), 161
  as source of errors, 272
  UPDATE statements (SQL), 207
  for using Web controls, 174
  validation controls, 180
System namespace, 117
  classes, 119–120
  exceptions, 119
  structures, 120
system requirements
  .NET Framework programs, 29–30
  SQL Server 2000 (Microsoft), 212
system usage. See scalability
System.Collections namespace, 117, 120
SystemCollections.Specialized
  namespace, 117
System.Configuration namespace, 118
System.Data namespace, 91
  data access classes, 239
  data access using, 238
  in data binding example, 226–228
  using in data-aware applications, 253
System.Data.OleDb namespace
  data access interface classes, 238–239
  in data-aware applications, 253
  in data binding example, 226–228
  DataView class, using with DataGrid
    control, 230–231
  update code classes, 254–256

System.Data.SqlClient namespace
data access interface classes, 239
data access using, 238
System.Decimal namespace, 147
exceptions, 152
System.IO namespace, 80, 81–83, 118
classes, 121
exceptions, 120–121
System.Text namespace, 118
System.Text.RegularExpressions namespace,
118
System.Web namespace, 80, 91, 118
classes, 121–122
System.Web.Caching namespace, 118
System.Web.Mail namespace, 77
System.Web.Security namespace, 118
System.Web.SessionState namespace, 118
System.Web.UI namespace, 118, 122
System.Web.UI.HtmlControls namespace,
80, 118, 122
classes exposed by, 162
System.Web.UI.WebControls namespace,
118, 122, 167–168
DataGrid base control, 230–233
DataList base control, 233

T

TabIndex property (WebControl base
class), 169
Table control, 173
tables, database, 202
accessing/managing records in, 204
in ASP.NET WCC database, viewing, 221
displaying records in using DataGrid
control, 230–231
naming, in Enterprise Manager, 222–223
relationships among, 203
tags, HTML, System.Web.UI.HtmlControls
classes for, 162
tags, XML, 57. *See also XML*
language/documents
in well-formed XML, 59
tags, XTML, Web.config file, 264–269
template element (XLST), 65–66
TemplateColumn control (data controls), 229
templates, DataList control (data controls),
233

testing SQL statements, 207
text boxes (Web controls), 167
adding to ASP.NET pages, 82
adding to math form, 190
validating, 194
text displays, Web controls for, 170
text files
ASP pages as, 15
Web.config, 264
XML-based configuration files, 101
TextBox control, 170
TextReader/TextWriter classes (System.IO
namespace), 121
third-generation languages, 87–88
third-part .NET services, 5
toolbox, Visual Studio .NET, Web form
controls, 160
ToolTip property (WebControl base class),
170
trace facility (ASP.NET), 104
Trace object
properties and methods, 279
using with page-level tracing, 278–279
<trace> tag (Web.config), 264, 276–277
trace utility (ASP.NET), 275
application-level tracing, 276–277
page-level tracing, 278–279
Trace.axd output, 277
Trace=On output, 278–279
TracerContext class (System.Web
namespace), 122
transactions, database
atomicity, 236
consistency, 236
durability, 236
isolation, 236
transforming XML documents
XPath language, 65
XSLT (Extensible Stylesheet Language
Transformation), 64
translating XML documents
XPath language, 65
XSLT (Extensible Stylesheet Language
Transformation), 64
Try...Catch...Finally..End Try syntax, 71–72
ASP.NET support for, 104–105
types, of variables, 24–25
<types> element (WSDL/WSML), 285
typographical errors, 272

U

Uniform Resource Identifiers (URIs), 62
Uniform Resource Locators (URLs), 62
Universal Resource Names (URNs), 62
unmanaged code, 44
unsafe code, 44
UPDATE statements/queries (SQL), 204,
207–208
updating recordsets, ADO for, 236–238
upgrading software, 7
uploading files
    HTML standard method, 78
    HttpPostedFile class, 78
Uri class (System namespace), 120
URIs (Uniform Resource Identifiers), 62
URLs (Uniform Resource Locators), 62
    reading using ASP, 17
    URL authorization, 131–132
URNs (Universal Resource Names), 62
user input
    ASP.NET validation controls, 178–180
    input validation, 177–178
user interfaces
    classes for, 122
    data access, 238–239
    Web controls for, 173–174
    Web forms, 160
UserControl class (System.Web.UI
namespace), 122
user-defined type variables, 25
username variable (ASP Session object), 17

V

validating XML documents, processing
options, 65
validation controls, for math form
    first value, 193–194
    second value, 194
validation controls, input validation,
177–178
    automatic implementation, 178–179
    CompareValidator, 179, 180–181
    CustomValidator, 179, 181–182
    linking HTML forms to, 178
    RangeValidator, 179, 182–183

    RegularExpressionValidator, 179, 183
    RequiredFieldValidator, 180, 183–184
    separating from validation messages, 179
    ValidationSummary, 180, 184
validation messages, separating from
validation controls, 179
ValidationSummary control, 180
    with mathform, 195
    using, 184
value-of select element (XSLT), 65–66
variable types
    Boolean, 24
    byte, 24
    char, 24
    date, 25
    decimal, 25
    double, 25
    integer, 25
    length of, 24–25
    long, 25
    object, 25
    short, 25
    single, 25
    string, 25
    user-defined, 25
variables
    constants, 70
    initializing/declaring, 69–70, 147
    session variables, 129, 135
VBScript, 17
    ASP support for, 15
versioning, ASP.NET vs. ASP
applications, 102
Very High Level Languages (VHLL), 52–53
View Details output (Trace.axd), 277
view state (Web forms), 161
viewing, database tables, 221
virtual directories, copying .NET files to,
126–127
Visual Basic, previous versions, 68
    Visual Basic .NET comparison, 55
    Visual Basic .NET compatibility, 72–73
Visual Basic .NET, 50, 54
    CLR (Common Language Runtime) support
        for, 42
    comments in, 68–69
    compiler component, 20–21
    constants, 70
    error handling, 71

IsNumeric function, with mathform, 194
origins of, 67–68
as strongly typed language, 24
sub procedures, 70–71
variables, 69–70
VB6 compatibility issues, 72–73
Visual Basic 6 comparison, 55
visual component (Web forms), 160
Visual Studio .NET
  ASP.NET support for, 108
  building Web forms using, 160
  debugging/error handling tools, 104
  integration with Eiffel, 52–53
VisualStudio .NET, 5

Web applications, 11
Web controls, 167–168
  action-performing, 172
  adding to ASP.NET applications, 77, 80,
    82–83
  binding to databases, 225–226
  data input, 170–172
  image controls, 173
  for layout and interface, 173
  text displays, 170
  using, 174
Web development tools, 6–8
Web farms
  ASP objects on, 102
  ASP.NET objects on, 103
Web forms
  ASP form, creating, 162–163
  building using Visual Studio .NET, 160
  code for, 165–166, 192–193
  controls on, 159–160
  converting XML page to, 189–190
  defined, 159–160
  dropdown list, adding, 190–191
  HTML controls, 161–162
  processing of, 160–161
  state preservation/management, 161
  submit button, adding, 191
  text boxes, adding, 190
  using data controls on, 229–233
  validation, 193–195
  visual/logical components, 160, 165–166

Web forms, math application example
  adding dropdown lists, 190–191
  adding submit buttons, 191
  adding text boxes, 190
  code for, 192–193
  specifications for, 189–190
  validating, 193–195
Web gardens, ASP.NET objects on, 103
*Web pages, data aware (ASP.NET Math
    Program example)*
  connection code, 253–254
  defining, requirements for, 252–253
  integrating code elements, 256–259
  statelessness of, 161
  updating, code for, 254–256
Web servers
  ASP.NET vs. ASP, 97–98
  handling of ASP.NET applications, 109–110
  HTTP compliant, running programs from, 11
Web services, 6, 281–282
  supported protocols, 282
*Web Services Description Language (WSDL),
    285*
Web Services Meta Language (WSML), 285
Web sites
  Annotated XML Specification, 58
  Extensible Schema Description (XSD), 61
  SOAP (Simple Object Access Protocol), 283
  SQL Server 2000, 211–212
  W3C Recommendation of the XML-Data
    Note, 60
  XPath recommendation, 65
Web.config file, 101, 108, 137–138
  <assemblies> subelement, 265
  <authentication> element, 267
  <authorization> element, 266–267
  <browserCaps> element, 268–269
  <compilation> element, 265
  <compiler> element, 265
  <compilers> element, 265
  <configsections> element, 264
  <configuration> element, 264, 269
  custom error pages, definition for, 273–274
  <customErrors> element, 265–266
  <globalization> element, 264
  <httpHandlers> element, 267
  <httpModules> element, 267–268
  <identity> element, 267
  <processmodel> element, 268

Continued

Web.config file (continued)
  purpose/contents of, 263
  <security> element, 266
  <sessionState> element, 267
  <trace> element, 264, 276
  with Web forms, 160
WebControl base class, 167
  action-performing controls, 172
  common properties, 168–170
  image display control, 173
  input controls, 170–172
  layout and interface controls, 173–174
  using Web controls, 174
well-formed XML, 59
Width property (WebControl base class), 170
Windows authentication, 130
  ASP.NET support for, 108
Windows Authentication Mode (SQL Server 2000), 218
Windows NT, ASPState service for, 139
Windows NT Option Pack, ASP 2.0 as part of, 15
wrappers, for legacy COM objects/classes, 76
Write method
  Response object, 17
  Stream object, 83
  Trace object, 279
WriteIf method (Trace object), 279
WriteLine method (Trace object), 279
WriteLineIf method (Trace object), 279
WSDL (Web Services Description Language), 285
WSML (Web Services Meta Language), 285

  data, 58
  document features, 58
  Document Type Definitions (DTD), 60
  DOM (Document Object Model) for, 63
  double quotes ("") in, 58
  elements, 58
  Extensible Stylesheet Language (XSL), 64
  functional validation standards, 61
  namespaces, 62
  in .NET Framework applications, 63
  nodes, 58
  processor instructions, 58
  referencing namespaces, 61
  referencing node relationships, 61
  short names, 62
  Simple API for XML (SAX) for, 63–64
  structural validation standards, 59–61
  tools for interacting with, 63–66
  translation tools, 65–66
  URN references, 62
  Web.config file, 263
  well-formed XML, 59
XML parser, instructions to, 62–63
XML Schema (XDR), 60–61
XML streams, ASP.NET support for, 99
XML-Data Reduced Schema (XDR), 60–61
xmlns, XML namespace designation, 62
XPath language, 65
xsd prefix (XML documents), 62
XSL (Extensible Stylesheet Language), 64
XSLT (Extensible Stylesheet Language Transformation), 64

XCOPY command, 101
XML language/documents, 57
  advantages of using, 59
  ASP.NET tools for, 66
  attributes, 58
  comments, 58
  creating DataSet/DataTable objects using, 240

Hungry Minds, Inc.
End-User License Agreement

READ THIS. You should carefully read these terms and conditions before opening the software packet(s) included with this book ("Book"). This is a license agreement ("Agreement") between you and Hungry Minds, Inc. ("HMI"). By opening the accompanying software packet(s), you acknowledge that you have read and accept the following terms and conditions. If you do not agree and do not want to be bound by such terms and conditions, promptly return the Book and the unopened software packet(s) to the place you obtained them for a full refund.

1. **License Grant.** HMI grants to you (either an individual or entity) a nonexclusive license to use one copy of the enclosed software program(s) (collectively, the "Software") solely for your own personal or business purposes on a single computer (whether a standard computer or a workstation component of a multi-user network). The Software is in use on a computer when it is loaded into temporary memory (RAM) or installed into permanent memory (hard disk, CD-ROM, or other storage device). HMI reserves all rights not expressly granted herein.

2. **Ownership.** HMI is the owner of all right, title, and interest, including copyright, in and to the compilation of the Software recorded on the disk(s) or CD-ROM ("Software Media"). Copyright to the individual programs recorded on the Software Media is owned by the author or other authorized copyright owner of each program. Ownership of the Software and all proprietary rights relating thereto remain with HMI and its licensers.

3. **Restrictions on Use and Transfer.**

   (a) You may only (i) make one copy of the Software for backup or archival purposes, or (ii) transfer the Software to a single hard disk, provided that you keep the original for backup or archival purposes. You may not (i) rent or lease the Software, (ii) copy or reproduce the Software through a LAN or other network system or through any computer subscriber system or bulletin-board system, or (iii) modify, adapt, or create derivative works based on the Software.

   (b) You may not reverse engineer, decompile, or disassemble the Software. You may transfer the Software and user documentation on a permanent basis, provided that the transferee agrees to accept the terms and conditions of this Agreement and you retain no copies. If the Software is an update or has been updated, any transfer must include the most recent update and all prior versions.

4. **Restrictions on Use of Individual Programs.** You must follow the individual requirements and restrictions detailed for each individual program in Appendix B of this Book. These limitations are also contained in the individual license agreements recorded on the Software Media. These limitations may include a requirement that after using the program for a specified period of time, the user must pay a registration fee or discontinue use. By opening the Software packet(s), you will be agreeing to abide by the licenses and restrictions for these individual programs that are detailed in Appendix B and on the Software Media. None of the material on this Software Media or listed in this Book may ever be redistributed, in original or modified form, for commercial purposes.

8. **General.** This Agreement constitutes the entire understanding of the parties and revokes and supersedes all prior agreements, oral or written, between them and may not be modified or amended except in a writing signed by both parties hereto that specifically refers to this Agreement. This Agreement shall take precedence over any other documents that may be in conflict herewith. If any one or more provisions contained in this Agreement are held by any court or tribunal to be invalid, illegal, or otherwise unenforceable, each and every other provision shall remain in full force and effect.

CD-ROM Installation Instructions

The CD-ROM that accompanies this book includes the following:

- Wiz.NET, freeware
- Self-assessment software
- All the code and examples from the book

See Appendix B for details on installing items from the CD-ROM.

Get Up to Speed
in a Weekend!

Flash™ 5 Weekend Crash Course™
by Shamms Mortier
408 pages
ISBN 0-7645-3546-3

Red Hat® Linux® 7 Weekend Crash Course™
by Naba Barkakati
432 pages
Red Hat Linux 7 on 3 CDs
ISBN 0-7645-4741-0

Visual Basic® 6 Weekend Crash Course™
by Richard Mansfield
408 pages
ISBN 0-7645-4679-1

Dreamweaver® 4 Weekend Crash Course™
by Wendy Peck
408 pages
ISBN 0-7645-3575-7